2nd EDITION

# THE BEATLES BEST
## for EASY PIANO

Cover photo Getty Images, Bettmann Collection

ISBN 978-1-4950-9282-4

HAL•LEONARD®

7777 W. BLUEMOUND RD. P.O. BOX 13819 MILWAUKEE, WI 53213

Visit Hal Leonard Online at
**www.halleonard.com**

# ACROSS THE UNIVERSE

Words and Music by JOHN LENNON
and PAUL McCARTNEY

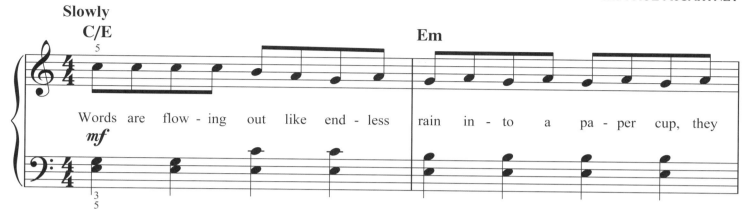

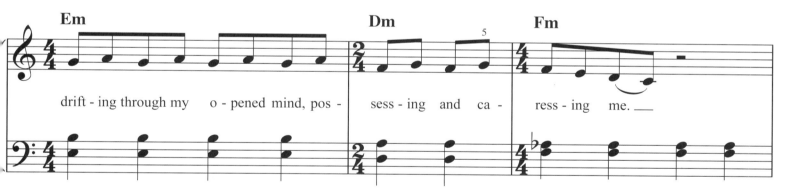

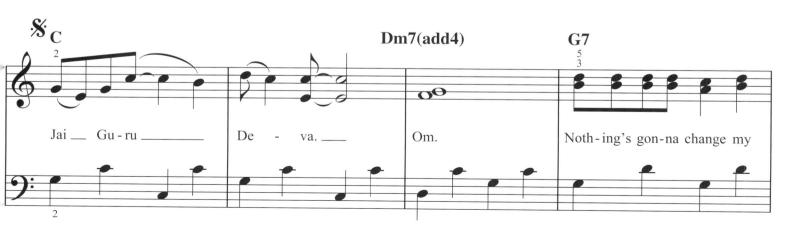

world. Noth - ing's gon-na change my world. Noth - ing's gon-na change my

To Coda

world. Noth - ing's gon - na change my world. Im-ag-es of bro-ken light which

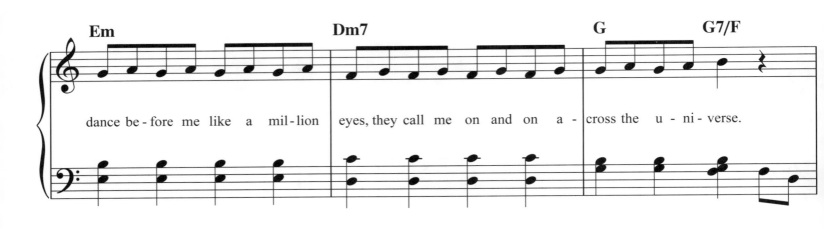

dance be - fore me like a mil-lion eyes, they call me on and on a - cross the u - ni - verse.

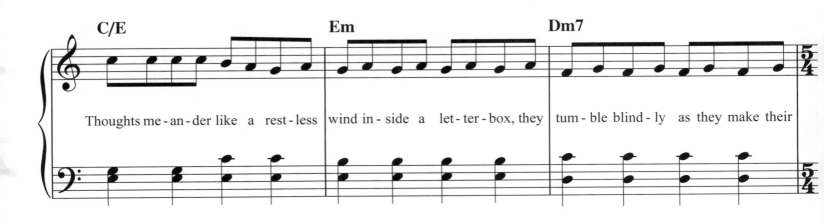

Thoughts me-an-der like a rest-less wind in-side a let-ter-box, they tum - ble blind-ly as they make their

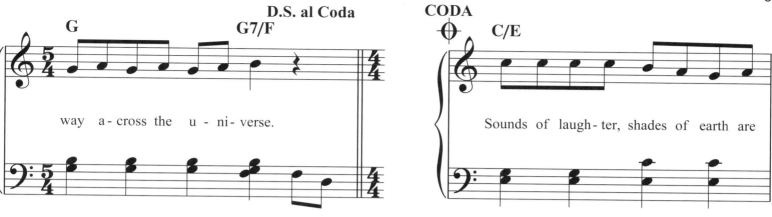

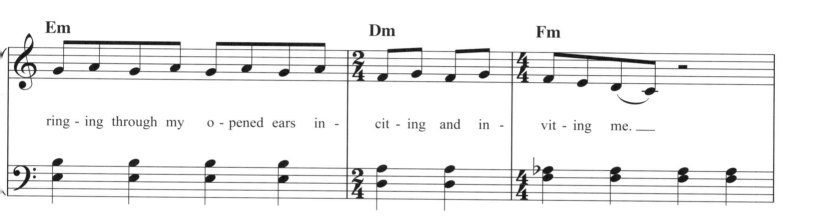

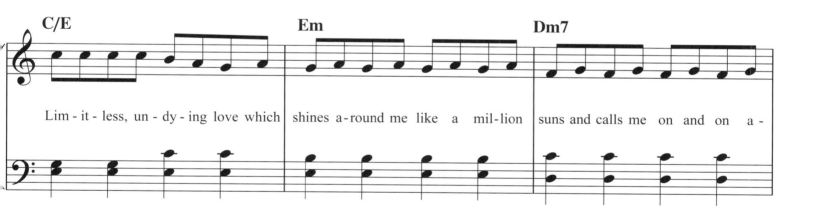

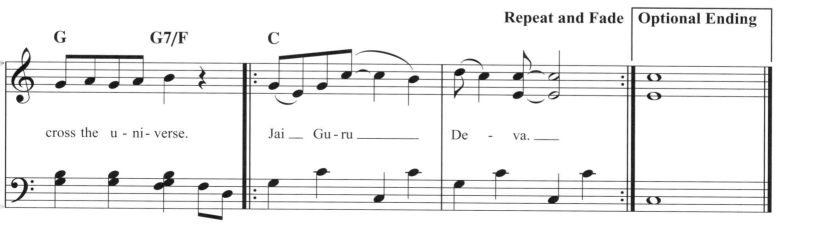

# ALL MY LOVING

Words and Music by JOHN LENNON
and PAUL McCARTNEY

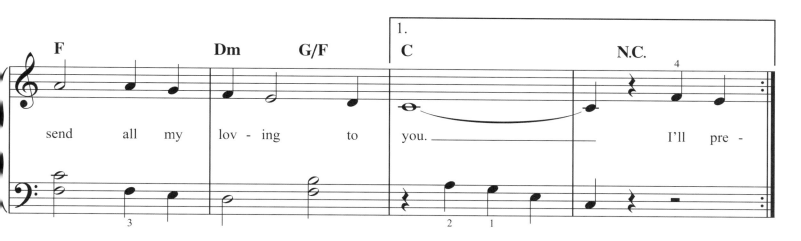

send all my lov - ing to you. ___ I'll pre -

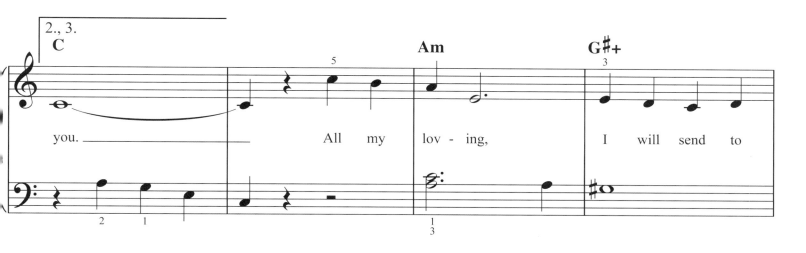

you. ___ All my lov - ing, I will send to

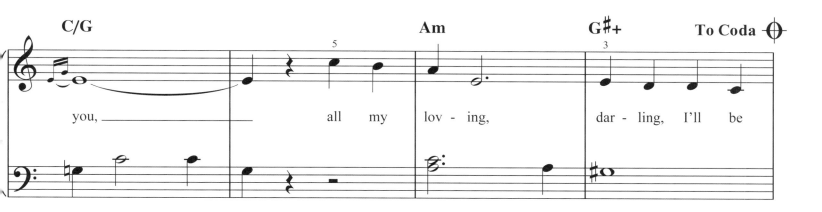

you, ___ all my lov - ing, dar - ling, I'll be

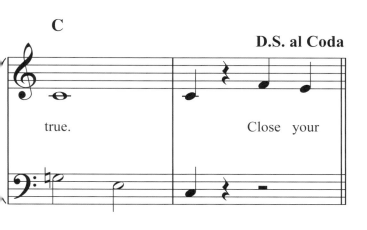

true. Close your

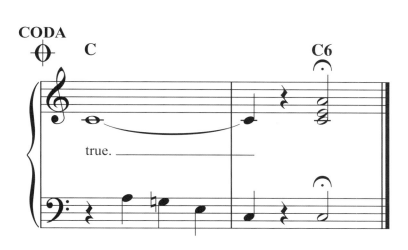

true. ___

# ALL YOU NEED IS LOVE

Words and Music by JOHN LENNON
and PAUL McCARTNEY

Moderately, not too fast

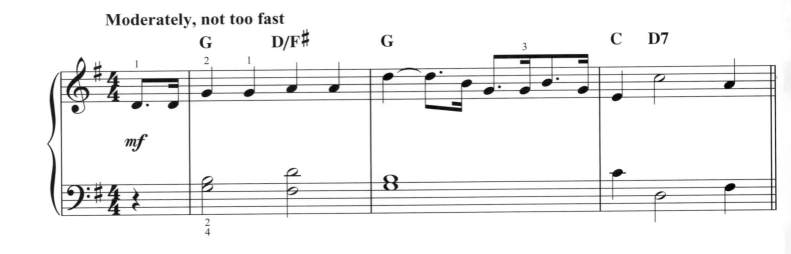

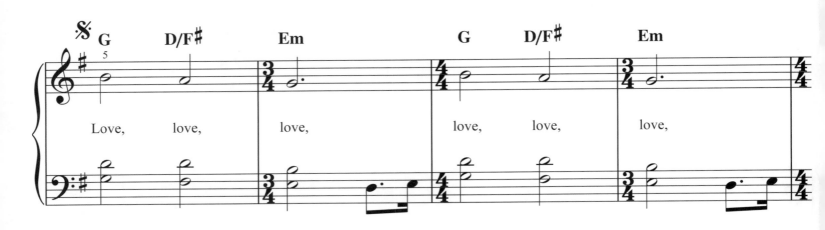

Love, love, love, love, love, love,

love, love, love...

There's noth - ing you can do that can't be done.
Noth - ing you can make that can't be made.
Noth - ing you can know that is - n't known.

Noth - ing you can sing that can't be sung.
No one you can save that can't be saved.
Noth - ing you can see that is - n't shown.

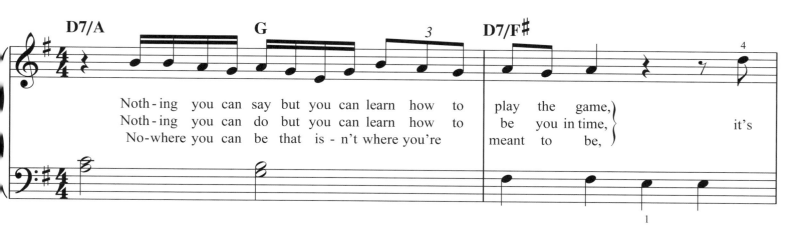

Noth - ing you can say but you can learn how to play the game,
Noth - ing you can do but you can learn how to be you in time,  it's
No - where you can be that is - n't where you're meant to be,

eas - y.

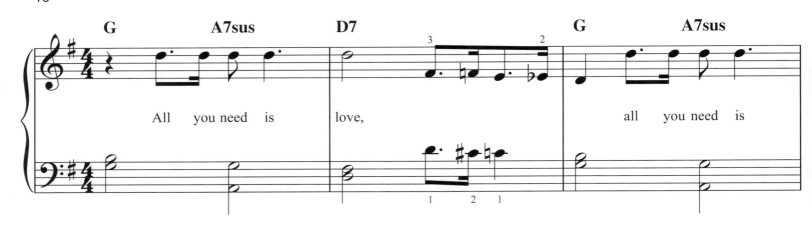

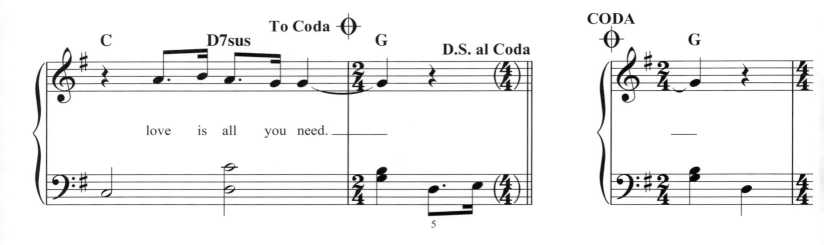

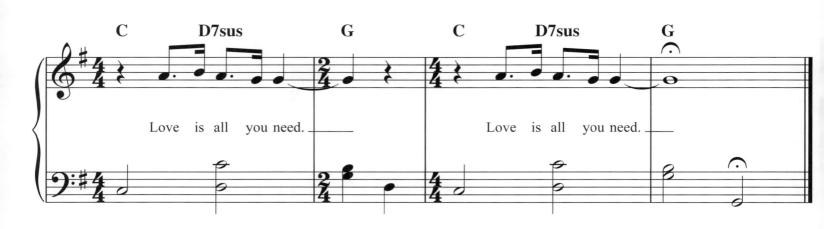

# ALL TOGETHER NOW

Words and Music by JOHN LENNON
and PAUL McCARTNEY

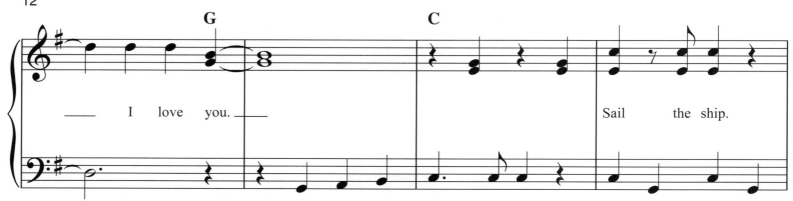

All to-geth - er now, all to-geth - er now.

now. Black, white, green, red, can I take my

friend to bed? __ Pink, brown, yel-low, or-ange and blue, __ I love you! __

**D.S. al Coda**

**CODA**

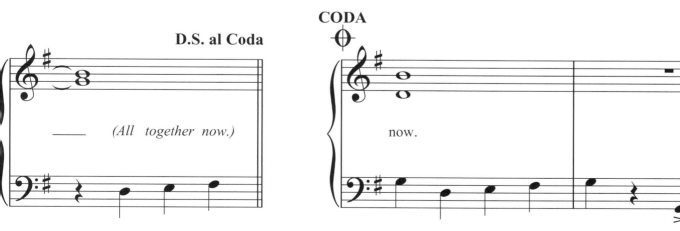

__ (All together now.)

now.

# AND I LOVE HER

Words and Music by JOHN LENNON
and PAUL McCARTNEY

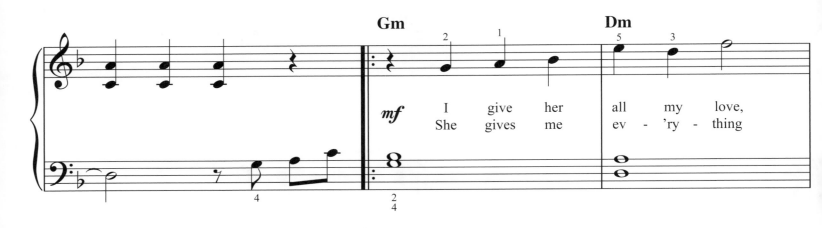

I give her all my love,
She gives me ev - 'ry - thing

that's all I do. ____
And if you saw my love,
and ten - der - ly. ____
The kiss my lov - er brings,

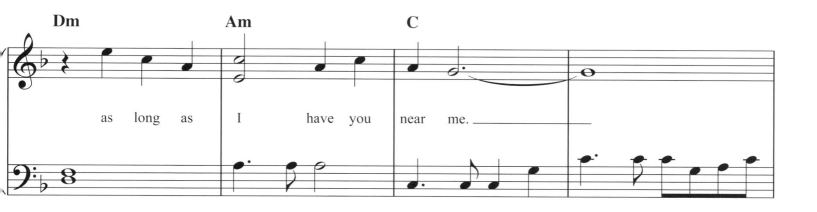

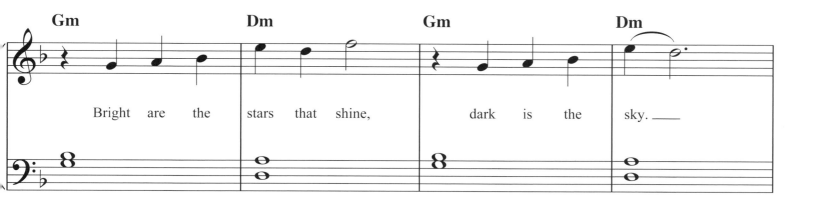

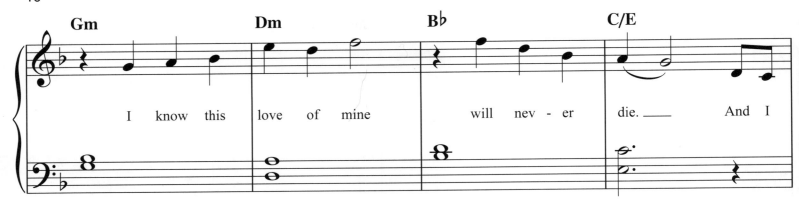

I know this love of mine will nev - er die. ____ And I

love her. ____

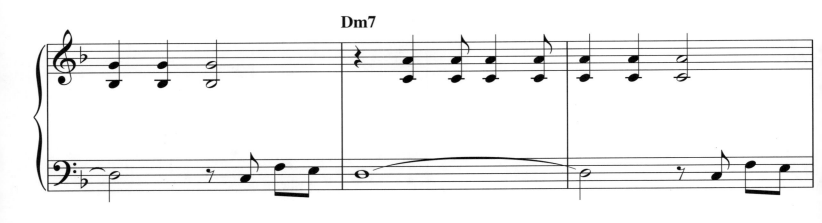

# ASK ME WHY

Words and Music by JOHN LENNON
and PAUL McCARTNEY

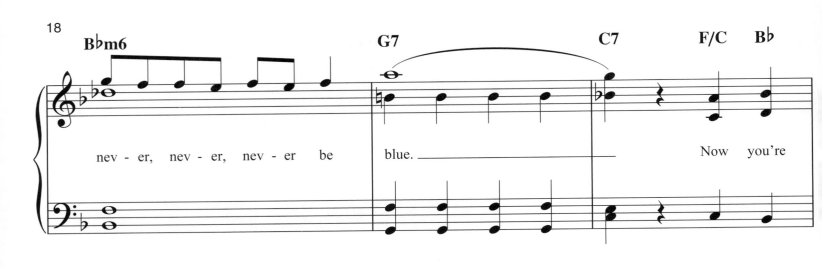

never, nev - er, nev - er be blue. Now you're

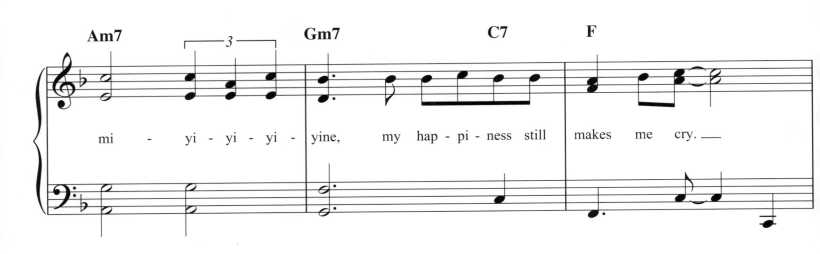

mi - yi - yi - yi - yine, my hap - pi - ness still makes me cry. ___

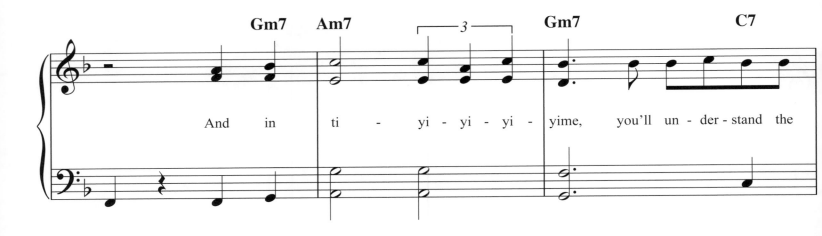

And in ti - yi - yi - yi - yime, you'll un - der - stand the

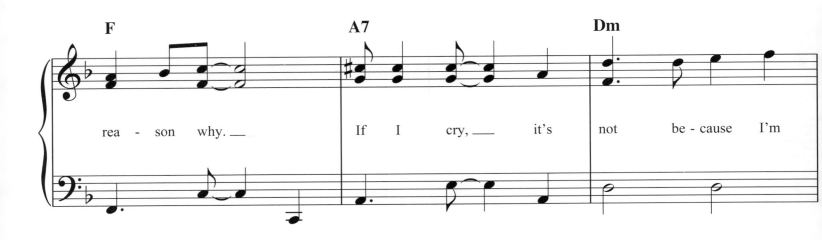

rea - son why. ___ If I cry, ___ it's not be - cause I'm

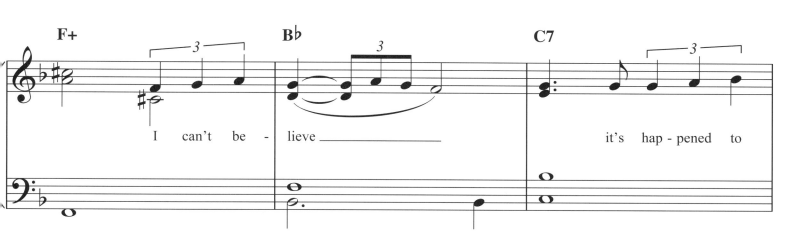

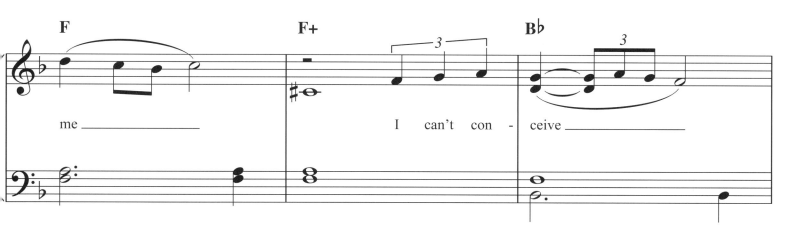

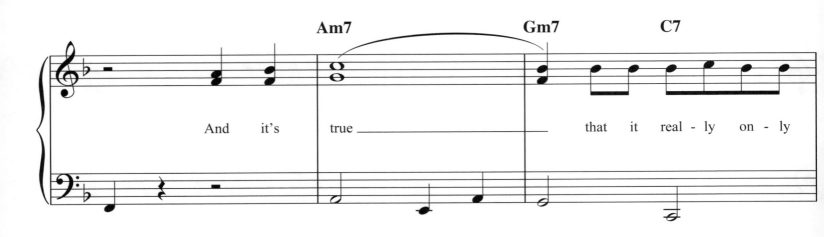

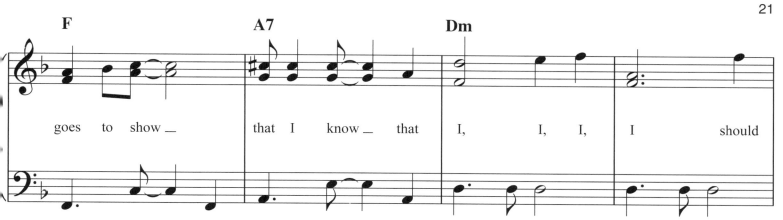

goes to show ___ that I know ___ that I, I, I, I should

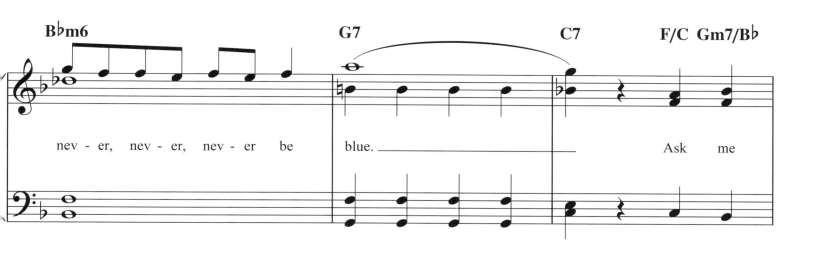

nev - er, nev - er, nev - er be blue. _____ Ask me

why, _____ I'll say I love you ___ and I'm al - ways think - ing of

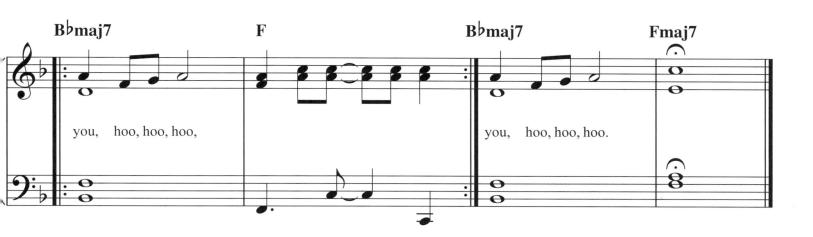

you, hoo, hoo, hoo, you, hoo, hoo, hoo.

# ANYTIME AT ALL

Words and Music by JOHN LENNON
and PAUL McCARTNEY

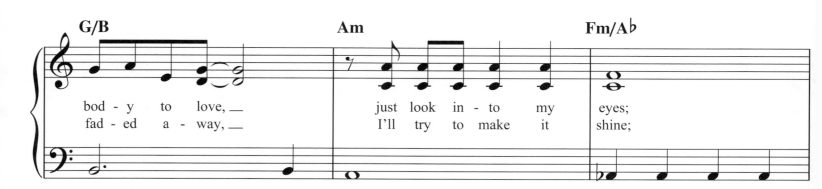

I'll __ be there __ to make you feel __ right. If you're feel - ing
there __ is noth - in' I _____ won't __ do. When you need a

sor - ry and sad, __ I'd real - ly sym - pa - thize;
shoul - der to cry on, I hope it will be mine;

don't you be sad, __ just call me to - night.
call me to - night __ and I'll come to __ you.

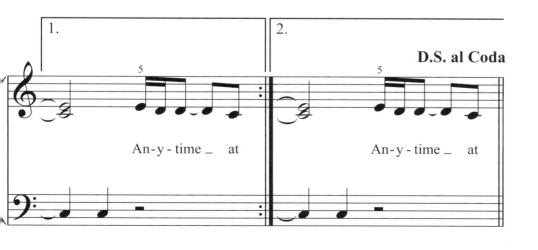

1.
An - y - time __ at

2.
**D.S. al Coda**
An - y - time __ at

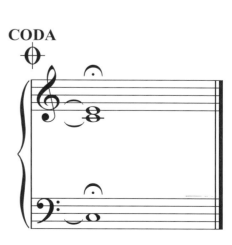

**CODA**

# BABY, YOU'RE A RICH MAN

Words and Music by JOHN LENNON
and PAUL McCARTNEY

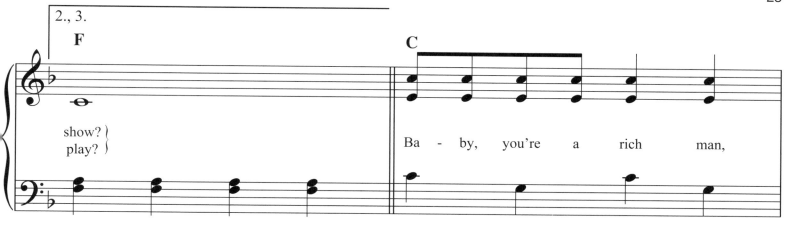

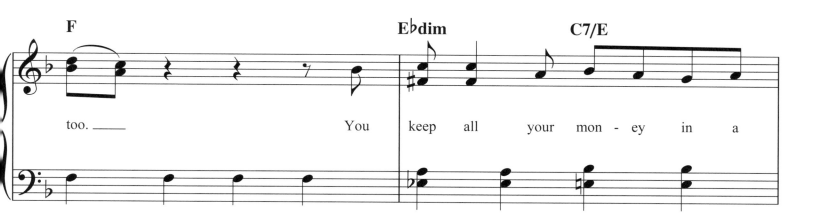

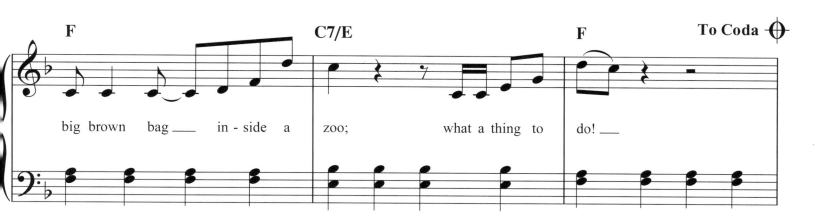

Ba - by, you're a rich man, ba - by, you're a rich man,

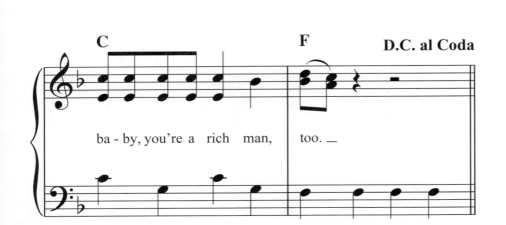

ba - by, you're a rich man, too. __

**D.C. al Coda**

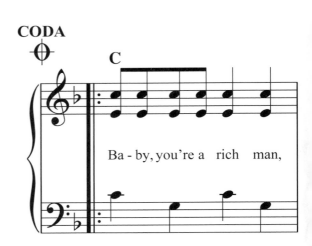

**CODA**

Ba - by, you're a rich man,

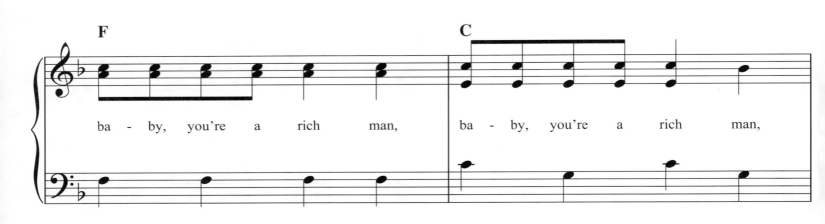

ba - by, you're a rich man, ba - by, you're a rich man,

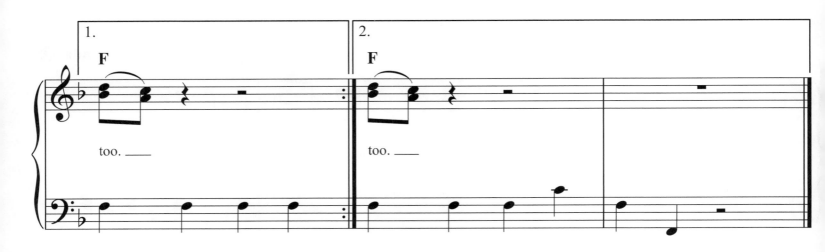

1.

too. __

2.

too. __

# BABY'S IN BLACK

Words and Music by JOHN LENNON
and PAUL McCARTNEY

Slowly, with a strong beat

Oh, dear, what can I do?

Ba-by's in black and I'm feel-ing blue. Tell me oh, what can I do?

She _____ thinks of him _____ and so she dress-es in black _____ and

I _____ think of her _____ but she thinks on-ly of him, _____ and

though he'll nev-er come back, she's dressed in black.

though it's on-ly a whim, she thinks of him.

Oh, how long will it take till she sees the mis-take she has

made? Dear, what can I do? Ba-by's in black and I'm feel-ing blue. Tell me

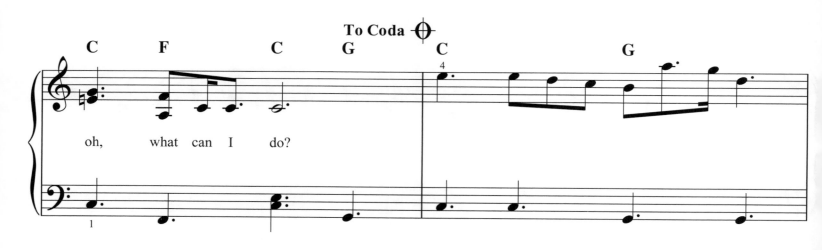

**To Coda** ⊕

oh, what can I do?

**D.S. al Coda**

**CODA**

She ___ thinks of him ___ and so she dress-es in black and

though he'll nev - er come back, she's dressed in black.

Oh, dear, what can I do? Ba - by's in black and I'm feel-ing blue. Tell me

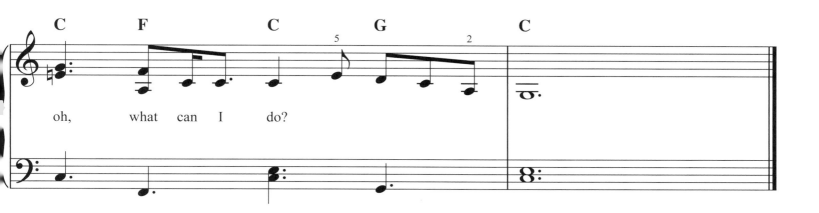

oh, what can I do?

# BACK IN THE U.S.S.R.

Words and Music by JOHN LENNON
and PAUL McCARTNEY

knock me out.___ They leave the ___ West be - hind.___ And Mos - cow girls make me

sing and shout ___ that Geor - gia's al - ways on my mi - mi - mi - mi - mi - mi - mi - mi - mind.

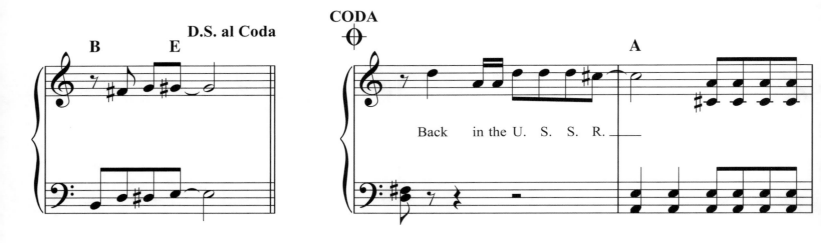

Back in the U. S. S. R. ___

# BIRTHDAY

Words and Music by JOHN LENNON
and PAUL McCARTNEY

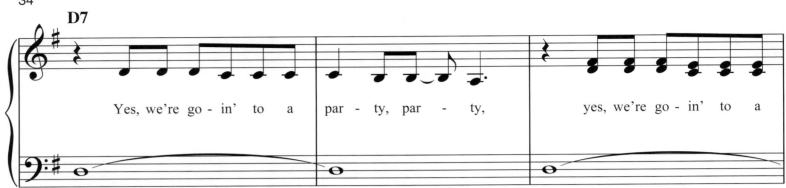

Yes, we're go - in' to a party, par - ty, yes, we're go - in' to a

par - ty, par - ty. Yes, we're go - in' to a par - ty, par - ty.

I would like you to dance, ___

take a cha - cha - cha - chance, ___

I would like you to dance, __

dance!

**D.C. al Coda**
**(no repeat)**

# THE BALLAD OF JOHN AND YOKO

Words and Music by JOHN LENNON
and PAUL McCARTNEY

last night the wife said, "Oh boy, when you're dead, you don't take noth-ing with you but your

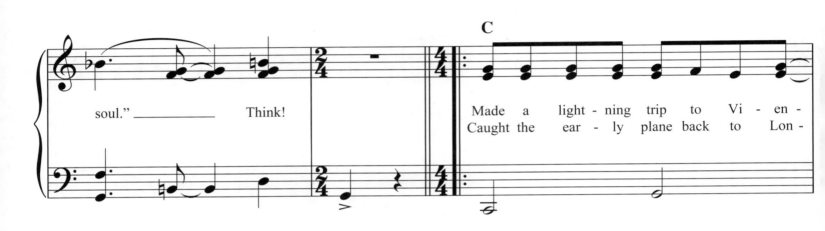

soul." _____ Think! Made a light-ning trip to Vi-en-
Caught the ear-ly plane back to Lon-

-na, \_\_\_ eat-ing choc-'late cake in a bag, \_\_\_\_\_ the
-don, \_\_\_ fif-ty a-corns tied in a sack, \_\_\_\_\_ the

news-pa-pers said, \_\_\_\_\_ "She's gone to his head; \_\_\_\_\_ they look just like two gu-rus in drag." \_
men from the press \_\_\_ said, "We wish you suc-cess; \_\_\_\_\_ it's good to have the both of you back." \_

Christ! You know it ain't eas - y, ___ you know how hard it can be. ___

The way things are go - ing, ___ they're gon-na cru - ci - fy ___

me. me, the way things are

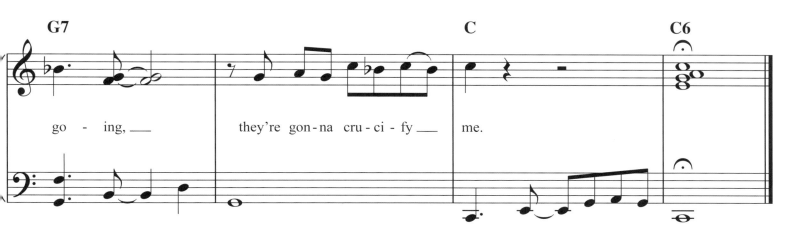

go - ing, ___ they're gon-na cru-ci-fy ___ me.

# BECAUSE

Words and Music by JOHN LENNON
and PAUL MCARTNEY

# COME TOGETHER

Words and Music by JOHN LENNON
and PAUL McCARTNEY

Here comes old flat-top, he come

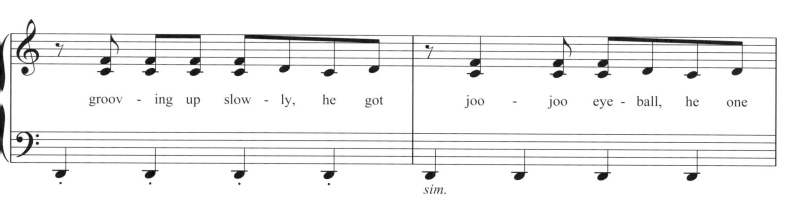

groov-ing up slow-ly, he got   joo - joo eye-ball, he one

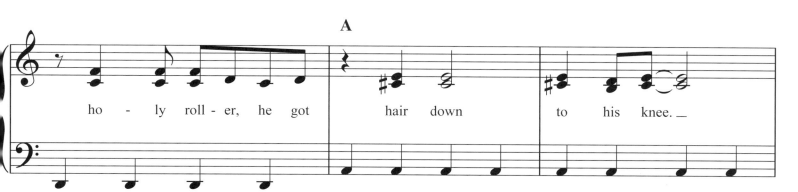

ho - ly roll-er, he got   hair down   to his knee. _

44

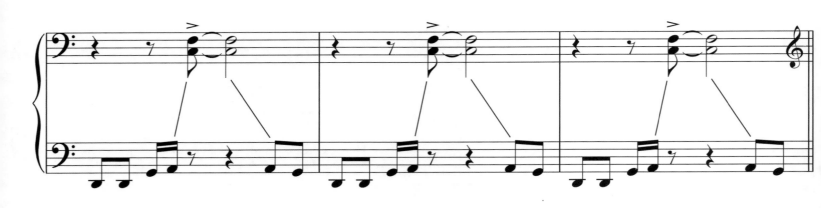

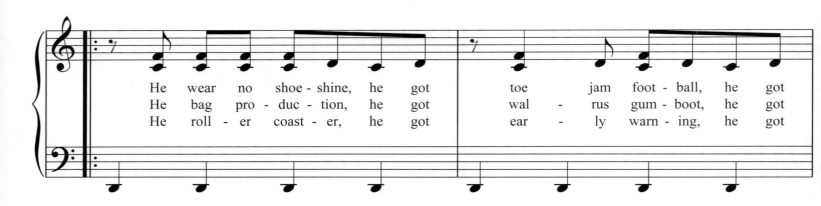

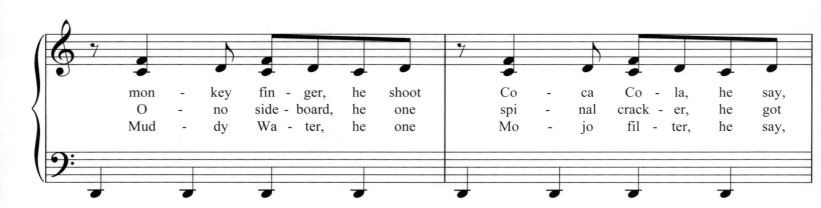

**A**

"I know ____ you; you know me. ____
feet down be - low ____ his knee. ____
"One and one and one ____ is three." ____

**G7**

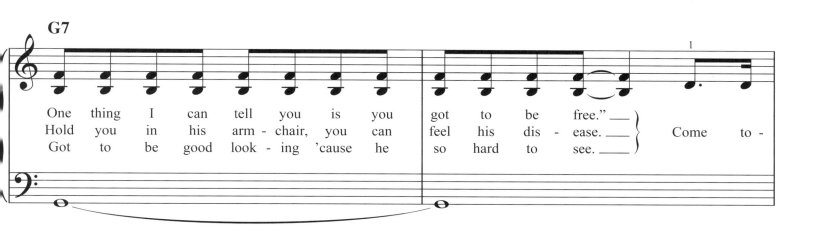

One thing I can tell you is you got to be free." ____ ⎫
Hold you in his arm - chair, you can feel his dis - ease. ____ ⎬ Come to -
Got to be good look - ing 'cause he so hard to see. ____ ⎭

**Bm**     **G**     **Dm7**

geth - er, right now, _ o - ver me!

**1., 2.**     **3.**

**Repeat and Fade**

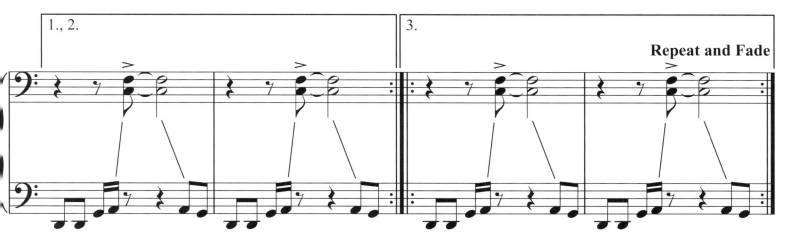

# BEING FOR THE BENEFIT OF MR. KITE

Words and Music by JOHN LENNON
and PAUL McCARTNEY

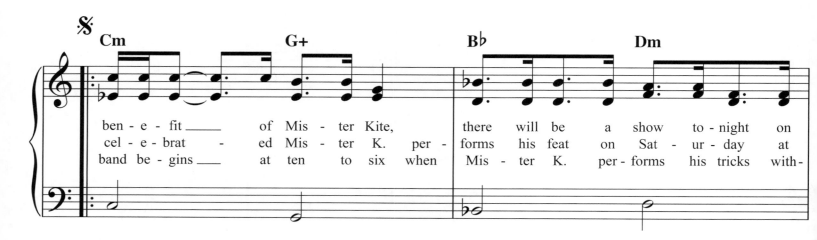

late of Pab - lo Fan - que's fair; / Mis - ter Kite flies through the ring; / som - er - saults he'll un - der - take on

what a scene. _____ / don't be late. _____ / sol - id ground. _____

O - ver / Mes - s'rs / Hav - ing

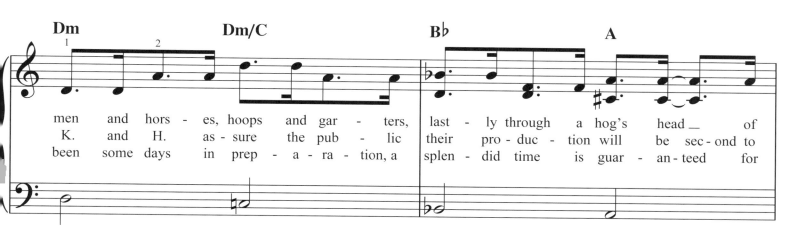

men and hors - es, hoops and gar - ters, / K. and H. as - sure the pub - lic / been some days in prep - a - ra - tion, a

last - ly through a hog's head _ of / their pro - duc - tion will be sec - ond to / splen - did time is guar - an - teed for

**To Coda** ⊕

real fire. / none. / all.

In this / And, of / And to -

way Mis - ter K. will chal - lenge the world!

The / course, Hen - ry the Horse danc - es the

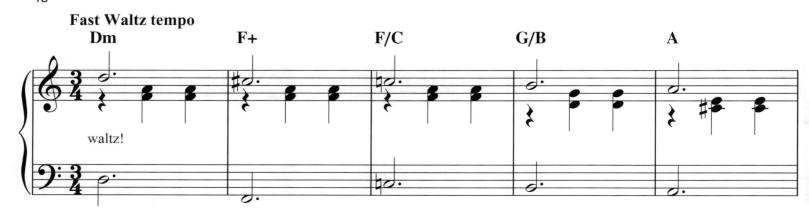

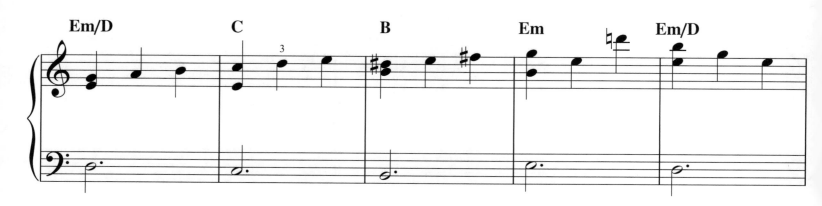

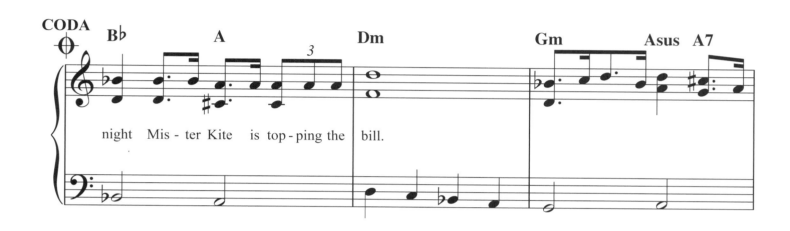

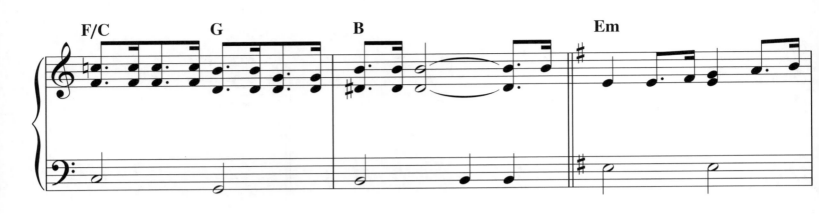

# DON'T LET ME DOWN

Words and Music by JOHN LENNON
and PAUL McCARTNEY

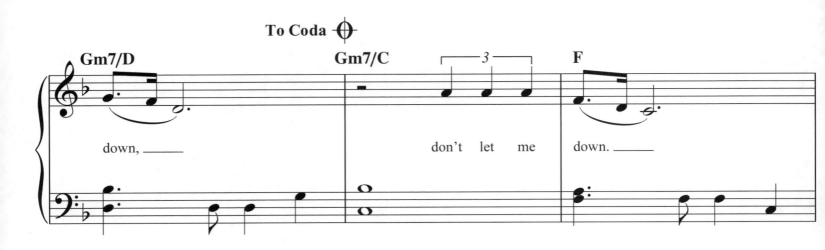

I'm in love for the first time. Don't you know it's gon - na

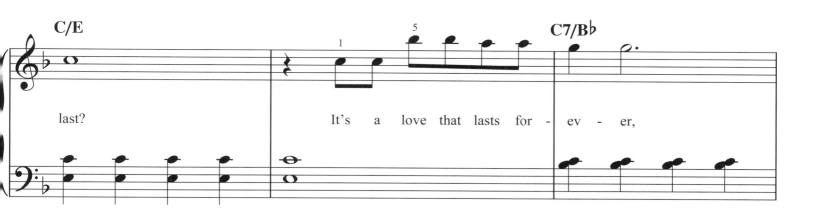

last? It's a love that lasts for - ev - er,

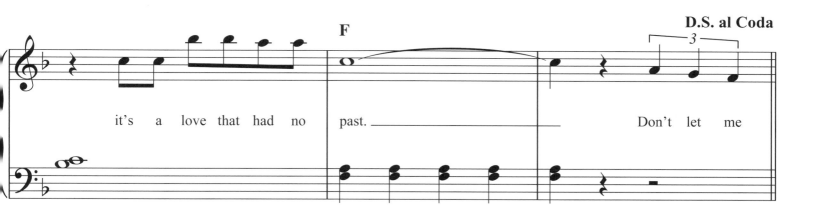

it's a love that had no past. Don't let me

don't let me down!

# BLACKBIRD

Words and Music by JOHN LENNON
and PAUL McCARTNEY

# CAN'T BUY ME LOVE

Words and Music by JOHN LENNON
and PAUL McCARTNEY

**C7**

thing, my friend, if it makes you feel al - right.  'Cause
lot to give, but what I've got I'll give to you.

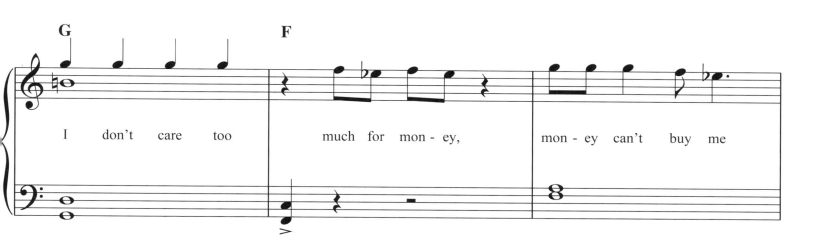

**G**  **F**

I don't care too much for mon - ey, mon - ey can't buy me

1.  **C7**  2.  **C**  **Em**

love.  I'll love. Can't buy me love, ___

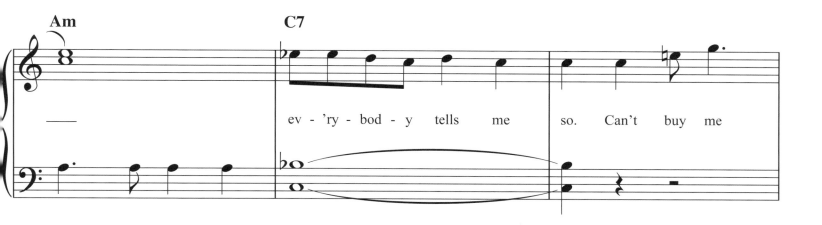

**Am**  **C7**

___  ev - 'ry - bod - y tells me so. Can't buy me

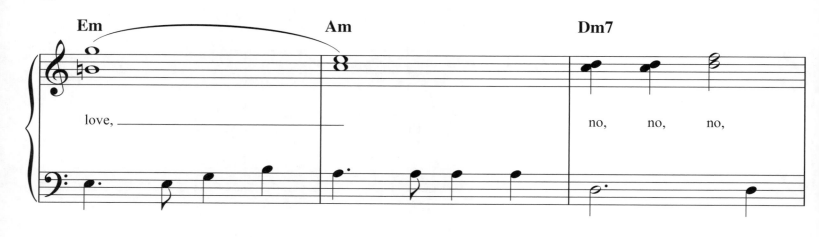

**Em** **Am** **Dm7**

love, _____ no, no, no,

**G** **C7**

no! Say you don't need no dia - mond rings and

**F7**

I'll be sat - is - fied. Tell me that you want the

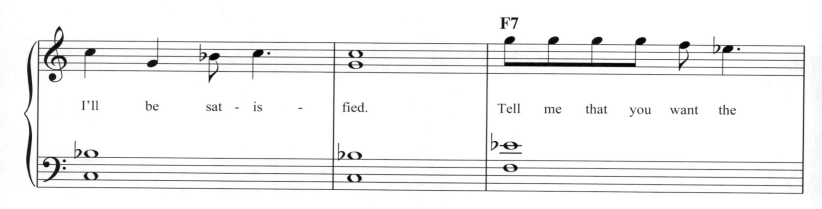

**C7**

kind of things that mon - ey just can't buy.

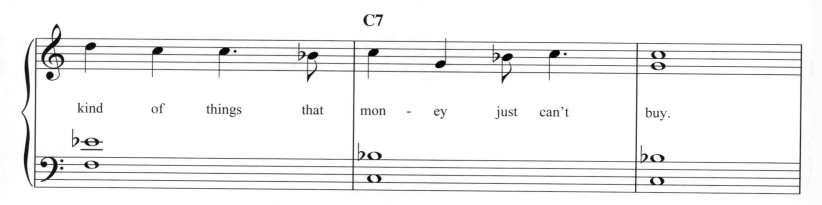

# CARRY THAT WEIGHT

Words and Music by JOHN LENNON
and PAUL McCARTNEY

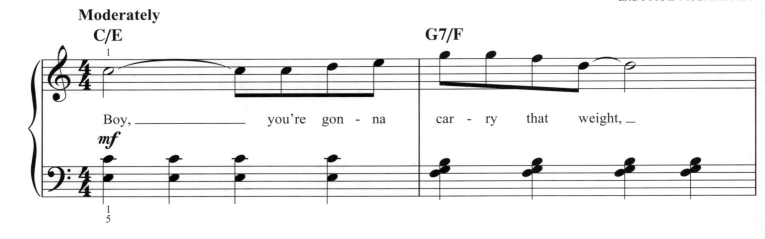

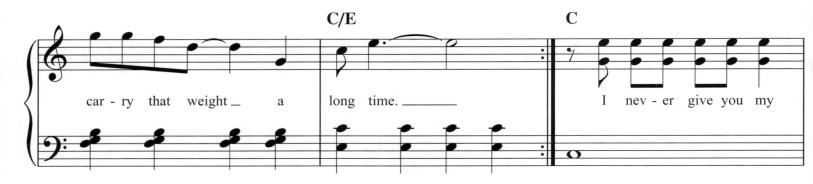

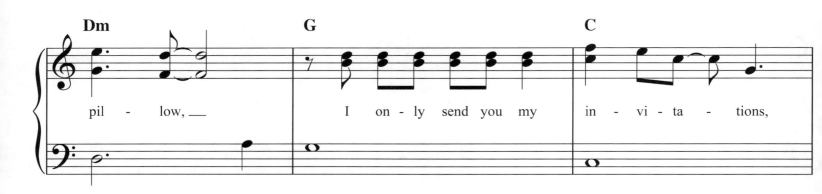

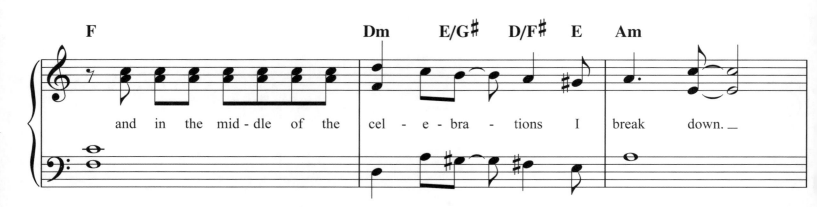

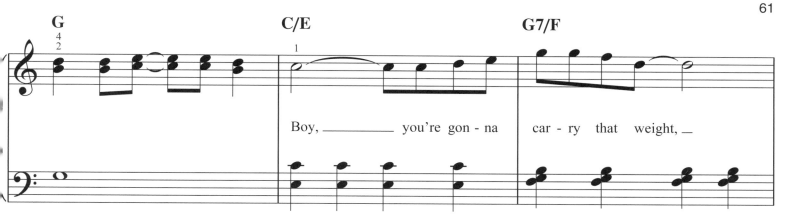

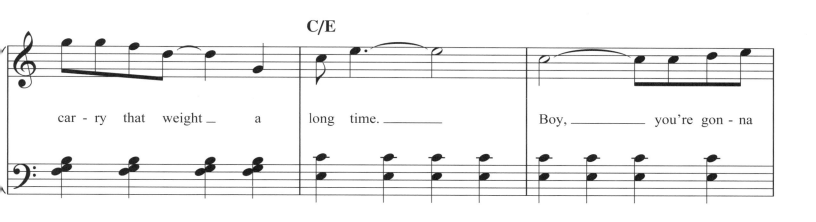

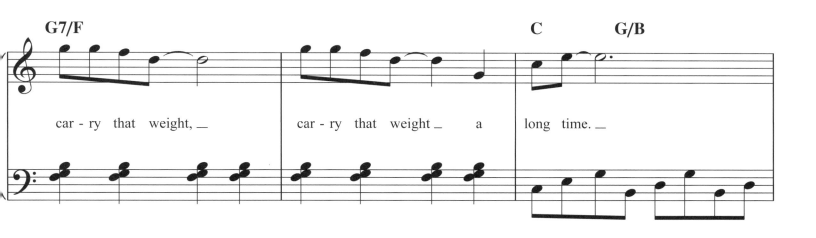

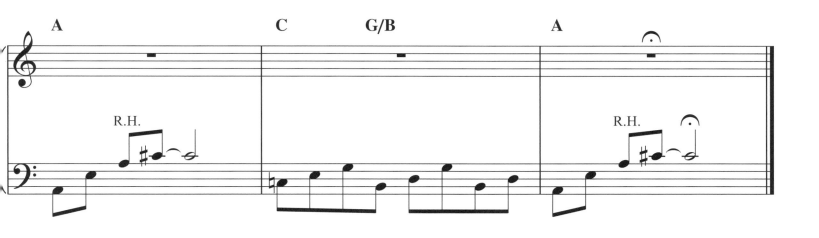

# A DAY IN THE LIFE

Words and Music by JOHN LENNON
and PAUL McCARTNEY

I read the news to-day, __ oh boy,

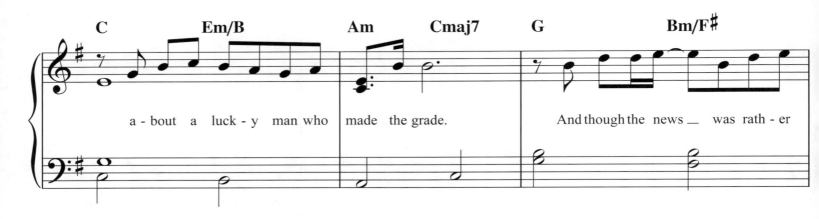

a-bout a luck-y man who made the grade. And though the news __ was rath-er

sad, well, I just had to laugh. _____

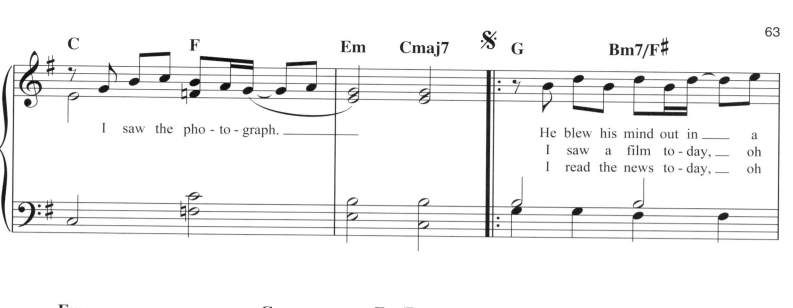

I saw the pho-to-graph. _____

He blew his mind out in ____ a
I saw a film to-day, __ oh
I read the news to-day, __ oh

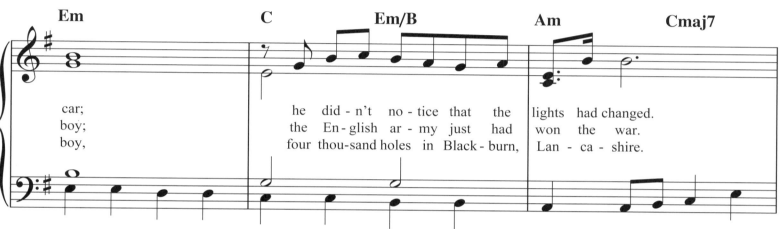

car;
boy;
boy,

he did-n't no-tice that the lights had changed.
the En-glish ar-my just had won the war.
four thou-sand holes in Black-burn, Lan-ca-shire.

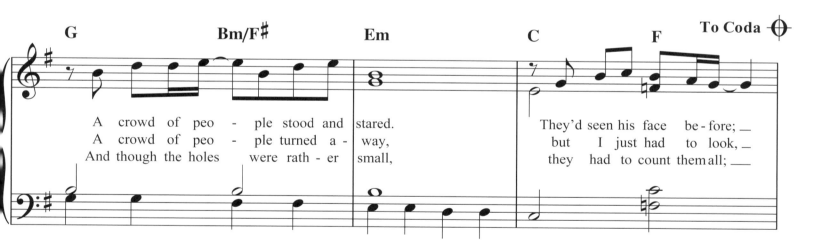

To Coda ⊕

A crowd of peo - ple stood and stared.
A crowd of peo - ple turned a - way,
And though the holes were rath-er small,

They'd seen his face be-fore; __
but I just had to look, __
they had to count them all; __

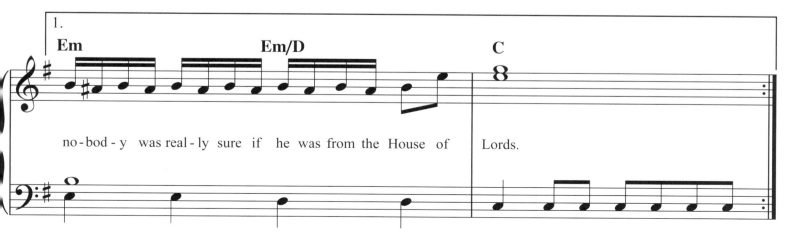

1.

no-bod-y was real-ly sure if he was from the House of Lords.

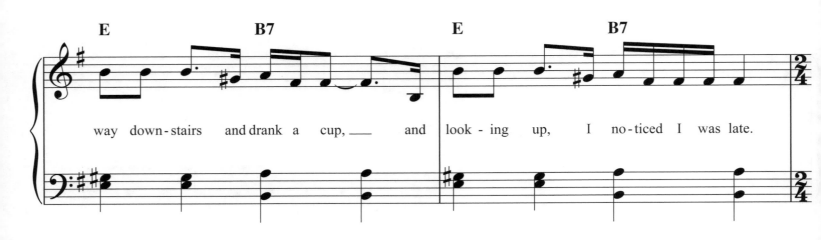

Found my coat and grabbed my hat made the bus in sec-onds

flat. Found my way up-stairs and had a smoke. And

some-bod-y spoke and I went in-to a dream. Ah. _____

# EIGHT DAYS A WEEK

Words and Music by JOHN LENNON
and PAUL McCARTNEY

**Brightly**

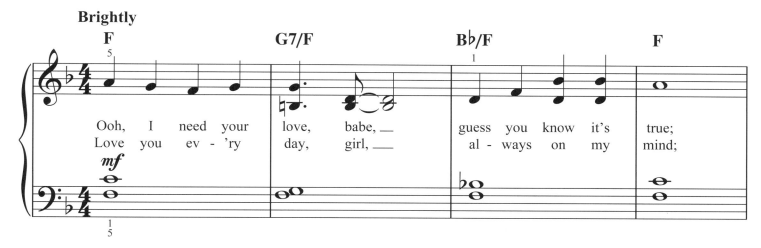

Ooh, I need your love, babe, __ guess you know it's true;
Love you ev - 'ry day, girl, __ al - ways on my mind;

hope you need my love, babe, __ just like I need you.
one thing I can say, girl, __ love you all the time.

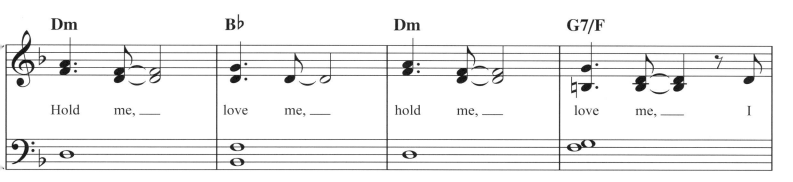

Hold me, __ love me, __ hold me, __ love me, __ I

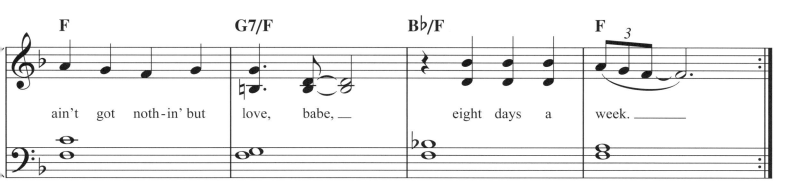

ain't got noth - in' but love, babe, __ eight days a week. __

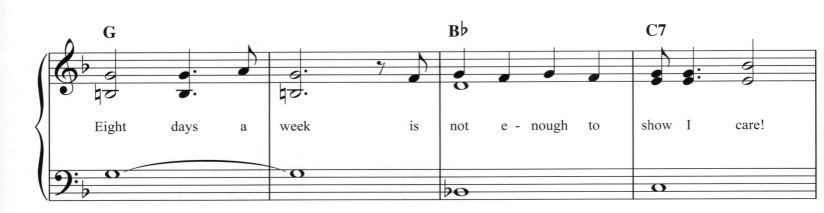

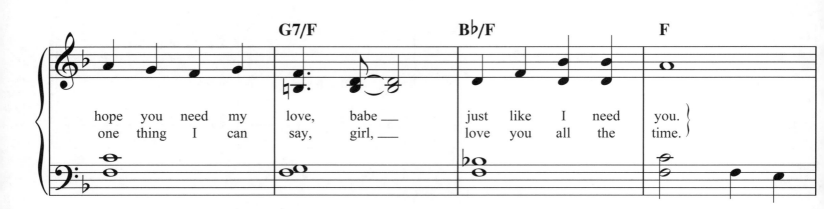

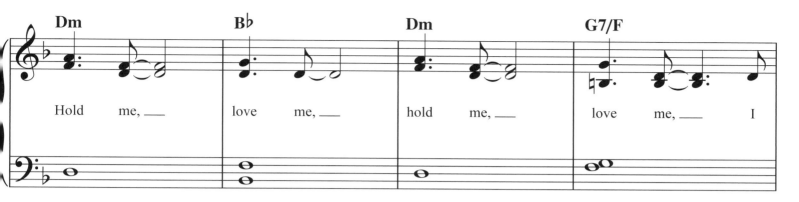

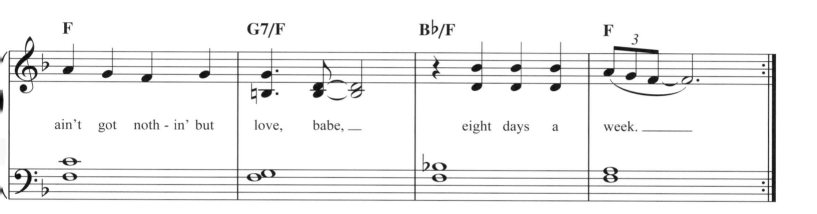

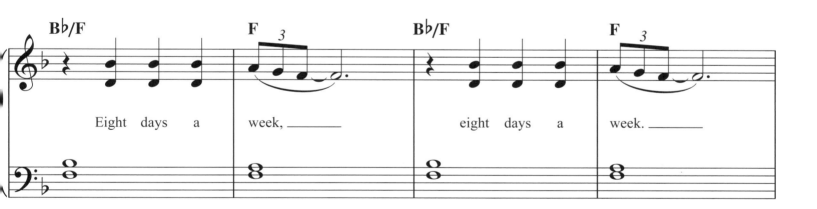

# DAY TRIPPER

Words and Music by JOHN LENNON
and PAUL McCARTNEY

Moderate Rock

Got a good rea - son
She's a big teas - er,
Tried __ to please __ her,

for

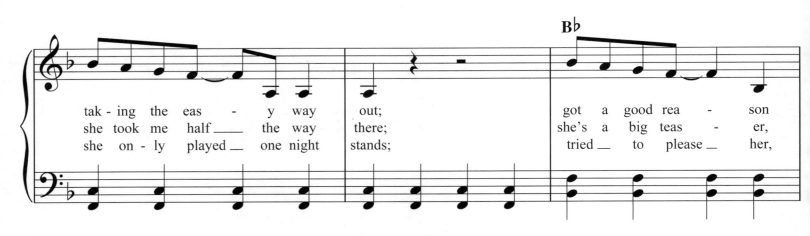

tak - ing the eas - y way out;
she took me half __ the way there;
she on - ly played __ one night stands;

got a good rea - son
she's a big teas - er,
tried __ to please __ her,

for / tak-ing the eas-y way / out, now; she was a
she took me half __ the way / there, now; she was a
she on-ly played one night / stands now; she was a

Day _____ Trip-per, one-way tick-et, yeah! __
Day _____ Trip-per, one-way tick-et, yeah! __
Day _____ Trip-per, Sun-day driv-er, yeah! __

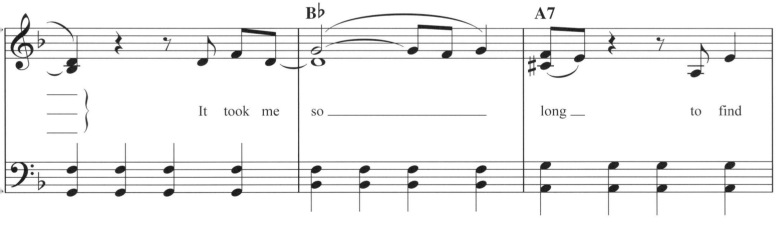

It took me so _____ long __ to find

**To Coda** ⊕

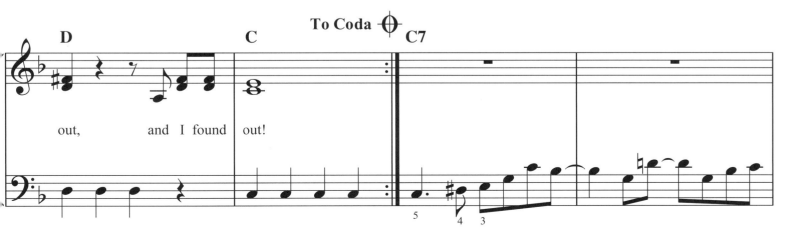

out, and I found out!

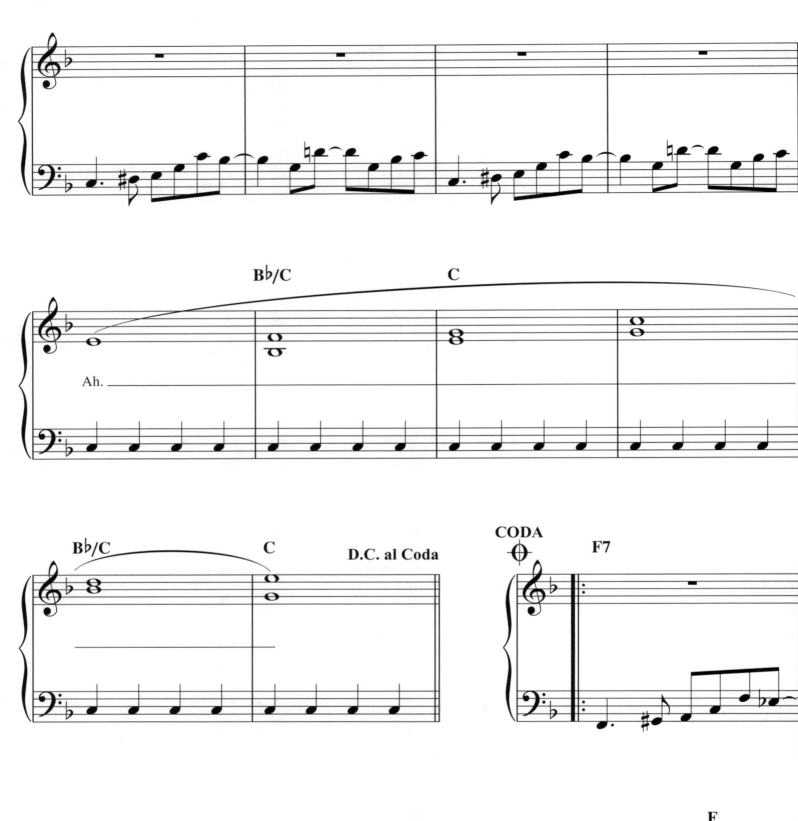

# THE END

Words and Music by JOHN LENNON
and PAUL McCARTNEY

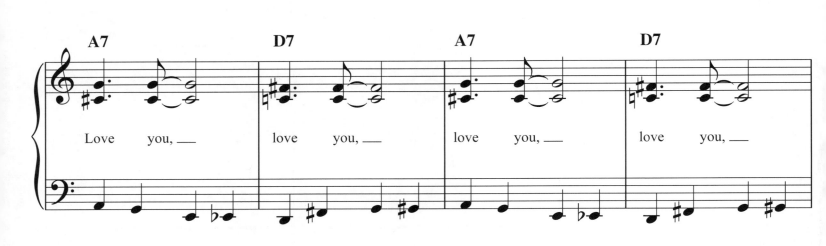

Love you, ___ love you, ___ love you, ___ love you, ___

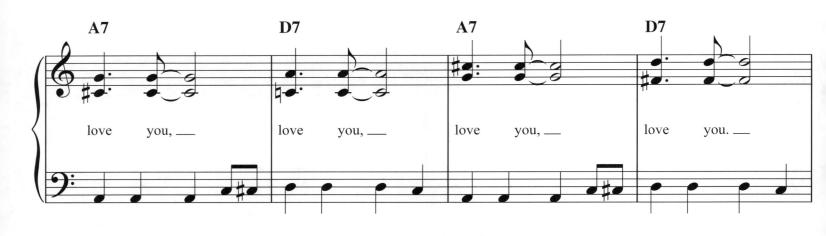

love you, ___ love you, ___ love you, ___ love you. ___

And in ___ the end, ___

# DEAR PRUDENCE

Words and Music by JOHN LENNON
and PAUL McCARTNEY

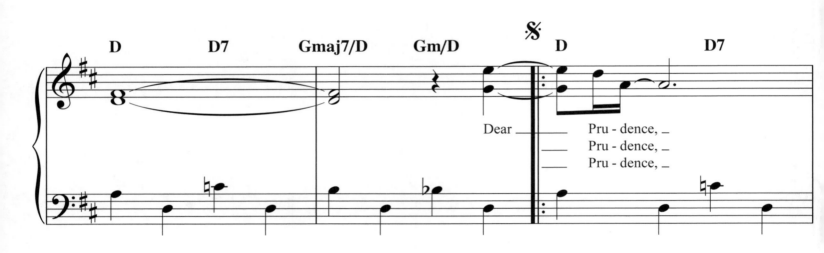

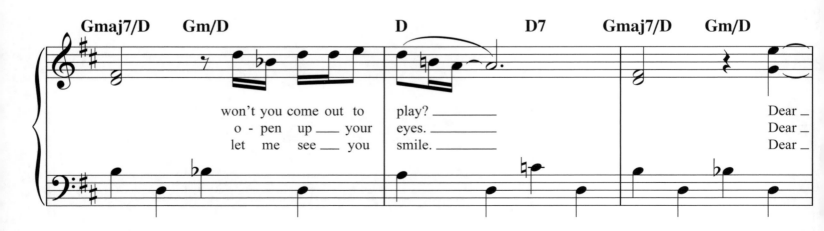

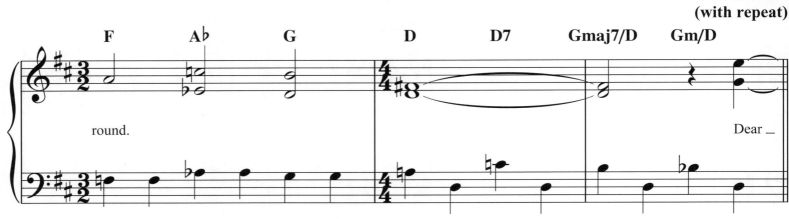

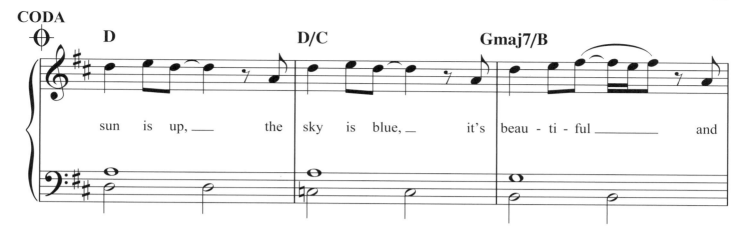

CODA

sun is up, ___ the sky is blue, __ it's beau - ti - ful ___ and

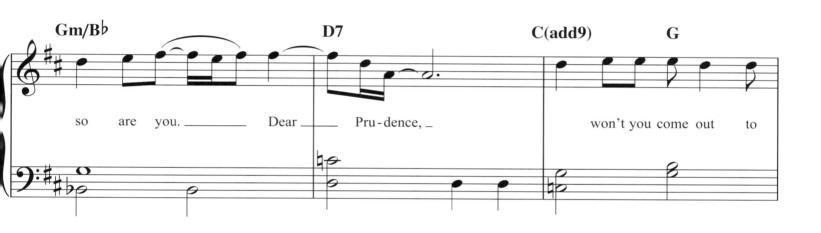

so are you. ___ Dear ___ Pru - dence, _ won't you come out to

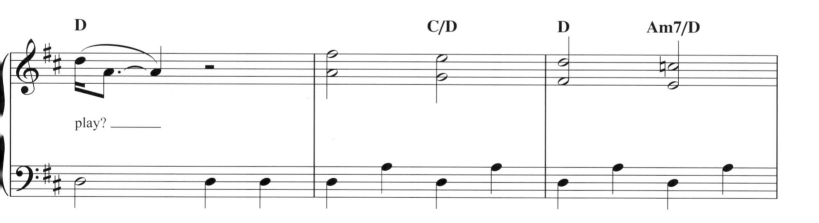

play? ___

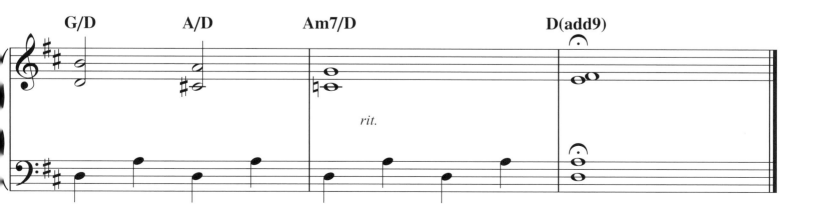

rit.

# DO YOU WANT TO KNOW A SECRET?

Words and Music by JOHN LENNON
and PAUL McCARTNEY

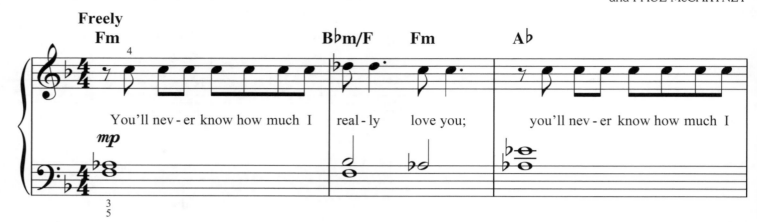

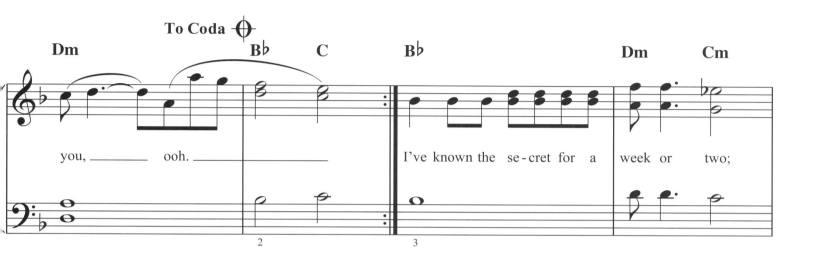

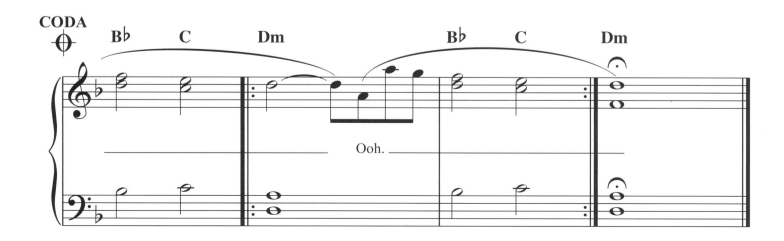

# DRIVE MY CAR

Words and Music by JOHN LENNON
and PAUL McCARTNEY

**Modedrately**

Asked a girl what she want - ed to be. ____
I told the girl what that my pros - pects were good, ____
I told that girl I could start right a - way, ____

She said, "Ba - by, can't you see? ____
and she said, "Ba - by, it's un - der - stood. ____
and she said, "Lis - ten, babe, I got some - thing to say.

I wanna be fa - mous, a star on the screen, __ but
Work - ing for pea - nuts is all ver - y fine, ___ but
I got no car and it's break - ing my heart, ___ but

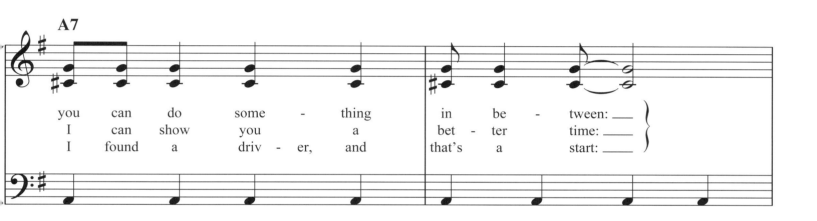

you can do some - thing in be - tween: __
I can show you a bet - ter time: ___
I found a driv - er, and that's a start: ___

Ba - by, you can drive my car. __ Yes, I'm gon - na be a star. _

__ Ba - by, you can drive my car, __ and may - be I'll

Yes, I'm gon-na be a star. ___ Ba-by, you can drive my car, ___

D.S. al Coda

___ and may-be I'll love ___ you.

CODA

play 3 times

Beep, beep, beep, beep. Yeah.

Beep, beep, beep, beep. Yeah.

# ELEANOR RIGBY

Words and Music by JOHN LENNON
and PAUL McCARTNEY

**Moderately, with a steady beat**

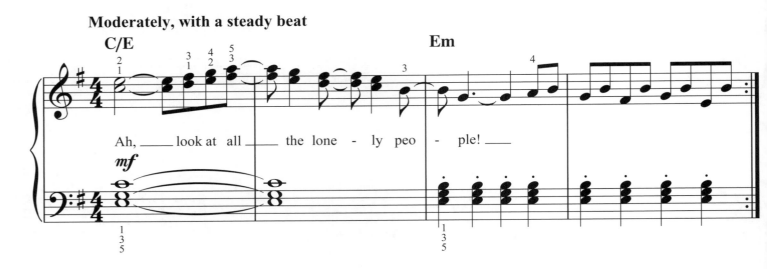

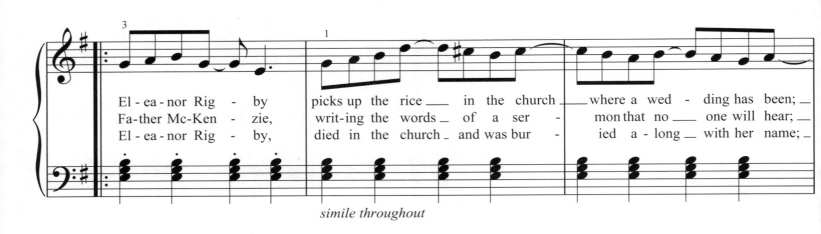

*simile throughout*

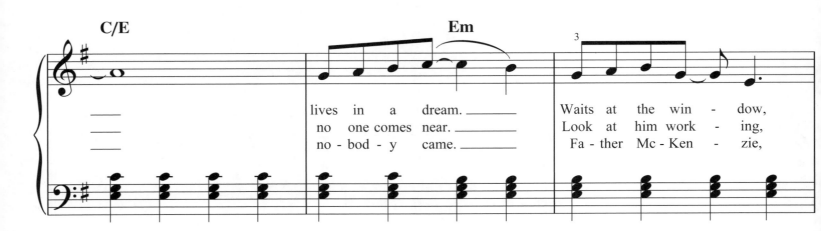

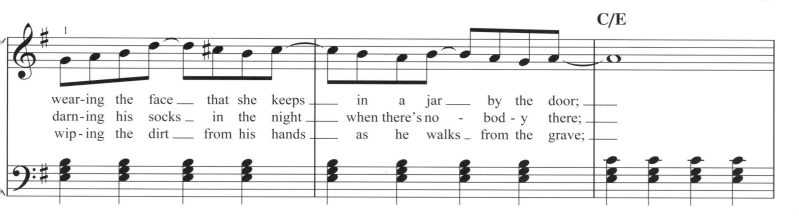

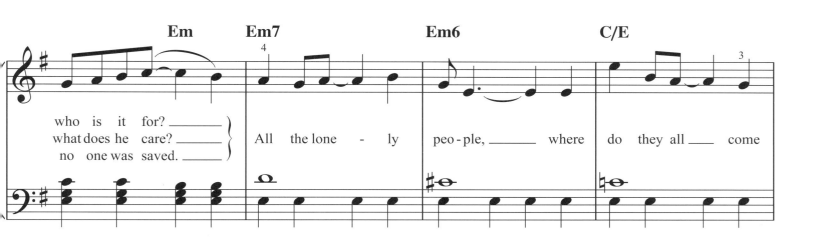

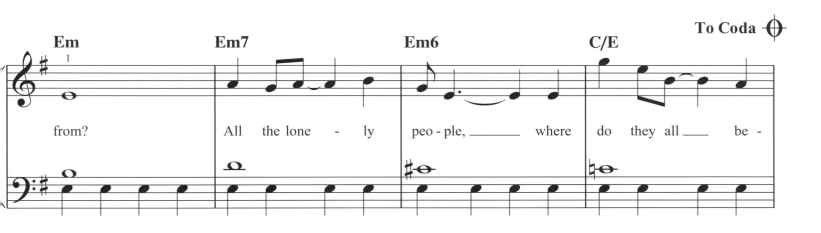

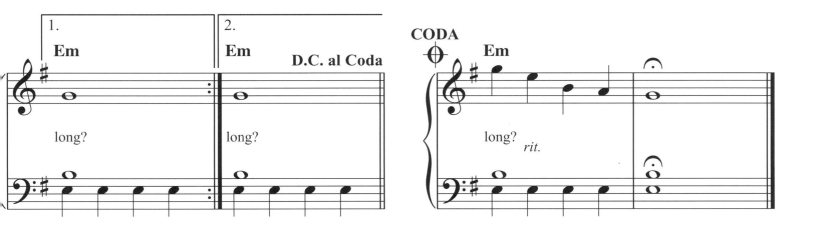

# FIXING A HOLE

Words and Music by JOHN LENNON
and PAUL McCARTNEY

See the peo-ple stand-ing there who dis - a - gree and nev-er win and won - der why they don't get in my
Sil - ly peo-ple run a-round who wor - ry me and nev-er ask me why they don't get past __ my __

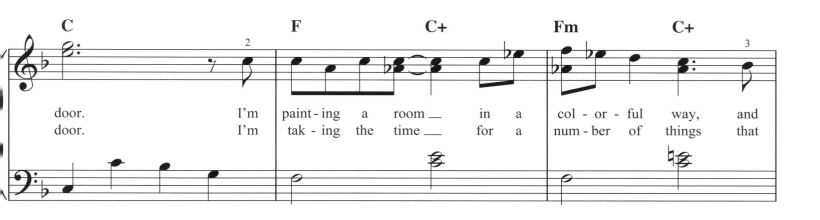

door. I'm paint-ing a room __ in a col-or-ful way, and
door. I'm tak-ing the time __ for a num-ber of things that

when my mind __ is wan-der-ing, there I will go. _____
weren't im-por - tant yes-ter-day, and I still go. _____

Oo oo oo ah ah... And it
oo.

# THE FOOL ON THE HILL

Words and Music by JOHN LENNON
and PAUL McCARTNEY

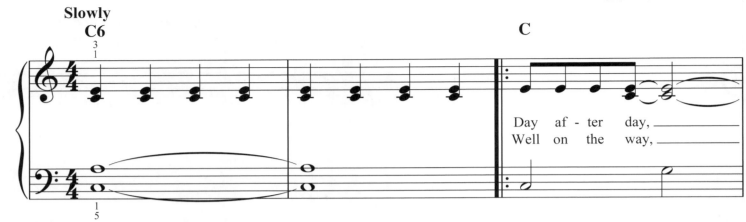

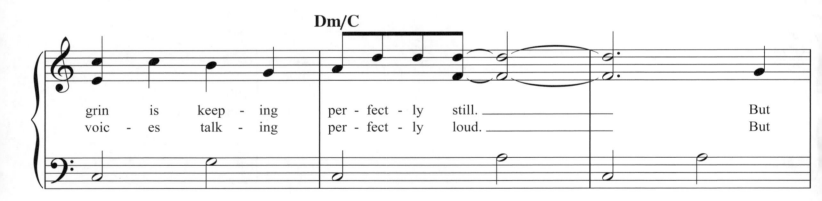

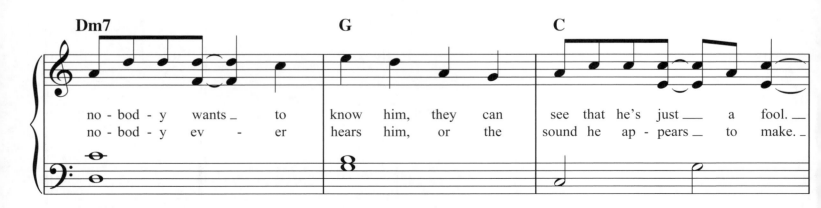

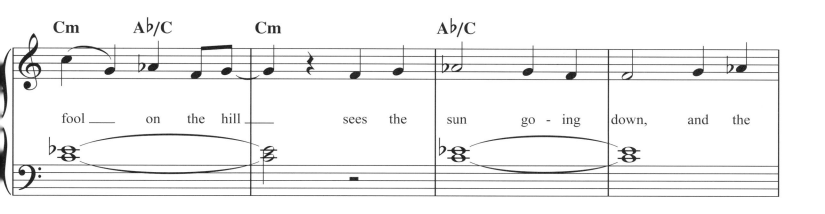

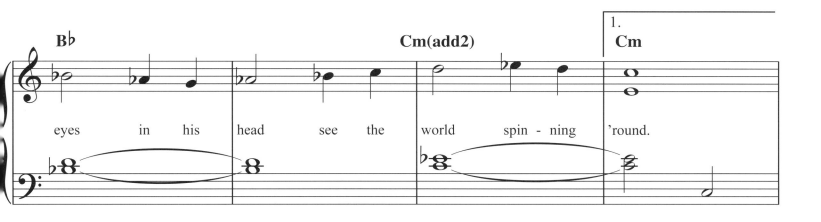

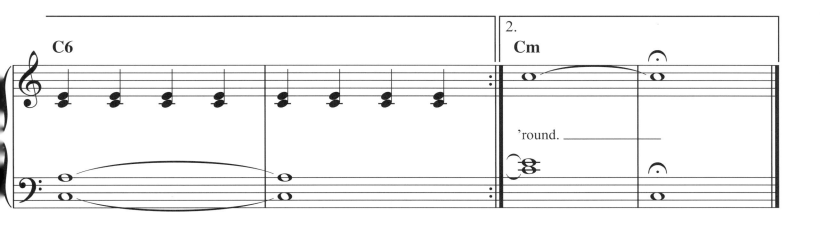

# FOR NO ONE

Words and Music by JOHN LENNON
and PAUL McCARTNEY

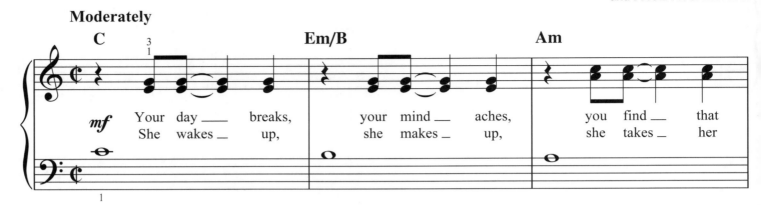

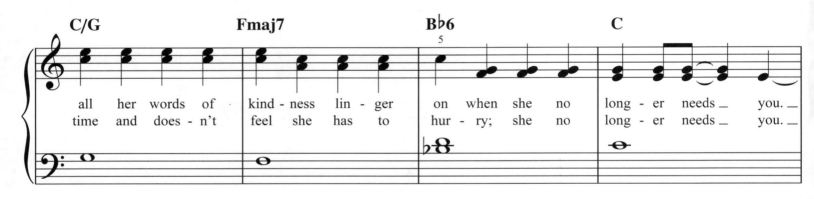

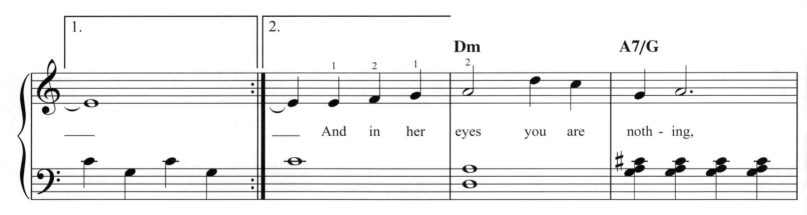

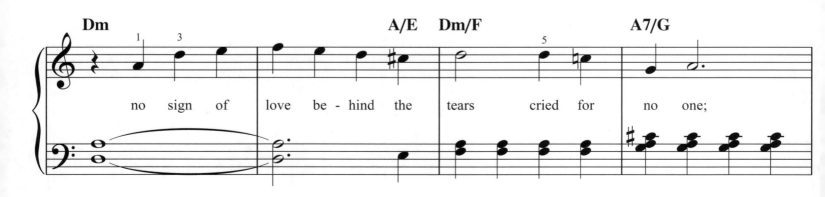

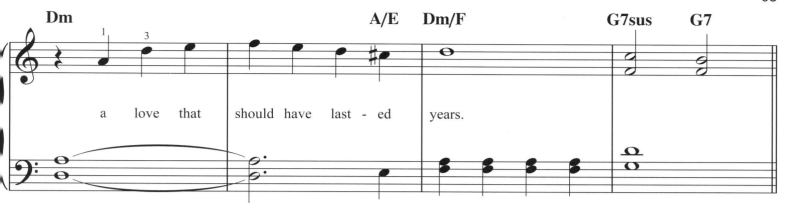

a love that should have last - ed years.

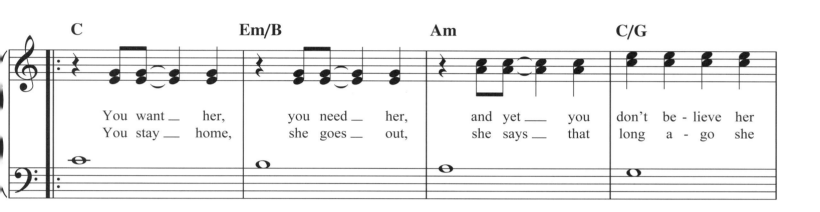

You want ___ her,    you need ___ her,    and yet ___ you    don't be - lieve her
You stay ___ home,    she goes ___ out,    she says ___ that    long a - go she

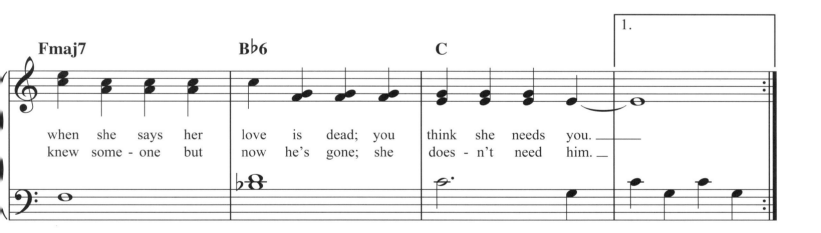

when she says her    love is dead; you    think she needs you. ___
knew some - one but    now he's gone; she    does - n't need him. ___

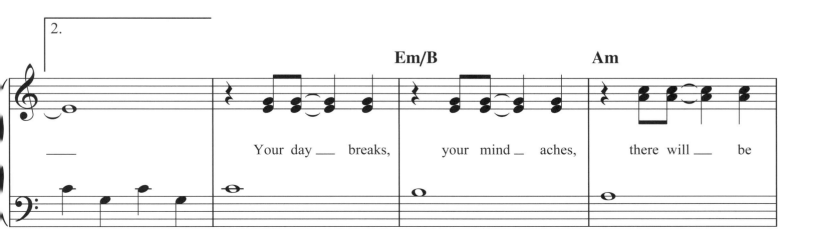

___    Your day ___ breaks,    your mind ___ aches,    there will ___ be

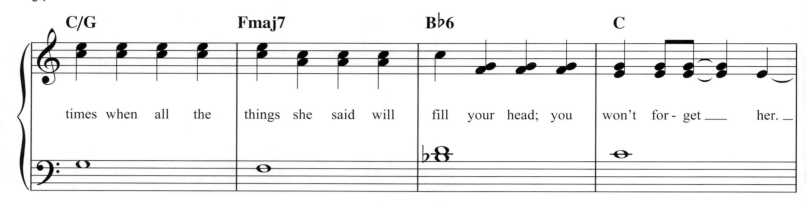

times when all the things she said will fill your head; you won't for-get \_\_\_ her. \_\_\_

And in her eyes you are noth - ing,

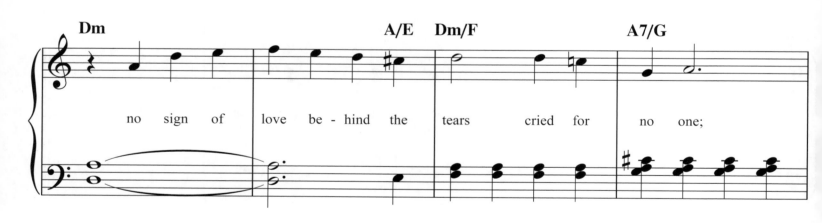

no sign of love be - hind the tears cried for no one;

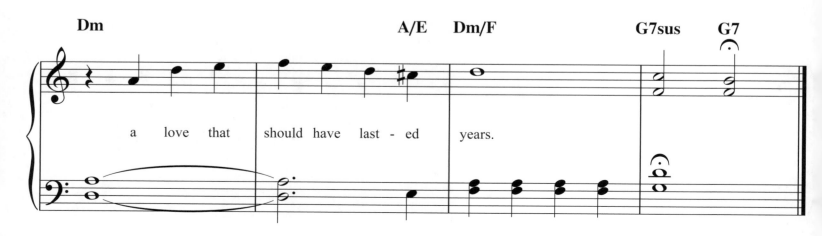

a love that should have last - ed years.

# Good Day Sunshine

Words and Music by JOHN LENNON
and PAUL McCARTNEY

good ____ in a | spe-cial way, | I'm in love, and it's a
good, ____ she knows she's | look-ing fine, | I'm so proud to know that

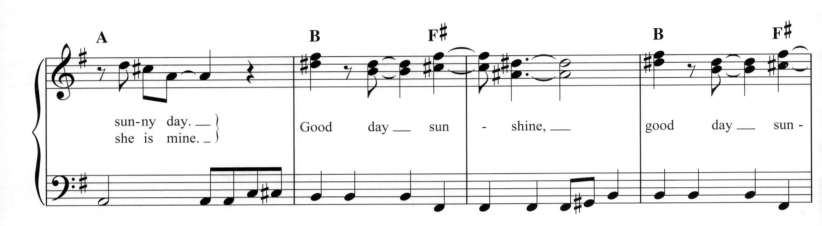

sun-ny day. ____ | Good day ____ sun - shine, ____ | good day ____ sun -
she is mine. ____ |

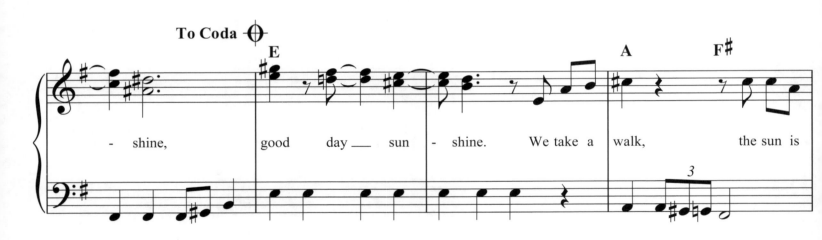

**To Coda** ⊕

- shine, | good day ____ sun - shine. | We take a walk, | the sun is

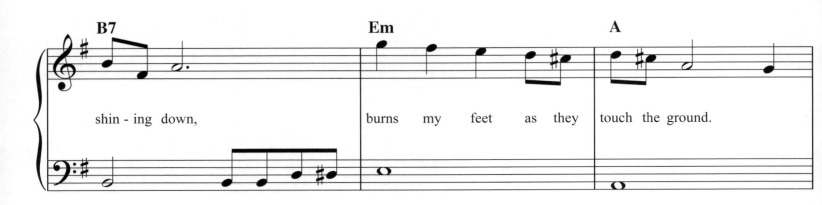

shin - ing down, | burns my feet as they | touch the ground.

D.S. al Coda

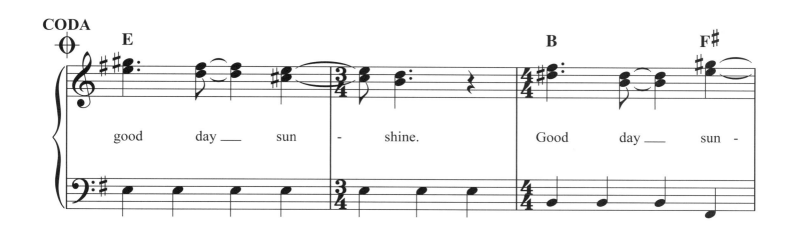

good day ___ sun - shine. Good day ___ sun -

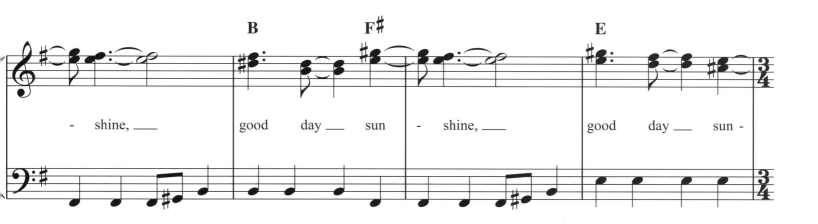

- shine, ___ good day ___ sun - shine, ___ good day ___ sun -

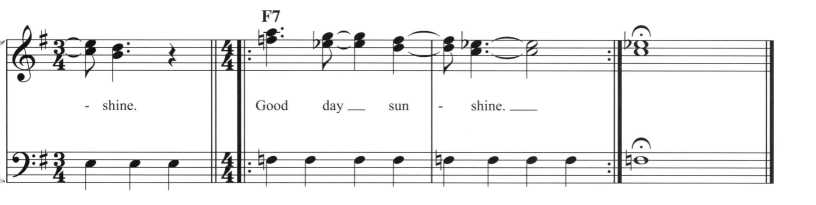

- shine. Good day ___ sun - shine. ___

# FROM ME TO YOU

Words and Music by JOHN LENNON
and PAUL McCARTNEY

**Moderately**

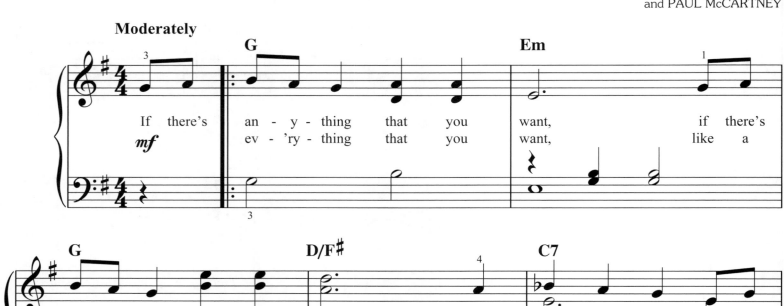

If there's an-y-thing that you want, if there's
ev-'ry-thing that you want, like a

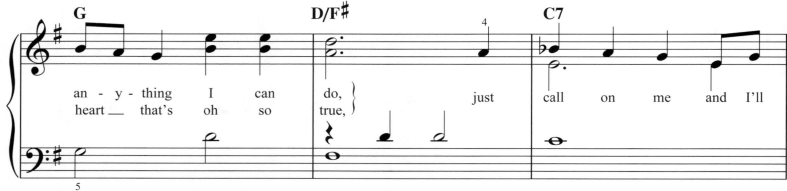

an-y-thing I can do, just call on me and I'll
heart ___ that's oh so true,

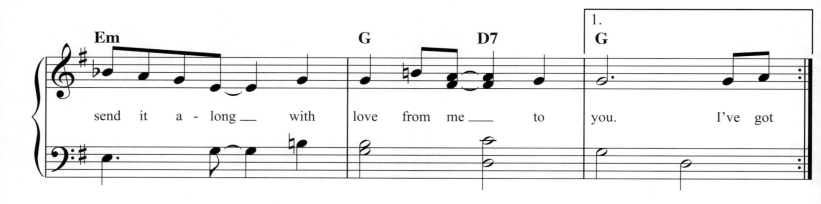

send it a-long ___ with love from me ___ to you. I've got

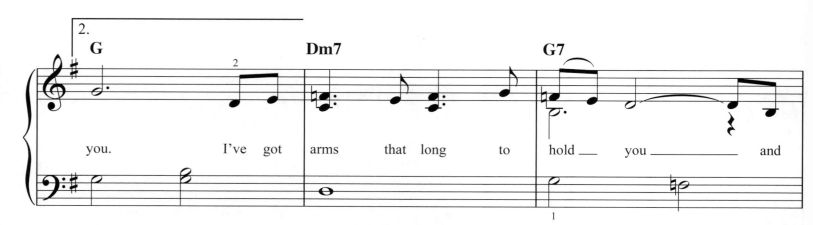

you. I've got arms that long to hold ___ you ___ and

keep you by my side, I've got lips that long to

kiss ___ you and keep you sat - is - fied. If there's

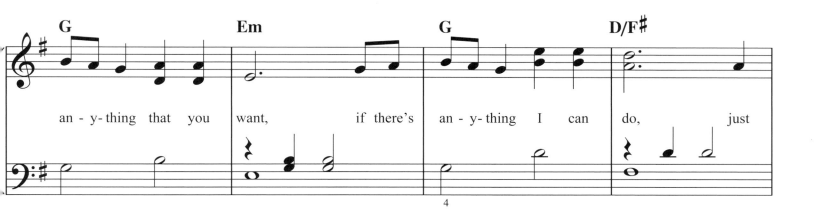

an - y-thing that you want, if there's an - y-thing I can do, just

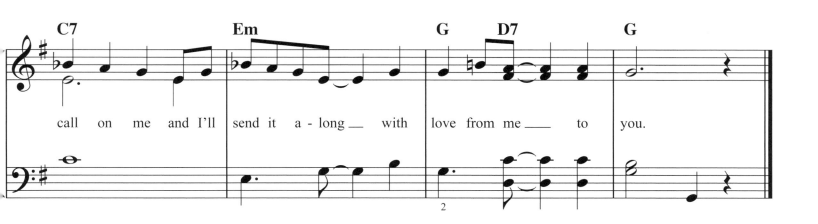

call on me and I'll send it a - long ___ with love from me ___ to you.

# GET BACK

Words and Music by JOHN LENNON
and PAUL McCARTNEY

_____ to where you once be - longed. _____ Get back! _____ Get back! _

_____ Get back ___ to where you once be - longed. _____

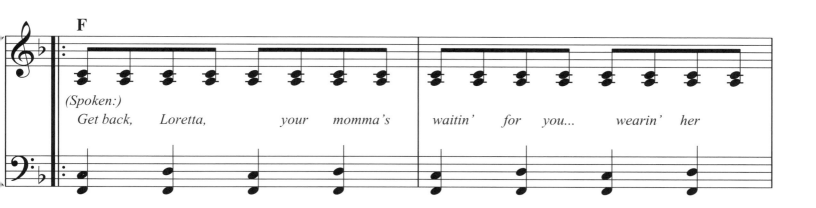

(Spoken:)
Get back, Loretta, your momma's waitin' for you... wearin' her

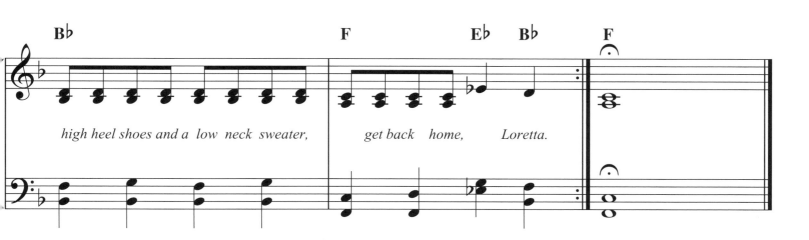

high heel shoes and a low neck sweater, get back home, Loretta.

# GETTING BETTER

Words and Music by JOHN LENNON
and PAUL McCARTNEY

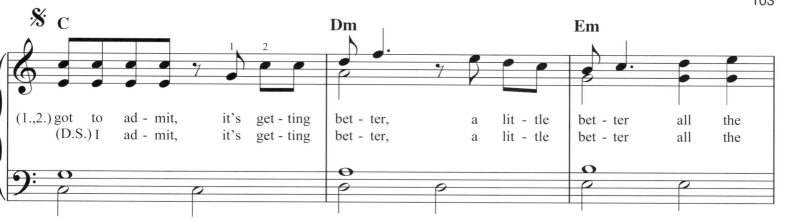

(1.,2.) got to ad - mit, it's get - ting bet - ter, a lit - tle bet - ter all the
(D.S.) I ad - mit, it's get - ting bet - ter, a lit - tle bet - ter all the

time. I have to ad - mit, it's get - ting bet - ter, it's get - ting
time. Yes, I ad - mit it's get - ting bet - ter, it's get - ting

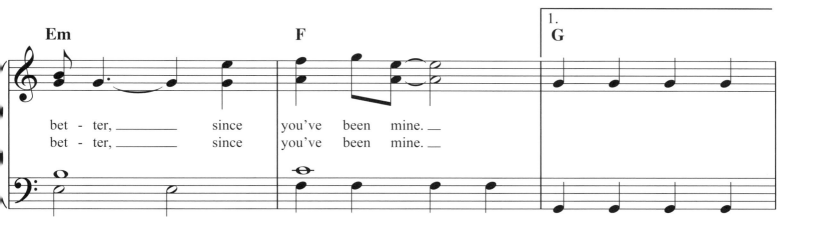

bet - ter, _____ since you've been mine. __
bet - ter, _____ since you've been mine. __

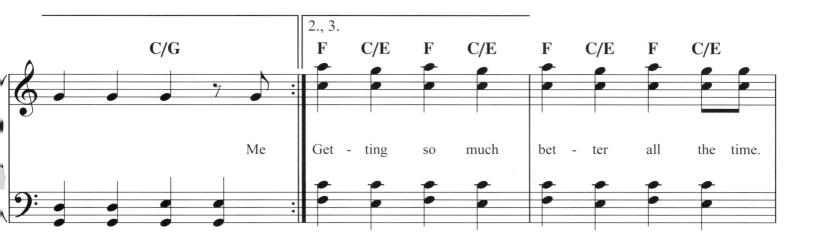

Me Get - ting so much bet - ter all the time.

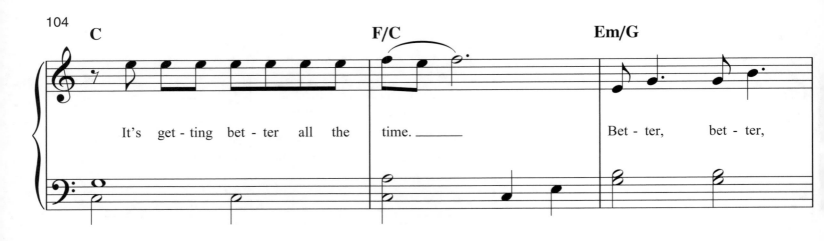

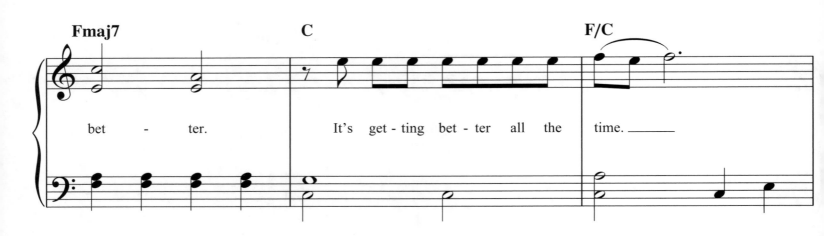

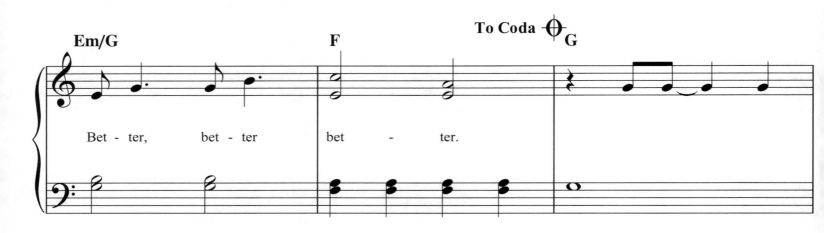

her a - part from the things that she loved.

Man, I was mean, but I'm chang - ing my scene, and I'm do - ing the best that I can.

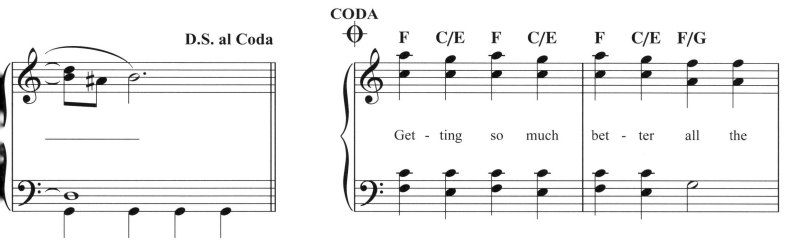

**D.S. al Coda**

**CODA**

F   C/E   F   C/E   F   C/E   F/G

Get - ting so much bet - ter all the

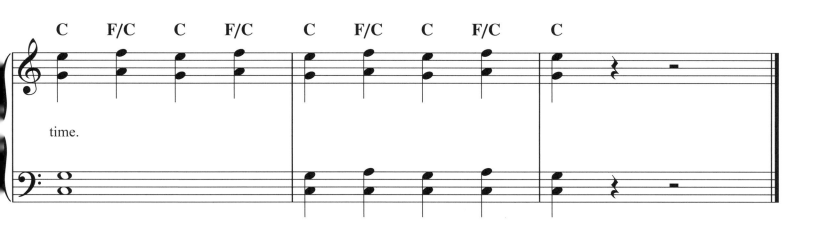

C   F/C   C   F/C   C   F/C   C   F/C   C

time.

# GIRL

Words and Music by JOHN LENNON
and PAUL McCARTNEY

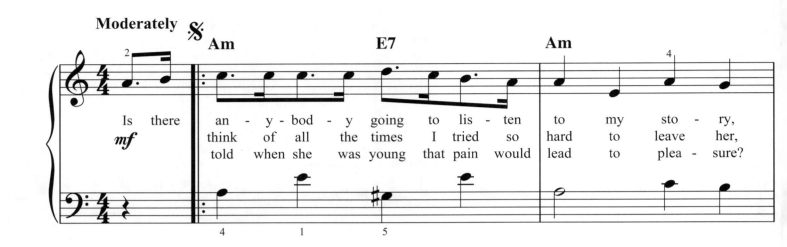

Is there an-y-bod-y going to lis-ten to my sto-ry,
think of all the times I tried so hard to leave her,
told when she was young that pain would lead to plea-sure?

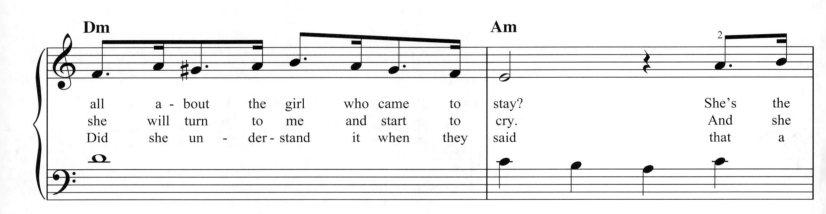

all a-bout the girl who came to stay? She's the
she will turn to me and start to cry. And she
Did she un-der-stand it when to they said that a

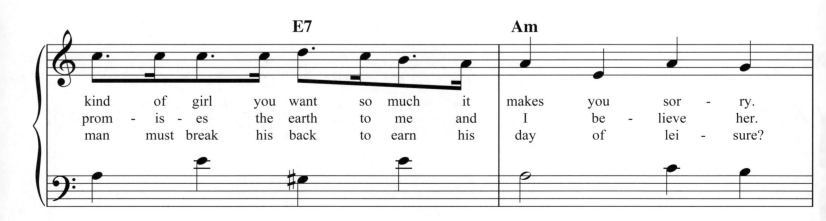

kind of girl you want so much it makes you sor-ry.
prom-is-es the earth to me and I be-lieve her.
man must break his back to earn his day of lei-sure?

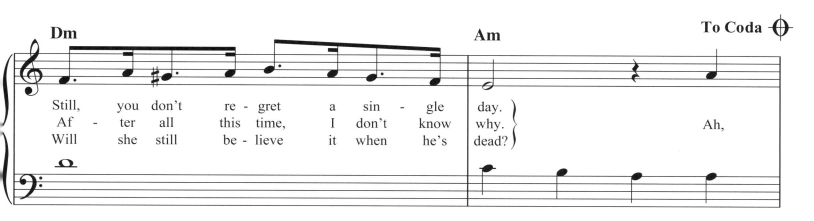

Still, you don't re-gret a sin-gle day.
Af-ter all this time, I don't know why.
Will she still be-lieve it when he's dead?

Ah,

girl, _____ girl, girl. _____

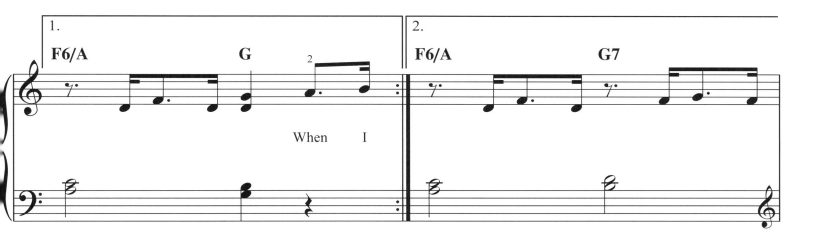

1.

When I

2.

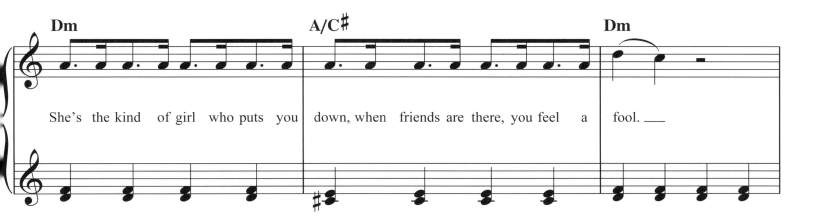

She's the kind of girl who puts you down, when friends are there, you feel a fool. ___

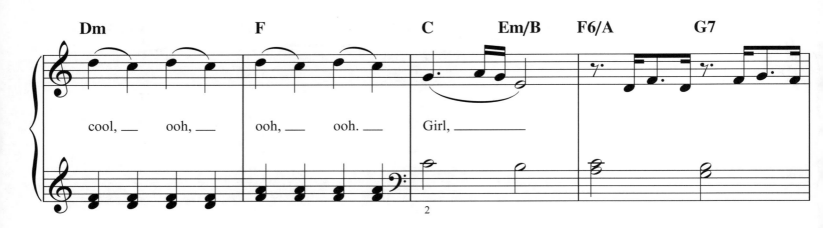

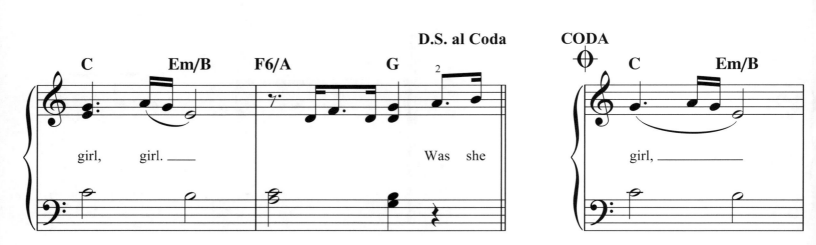

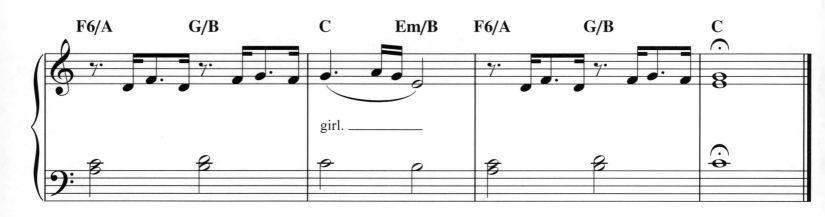

# GOT TO GET YOU INTO MY LIFE

Words and Music by JOHN LENNON
and PAUL McCARTNEY

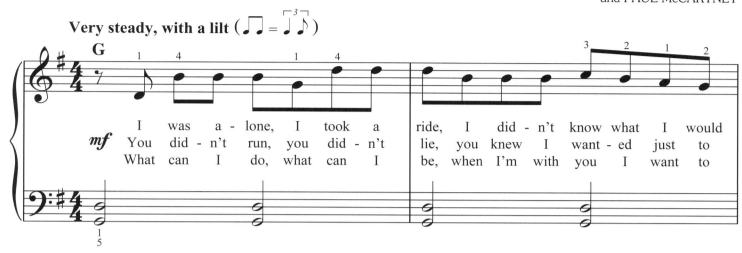

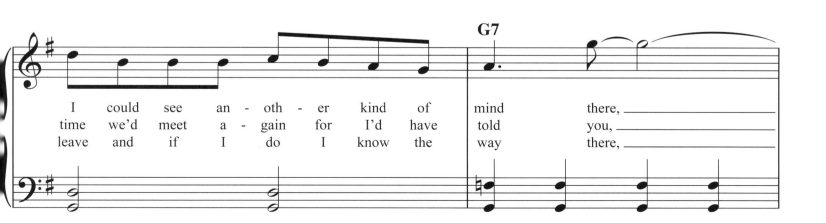

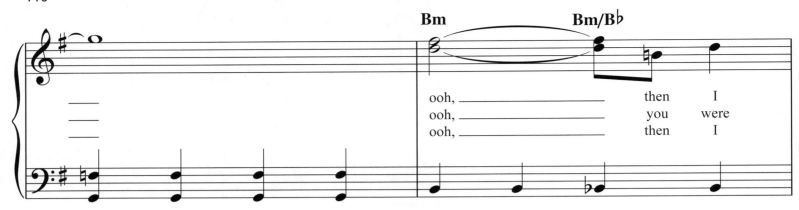

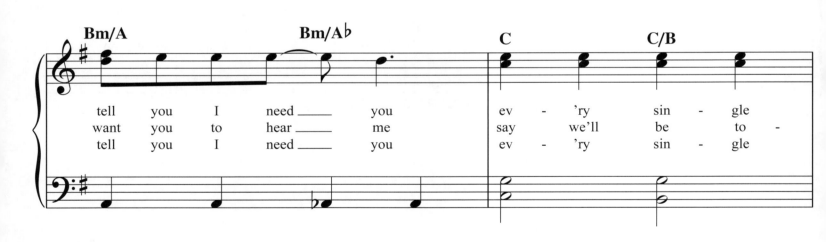

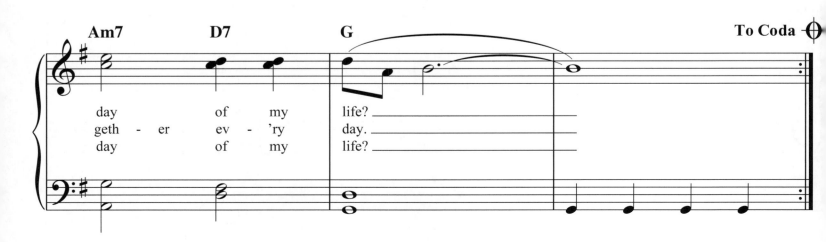

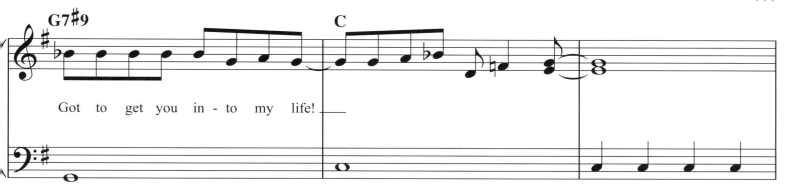

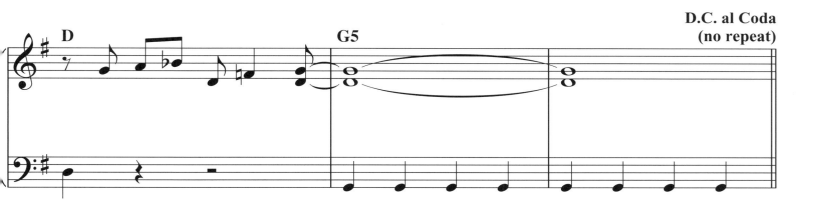

# GOLDEN SLUMBERS

Words and Music by JOHN LENNON
and PAUL McCARTNEY

and I will sing a lul - la - by. _____ Gold - en

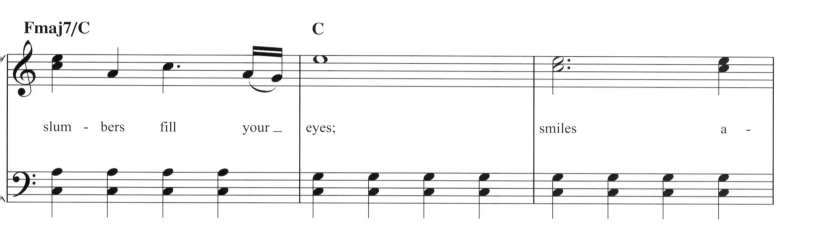

slum - bers fill your __ eyes; smiles a -

wake you when you __ rise. Sleep, pret - ty dar - ling, do not

cry, and I will sing a lul - la - by. _____

# A HARD DAY'S NIGHT

Words and Music by JOHN LENNON
and PAUL McCARTNEY

1.
F

right. You know I

2.
F    Am    Dm

K. When I'm home    ev-'ry-thing seems _ to be

Am        F    Dm

al - right,    when I'm home    feel-ing you hold - ing me

Bb    C    D.S. al Coda

tight.    Yeah! It's been a

CODA
F

right,    you know I

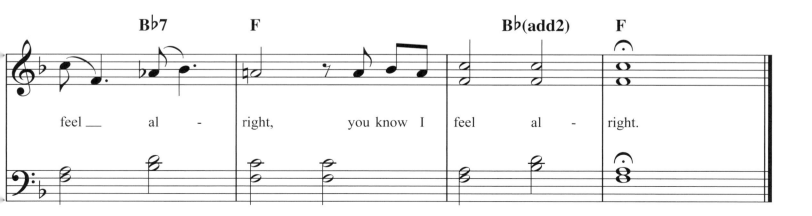

Bb7    F       Bb(add2)    F

feel _ al - right,    you know I    feel al - right.

# HELLO, GOODBYE

Words and Music by JOHN LENNON
and PAUL McCARTNEY

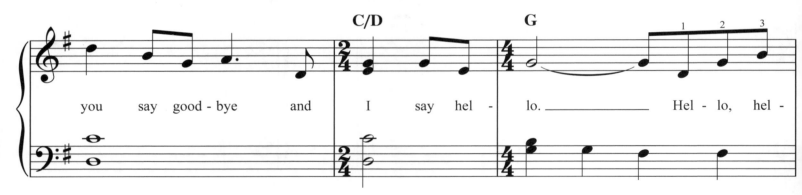

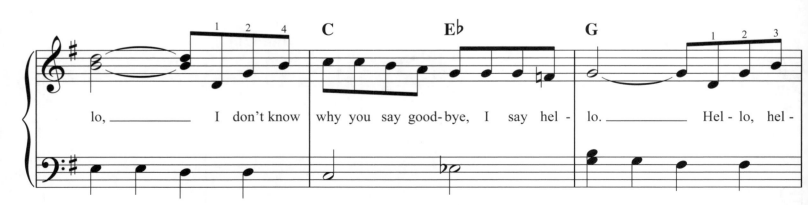

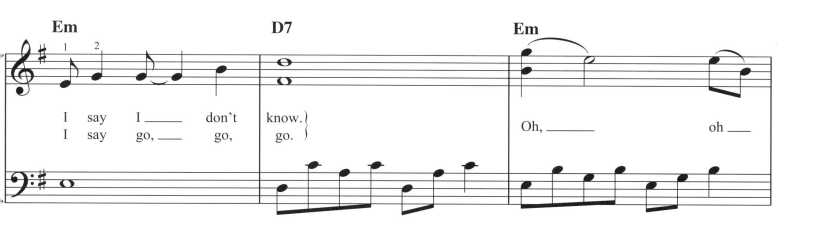

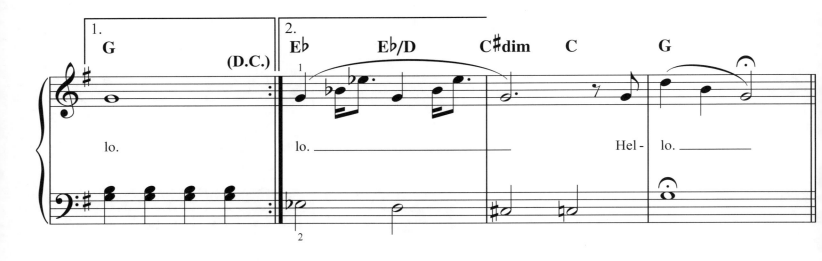

# HELP!

Words and Music by JOHN LENNON
and PAUL McCARTNEY

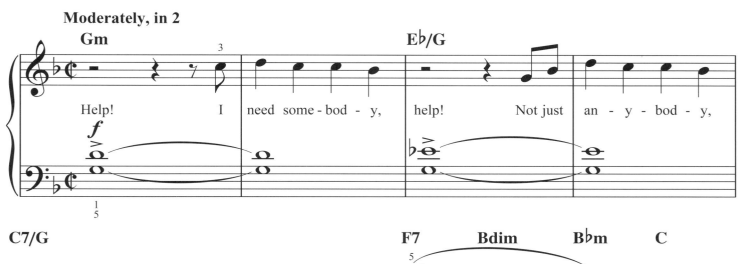

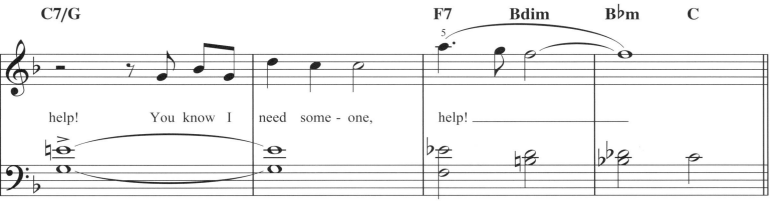

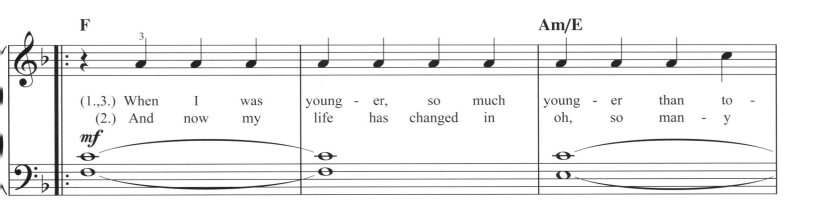

help in an-y way.
van-ish in the haze.

But now these days are gone, I'm
But ev-'ry now and then I

not so self as-sured, _____
feel so in-se-cure. _____

now I find I've
I know that I just

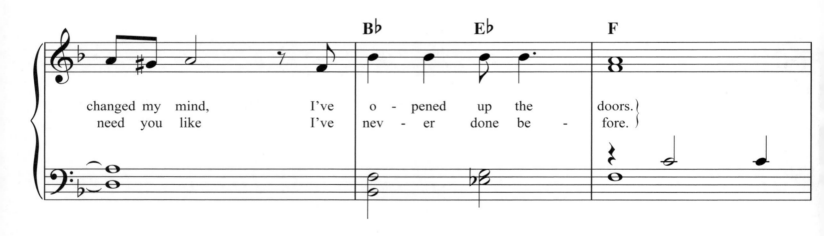

changed my mind, I've o-pened up the doors.
need you like I've nev-er done be-fore.

Help me if you can, I'm feel-ing down, _____ and I

do ap - pre - ci - ate you be - ing 'round. _____

Help me get my feet back on the ground; _____ won't you

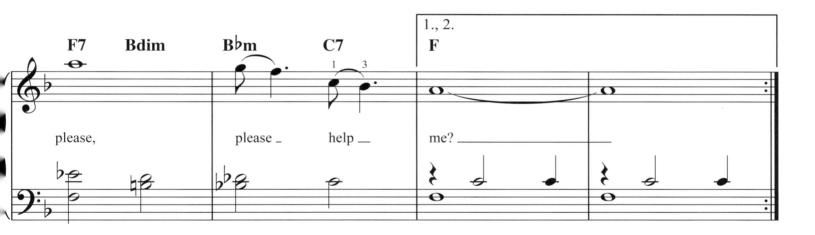

please, please ___ help ___ me? _____

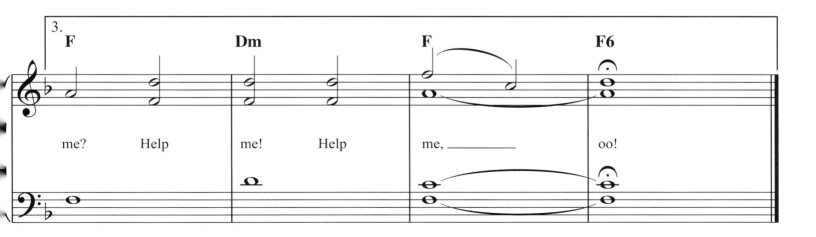

me? Help me! Help me, _____ oo!

# HERE, THERE AND EVERYWHERE

Words and Music by JOHN LENNON
and PAUL McCARTNEY

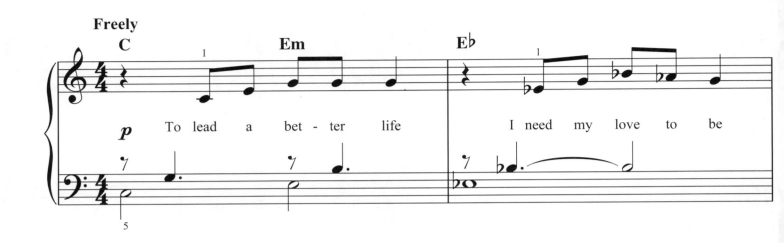

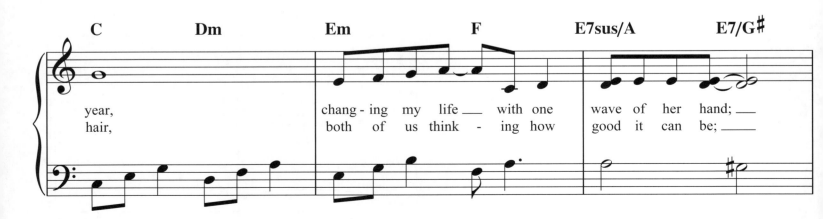

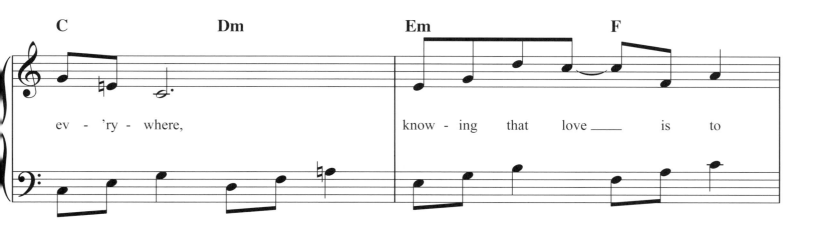

# HERE COMES THE SUN

Words and Music by
GEORGE HARRISON

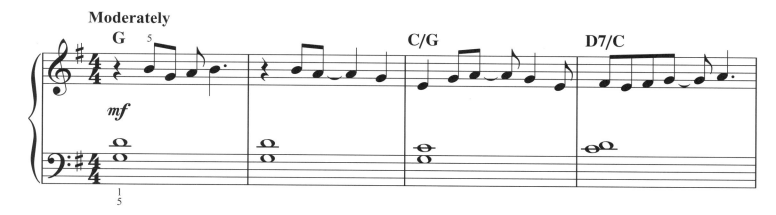

Here comes _ the sun, doo da doo doo. Here comes _ the

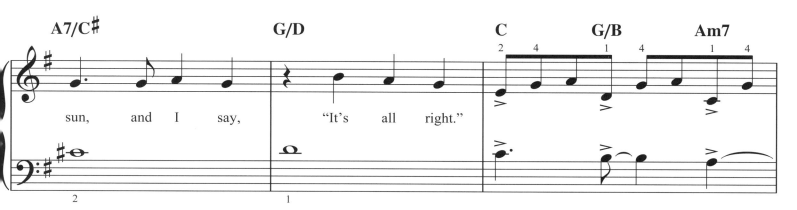

sun, and I say, "It's all right."

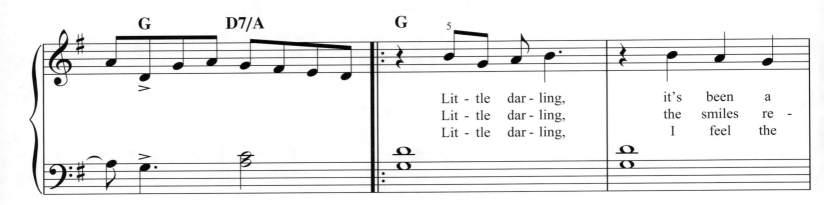

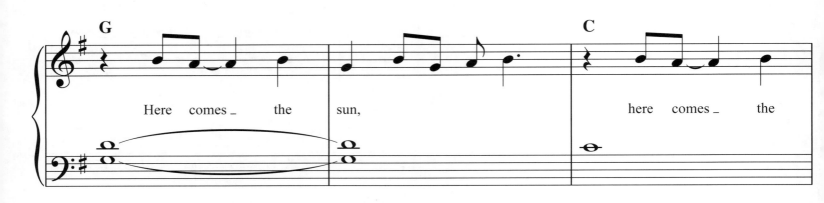

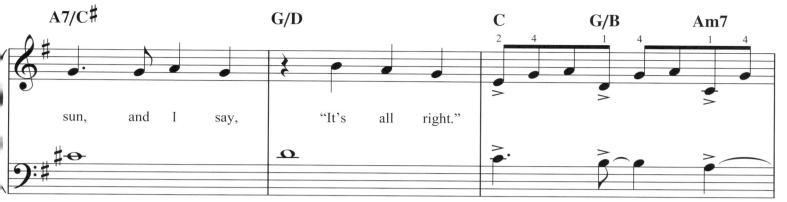

sun,     and I say,          "It's   all   right."

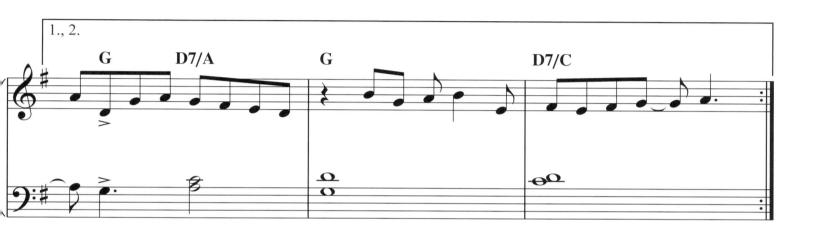

"It's   all   right."

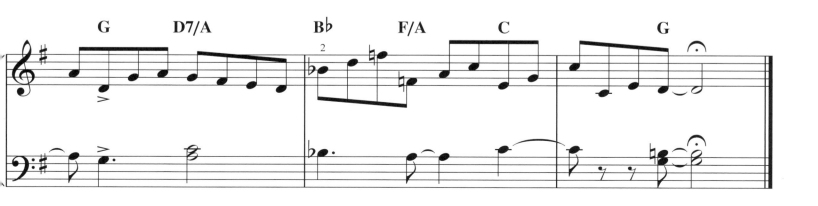

# HEY JUDE

Words and Music by JOHN LENNON
and PAUL McCARTNEY

**Slowly and steadily**

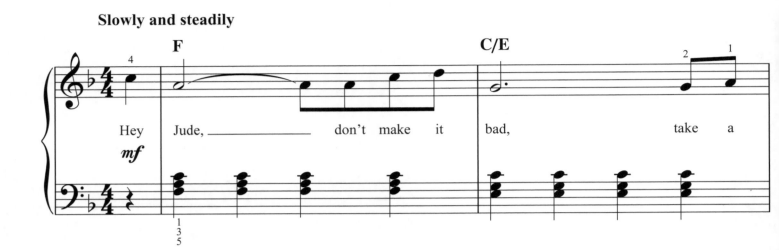

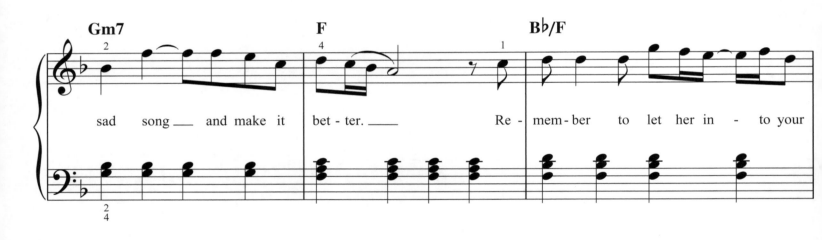

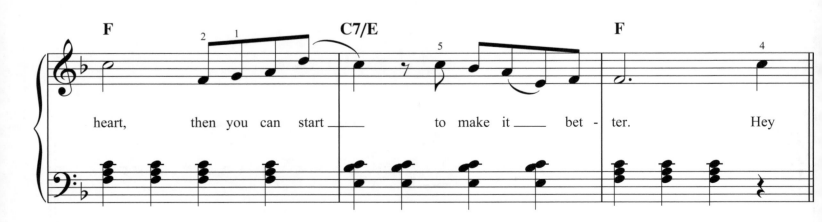

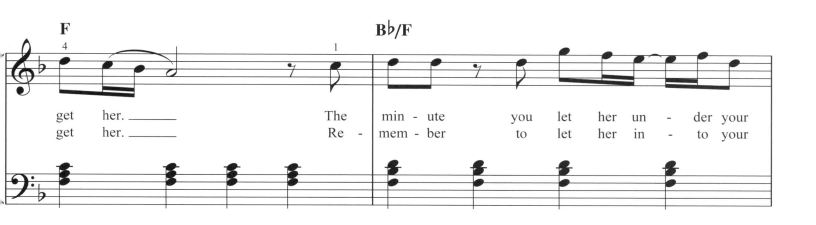

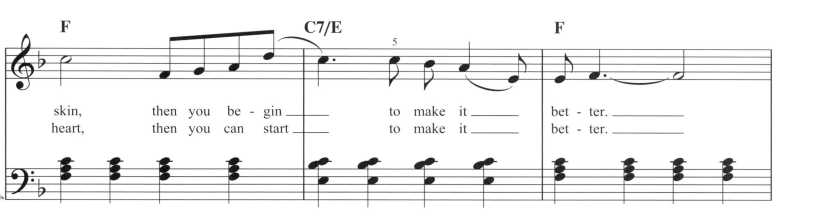

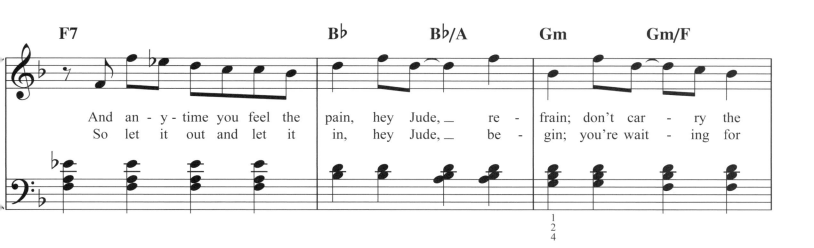

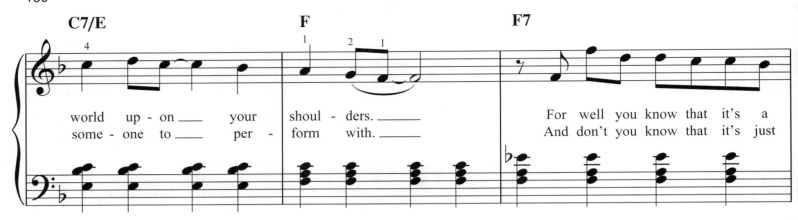

bad,      take a sad song ___ and make it bet - ter. ___     Re -

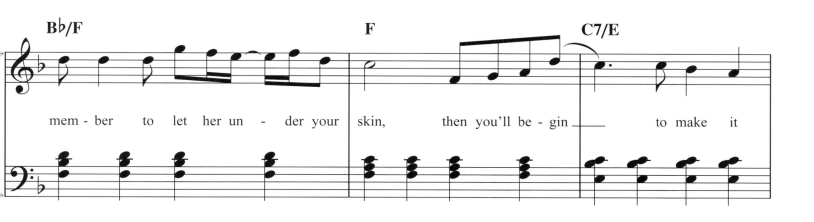

mem - ber to let her un - der your skin,    then you'll be - gin ___ to make it

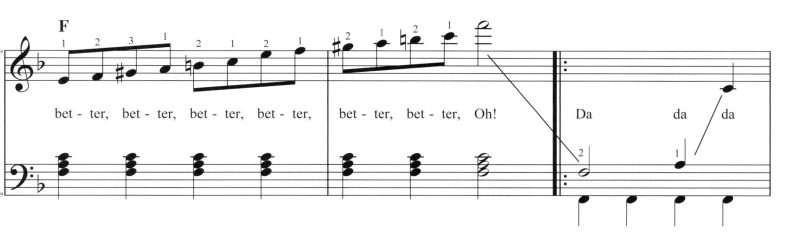

bet - ter, bet - ter, bet - ter, bet - ter,    bet - ter, bet - ter, Oh!    Da    da   da

**Repeat and Fade**      **Optional Ending**

da da da da      da da da da,    hey ___ Jude.

# HONEY PIE

Words and Music by JOHN LENNON
and PAUL McCARTNEY

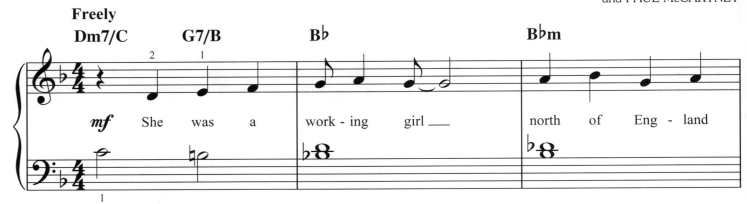

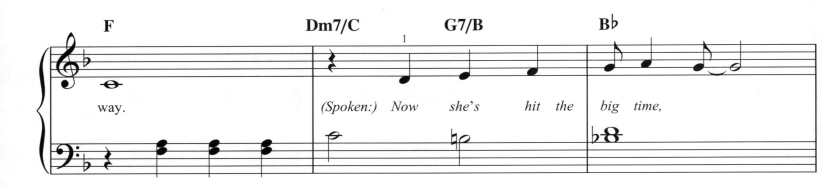

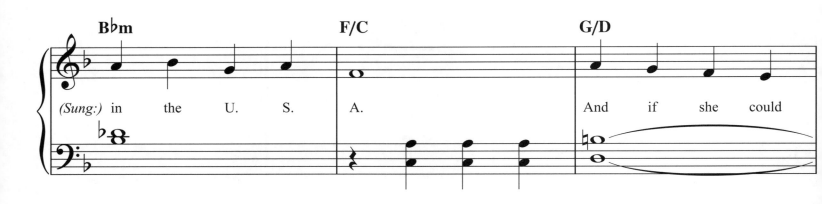

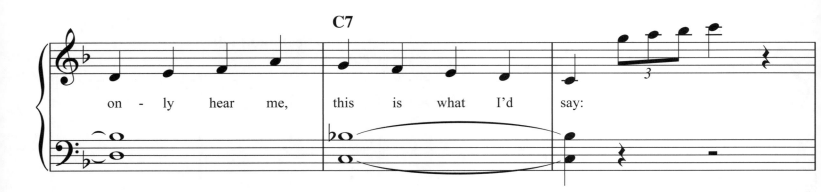

**Medium Bounce**

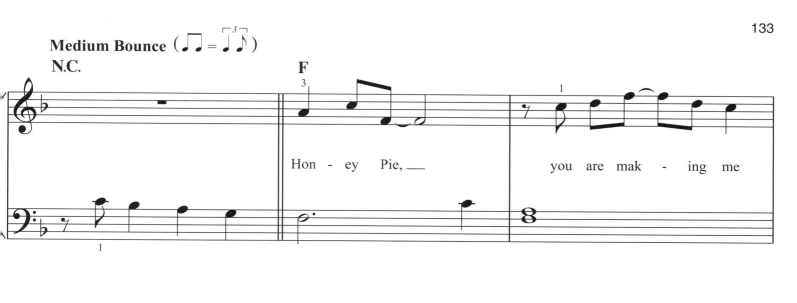

Hon - ey Pie, ___ you are mak - ing me

cra - zy, ___ I'm in love ___ but I'm la - zy, ___

so won't you please come ___ home? Oh,

Hon - ey Pie, ___ my po - si - tion is trag - ic, ___

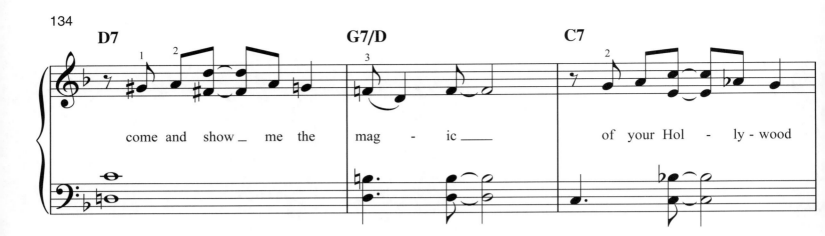

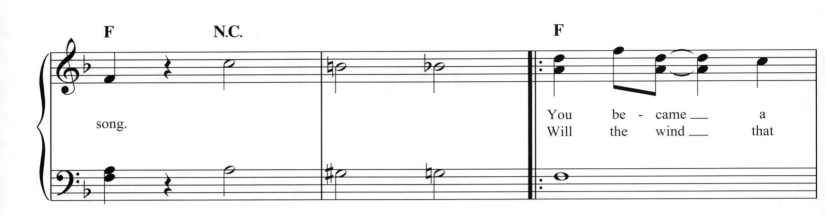

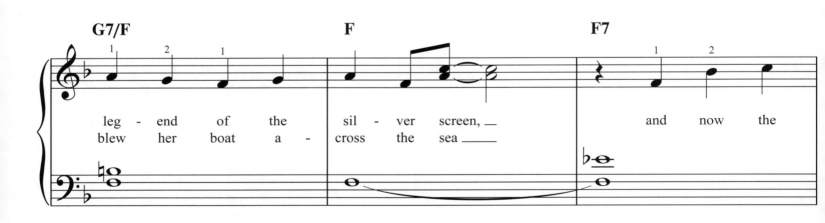

T - T - T - T - Tee! Oh Hon - ey Pie, ___ you are driv - ing me
T - T - T - T - Tee! Now Hon - ey Pie, ___ you are mak - ing me

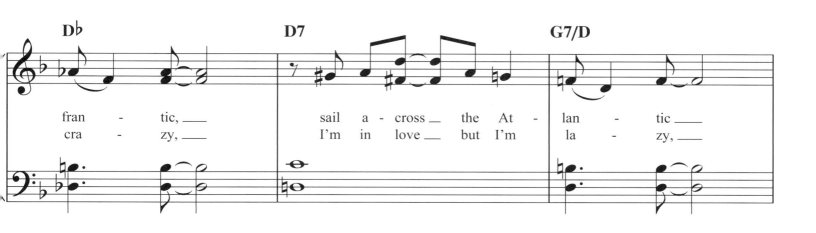

fran - tic, ___ sail a - cross ___ the At - lan - tic ___
cra - zy, ___ I'm in love ___ but I'm la - zy, ___

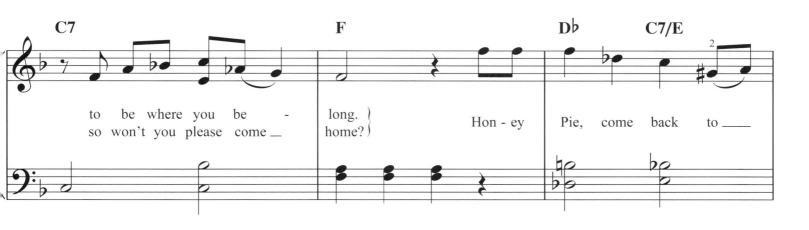

to be where you be - long. ) Hon - ey Pie, come back to ___
so won't you please come ___ home? )

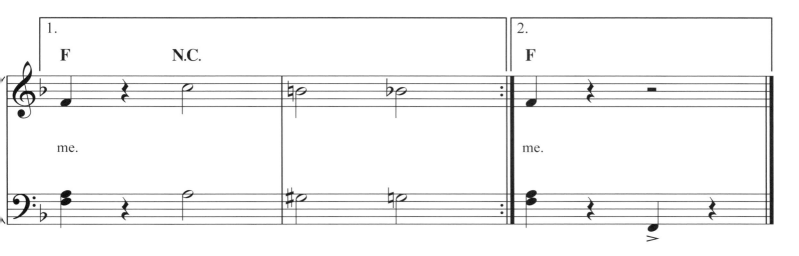

1.
F          N.C.

me.

2.
F

me.

# I AM THE WALRUS

Words and Music by JOHN LENNON
and PAUL McCARTNEY

I am he as you are he as you are me and we are all to-geth - er.
Ex-pert tex pert chok - ing smok - ers, don't you think the jok - er laughs at you?

See how they run, like pigs from a gun, see how they fly. I'm cry - ing.
See how they smile, like pigs in a sty, see how they snied. I'm cry - ing.

Sit - ting on a corn - flake, ___ wait - ing for the van to come.
Yel - low mat - ter cus - tard, ___ drip - ping from a dead dog's eye.
Sem - o - li - na pil - chards ___ climb - ing up the Eif - fel Tow -

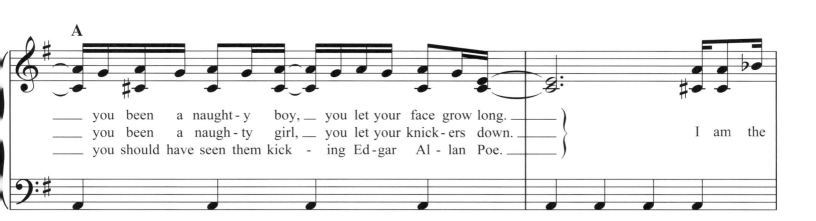

___ Cor - por - a - tion tee shirt, stu - pid blood - y Tues - day man, ___
___ Crab - a - lock - er fish - wife, por - no - graph - ic priest - ess, boy, ___
- er. El - e - men - try pen - guin sing - ing Ha - re Krish - na, man, ___

___ you been a naught - y boy, ___ you let your face grow long. ___
___ you been a naugh - ty girl, ___ you let your knick - ers down. I am the
___ you should have seen them kick - ing Ed - gar Al - lan Poe. ___

To Coda

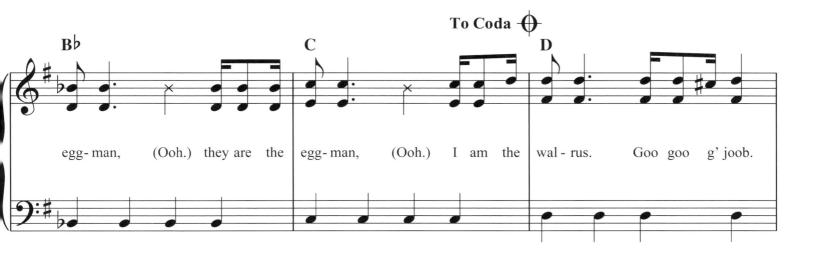

egg - man, (Ooh.) they are the egg - man, (Ooh.) I am the wal - rus. Goo goo g'joob.

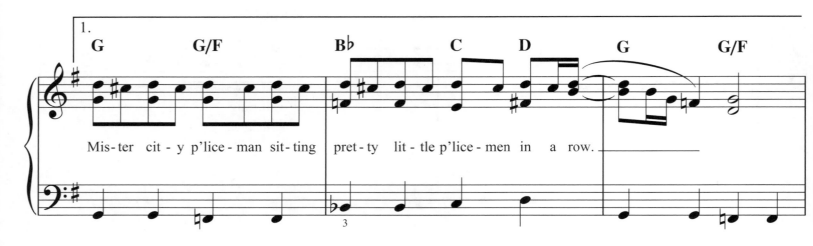

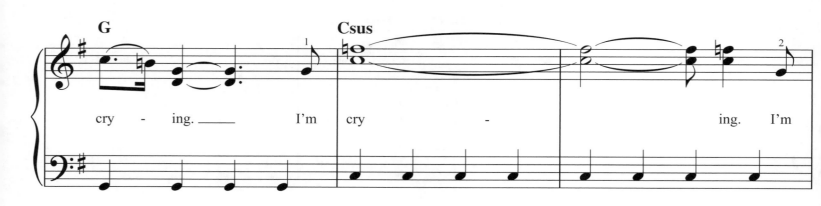

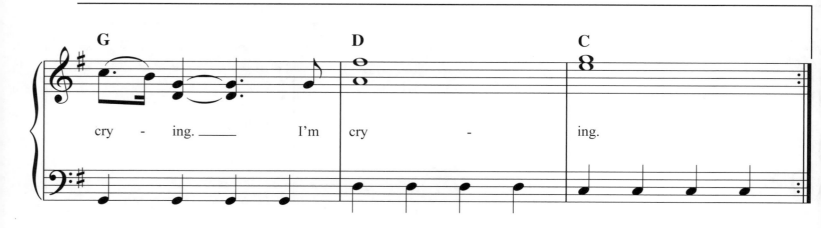

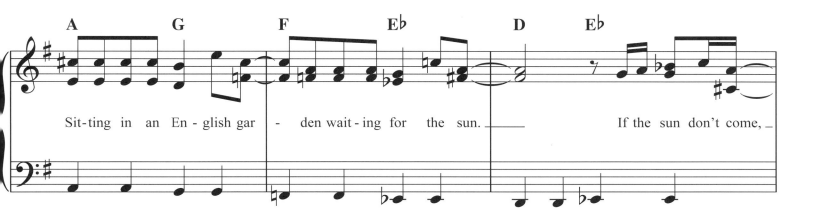

Sit-ting in an En - glish gar - den wait-ing for the sun. _____ If the sun don't come, _____

_____ you get a tan from stand - ing in the En - glish rain. _____ I am the

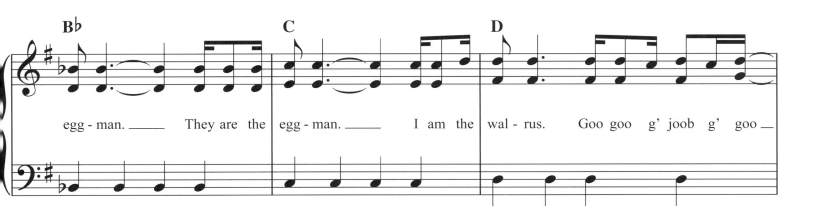

egg - man. _____ They are the egg - man. _____ I am the wal - rus. Goo goo g' joob g' goo _____

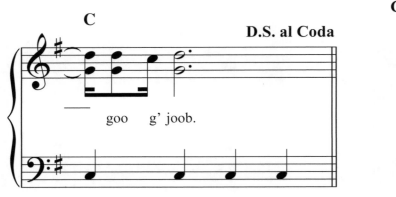

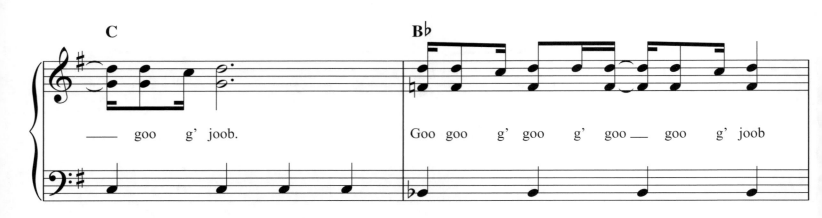

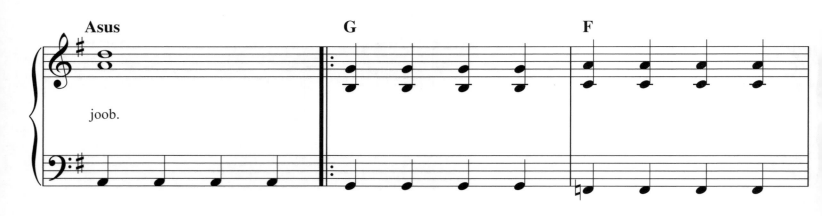

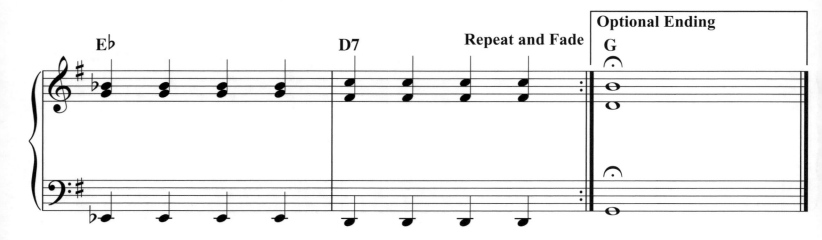

# I WANT TO HOLD YOUR HAND

Words and Music by JOHN LENNON
and PAUL McCARTNEY

**With a steady Rock beat**

hand.　　　　　　　And when I touch you I feel hap - py in -

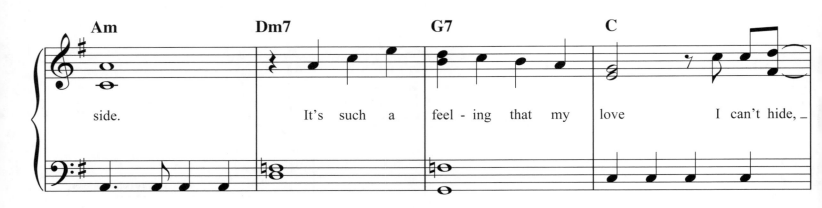

side.　　　　It's such a feel - ing that my love I can't hide, ＿

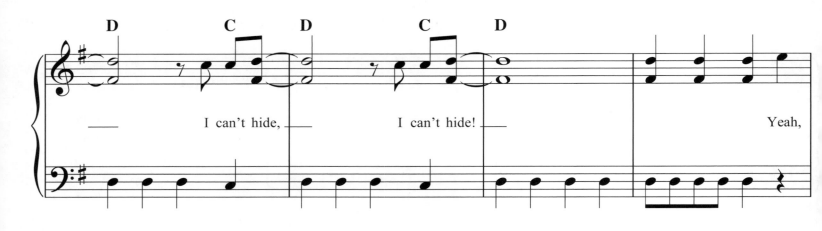

＿　I can't hide, ＿　I can't hide! ＿　　　　　Yeah,

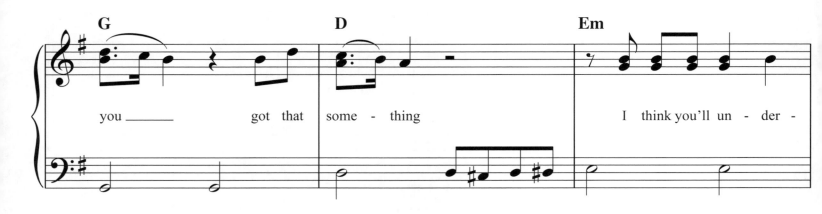

you ＿＿＿ got that some - thing　　　I think you'll un - der -

stand.    When    I _____  { say / feel } that   some - thing,

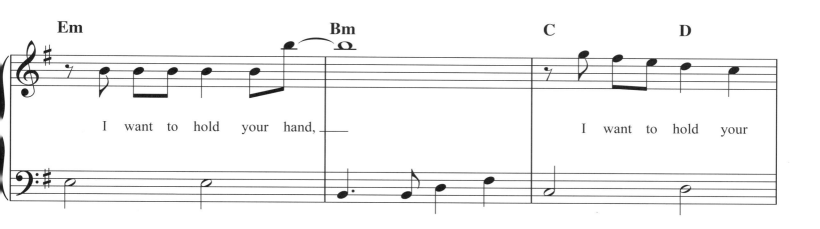

I  want  to  hold   your   hand, _____       I   want  to  hold   your

hand, _____    I  want  to  hold  your   hand.      I  want  to  hold  your

hand,         I  want  to  hold  your   hand.

# I FEEL FINE

Words and Music by JOHN LENNON
and PAUL McCARTNEY

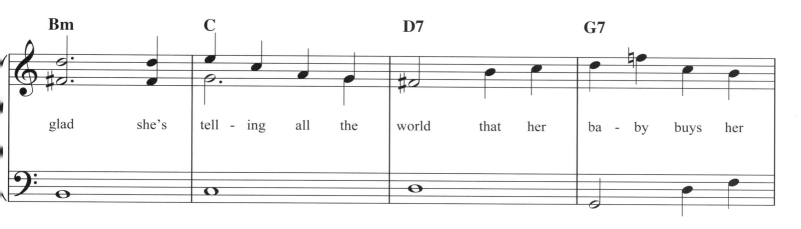

glad she's tell - ing all the world that her ba - by buys her

things, you know, ___ he buys her dia - mond rings, you know, ___ she said so. ___

___ She's in love with me and I ___ feel

fine. ___

# I SAW HER STANDING THERE

Words and Music by JOHN LENNON
and PAUL McCARTNEY

with an - oth - er, woo, when I saw her
with an - oth - er, woo, when I saw her

stand - ing there? Well, she —
stand - ing there. Well, my

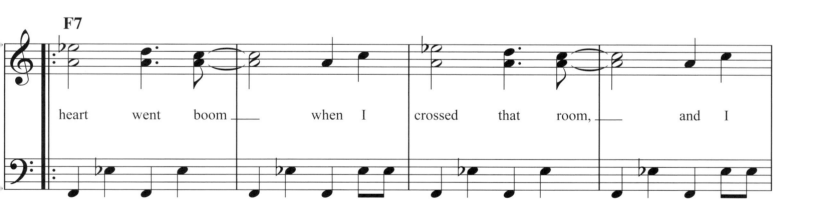

heart went boom — when I crossed that room, — and I

held her hand — in mine, —

mine. _____ Oh, we danced ____ through the night ____

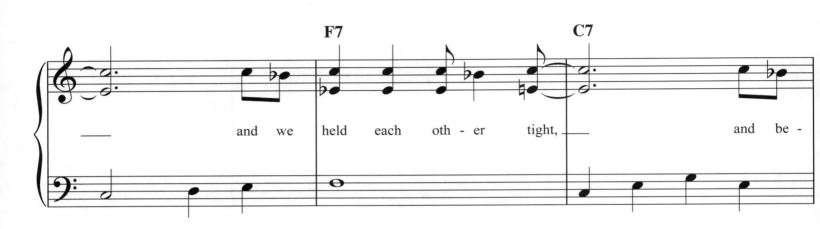

____ and we held each oth - er tight, ____ and be -

fore too long __ I fell ____ in love with her. ____ Now

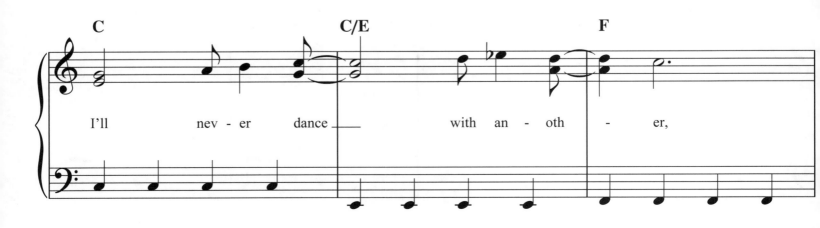

I'll nev - er dance ____ with an - oth - er,

# I SHOULD HAVE KNOWN BETTER

Words and Music by JOHN LENNON
and PAUL McCARTNEY

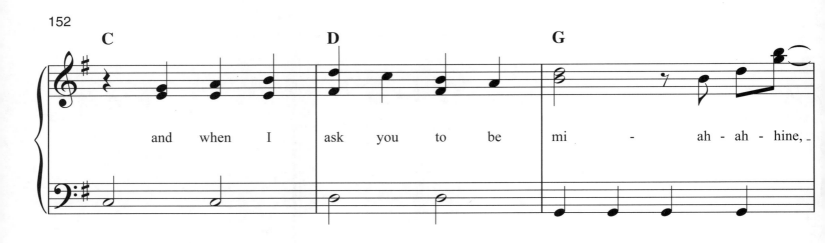

and when I ask you to be mi - ah - ah - hine,

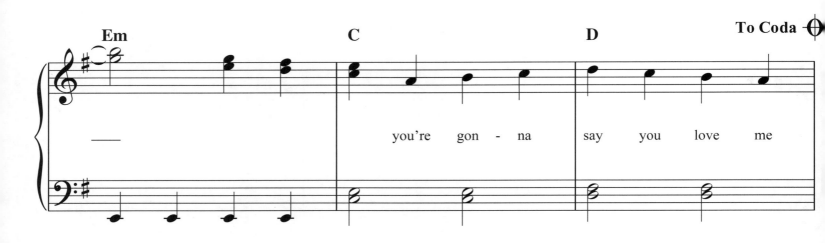

you're gon - na say you love me

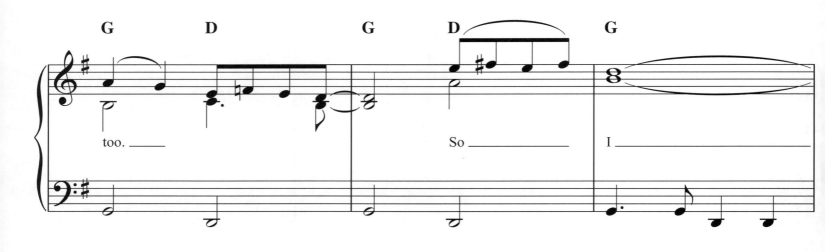

too. So I

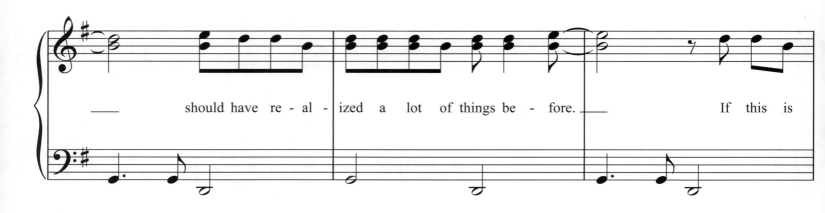

should have re - al - ized a lot of things be - fore. If this is

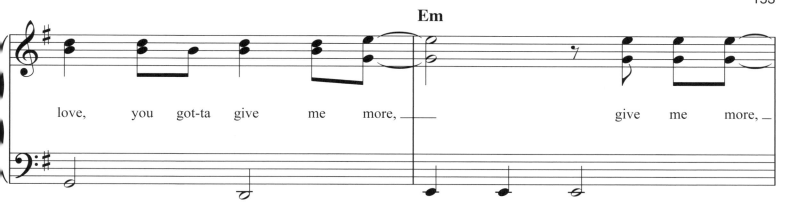

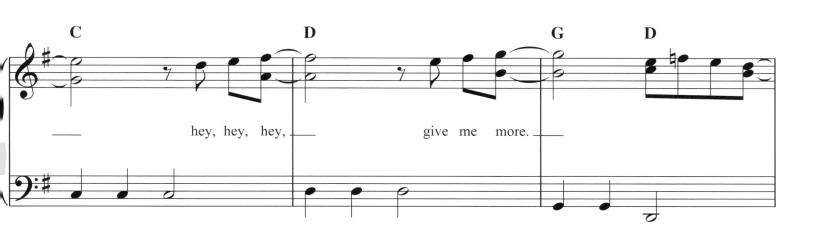

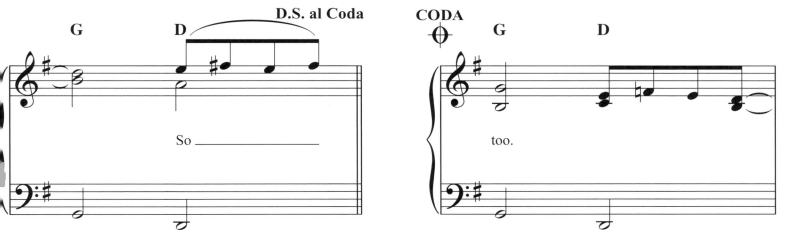

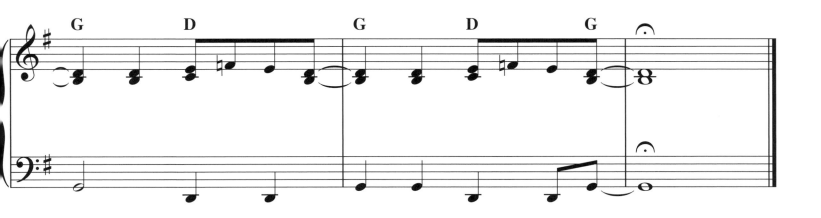

# I WANNA BE YOUR MAN

Words and Music by JOHN LENNON
and PAUL McCARTNEY

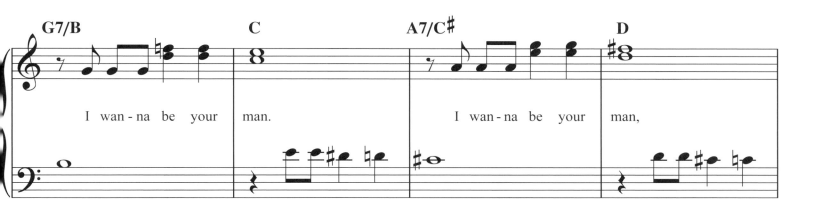

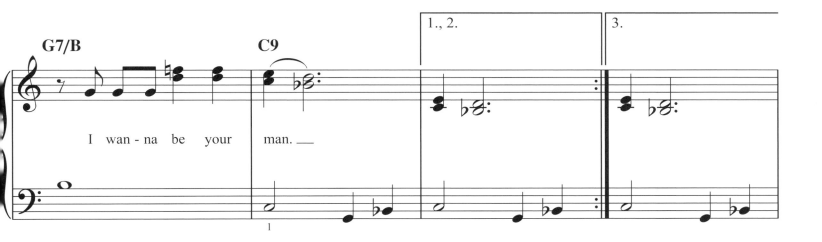

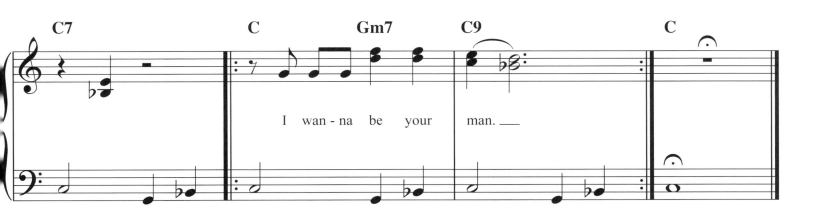

# I WANT YOU
## (She's So Heavy)

Words and Music by JOHN LENNON
and PAUL McCARTNEY

bad, _____ it's driv-ing me mad, it's driv-ing me mad.

I want you.

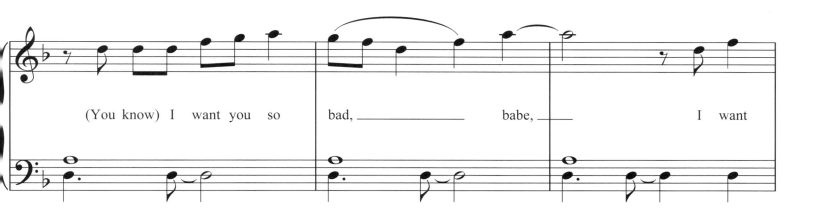

(You know) I want you so bad, _____ babe, _____ I want

you. _____ (You know) I want you so bad, _____ it's

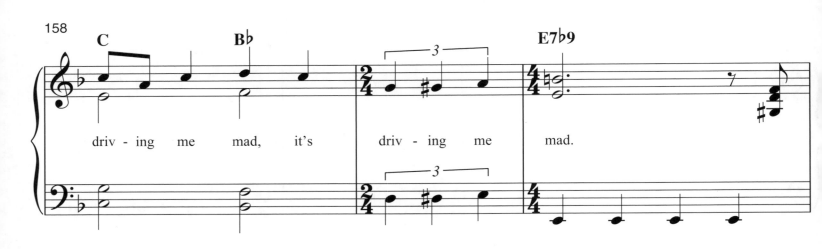

driv - ing me mad, it's driv - ing me mad.

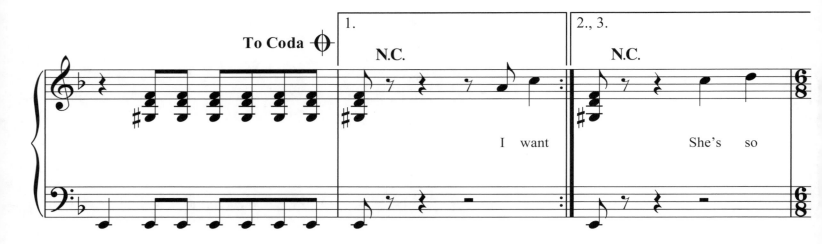

I want She's so

hea - vy. _____ (She's so) hea - vy, hea - vy, hea - vy. _____

**D.S. al Coda**
**Rock tempo**

*rit.*

I want

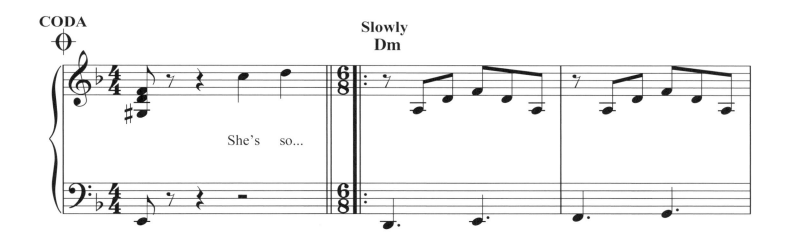

**CODA**
**Slowly**

She's so...

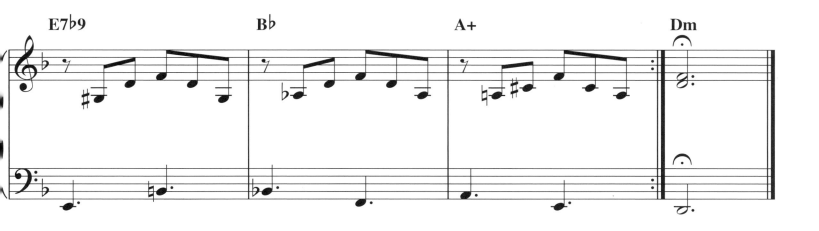

# I WILL

Words and Music by JOHN LENNON
and PAUL McCARTNEY

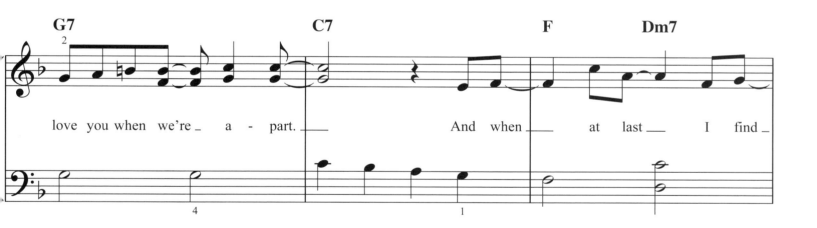

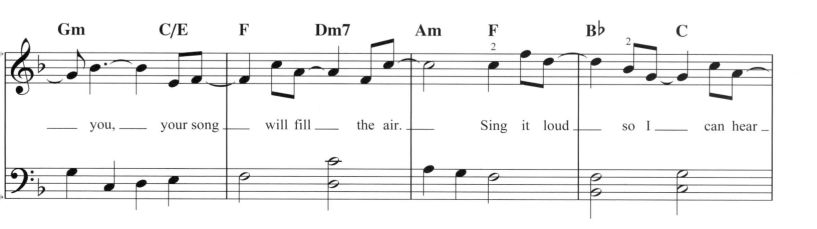

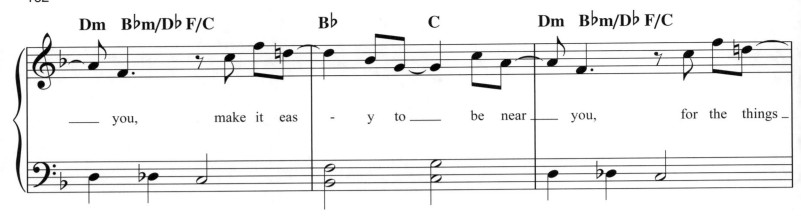

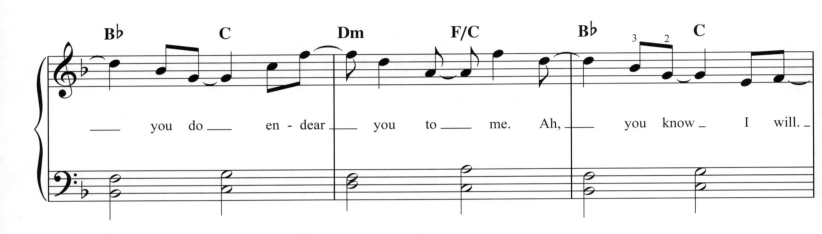

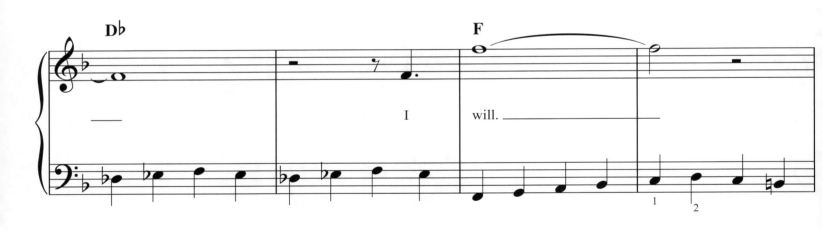

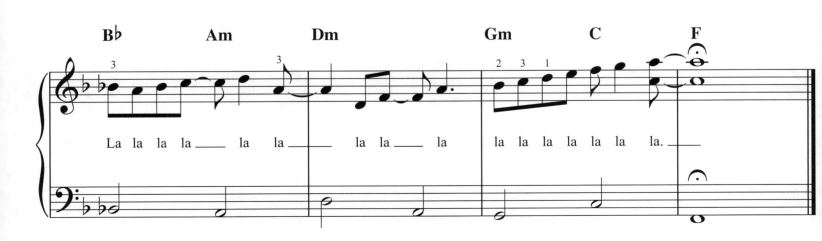

# I'LL BE BACK

Words and Music by JOHN LENNON
and PAUL McCARTNEY

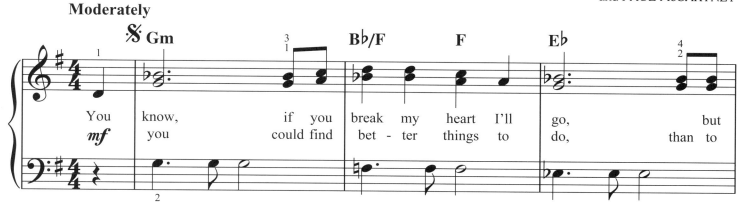

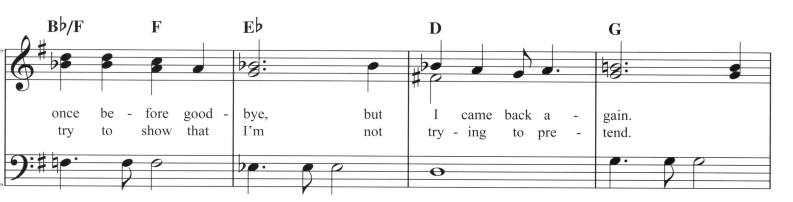

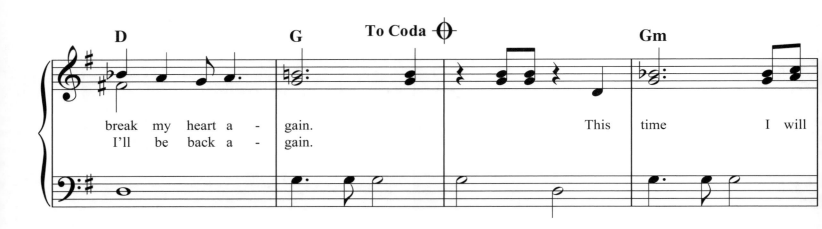

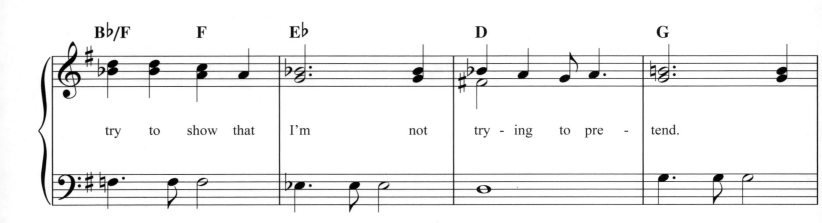

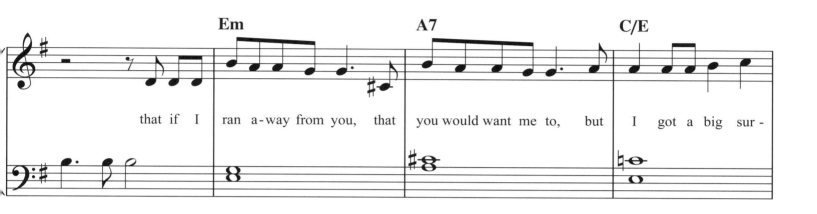

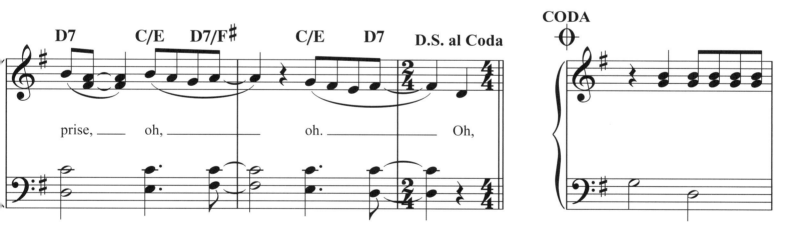

# I'LL CRY INSTEAD

Words and Music by JOHN LENNON
and PAUL McCARTNEY

I've got ev-'ry rea-son on earth to be mad,
chip on my shoul-der that's big-ger than my feet,

'cause I've just lost the on-ly girl I had.
I can't talk to peo-ple that I meet.

If I could get my way, I'd get my-self locked
If I could see you now, I'd try to make you

up to-day; but I can't, so I'll cry in-
sad some-how; but I can't so I'll cry in-

stead.
stead.
1. I've got a
2. Don't want to

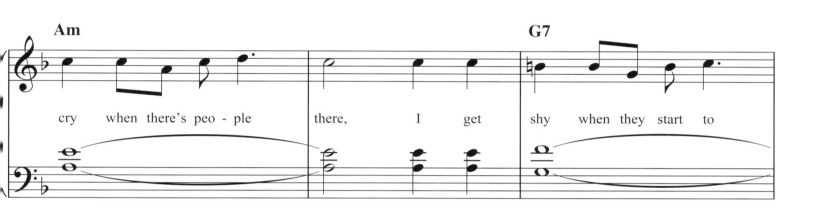

cry when there's peo - ple there, I get shy when they start to

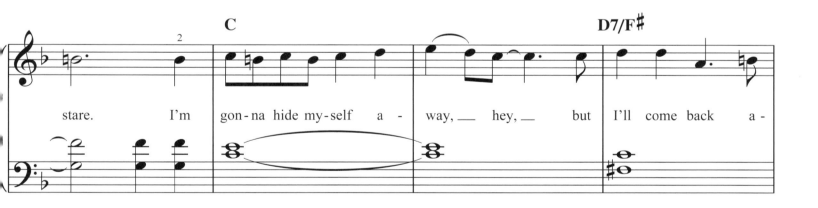

stare. I'm gon-na hide my-self a - way, __ hey, __ but I'll come back a -

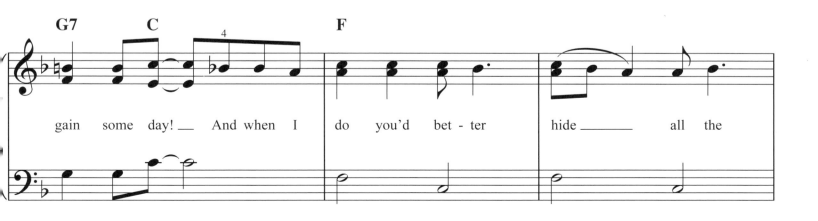

gain some day! __ And when I do you'd bet - ter hide _____ all the

girls ’cause I’m gon-na break their

hearts all ’round the world. Yes, I’m gon-na break ’em in

two, I’ll show you what your lov-in’ man can do.___ Un-til

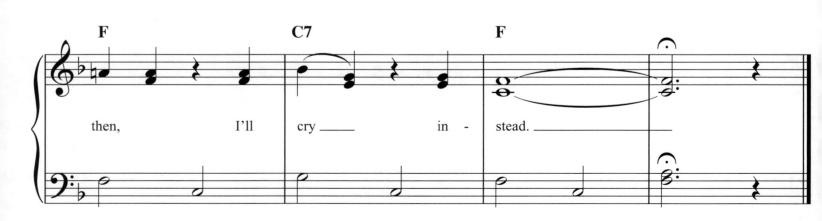

then, I’ll cry ___ in-stead. ___

# I'M HAPPY JUST TO DANCE WITH YOU

Words and Music by JOHN LENNON
and PAUL McCARTNEY

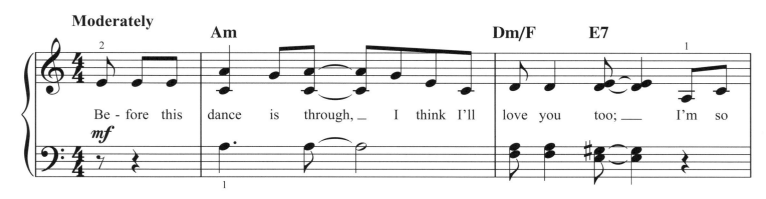

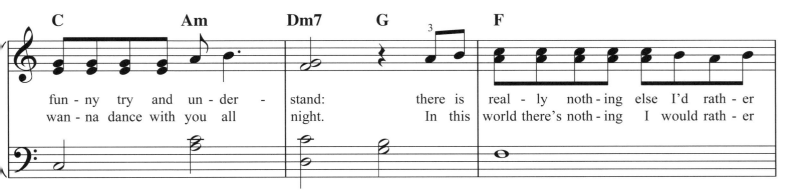

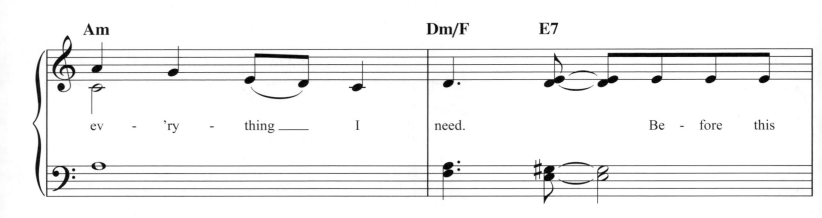

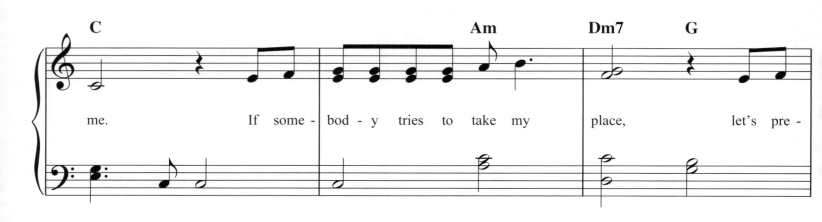

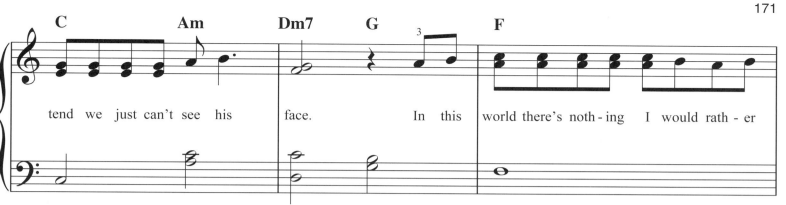

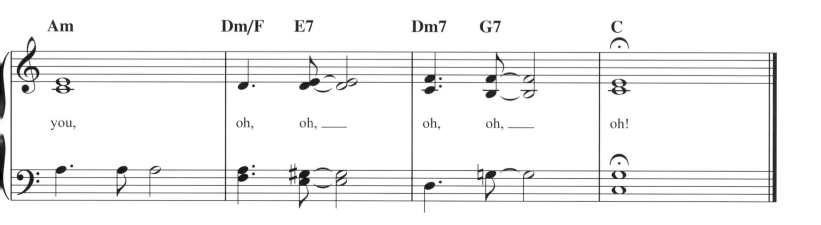

# I'LL FOLLOW THE SUN

Words and Music by JOHN LENNON
and PAUL McCARTNEY

And though I lose a friend _ in the end _ you will

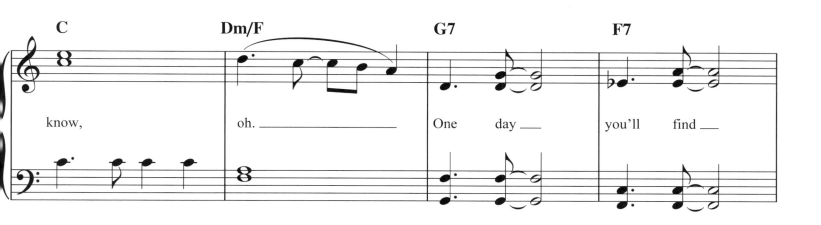

know, oh. _____ One day _ you'll find _

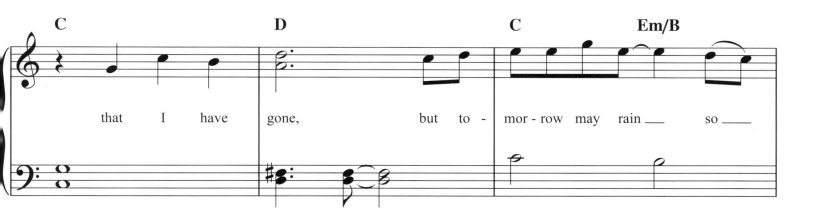

that I have gone, but to - mor - row may rain _ so _

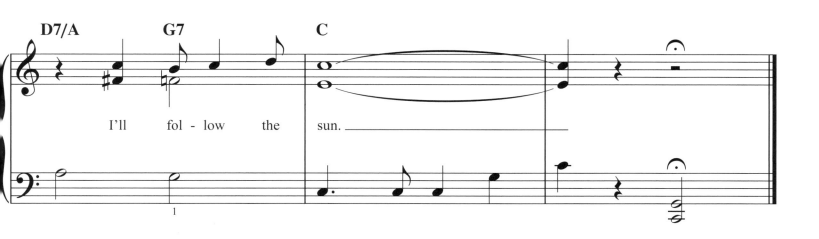

I'll fol - low the sun. _____

# I'M A LOSER

Words and Music by JOHN LENNON
and PAUL McCARTNEY

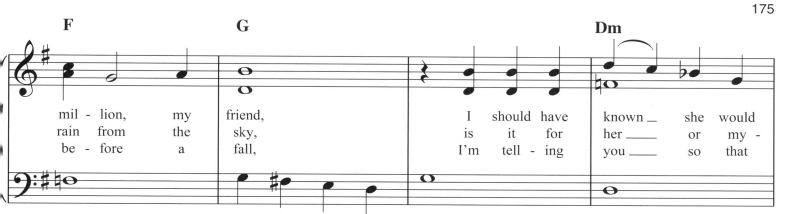

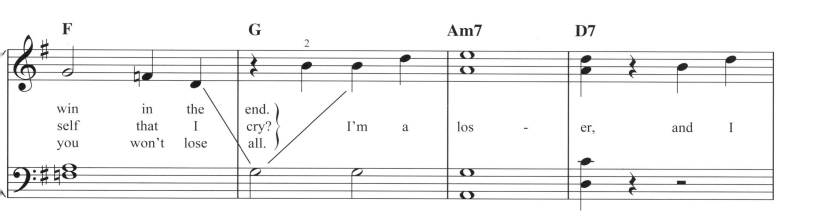

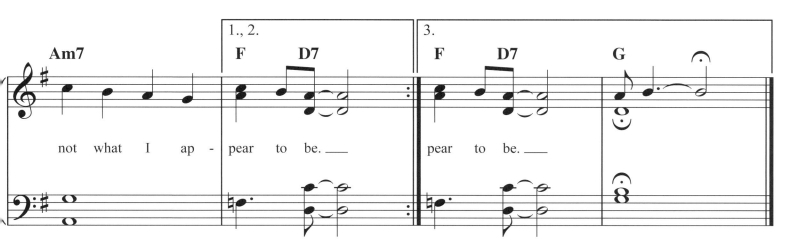

# I'M LOOKING THROUGH YOU

Words and Music by JOHN LENNON
and PAUL McCARTNEY

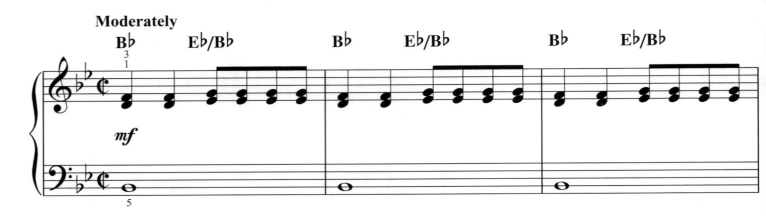

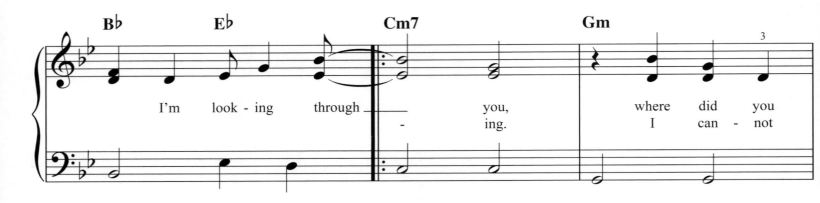

I'm look-ing through ____ you, ____ ing.

where did you I can - not

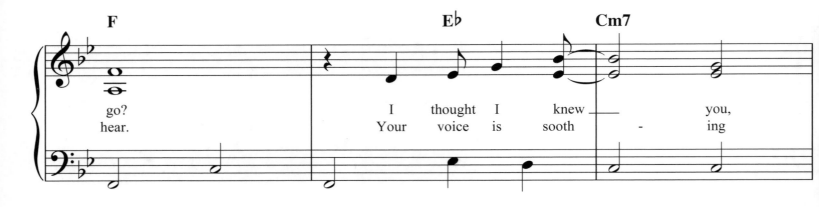

go? I thought I knew ____ you,
hear. Your voice is sooth - ing

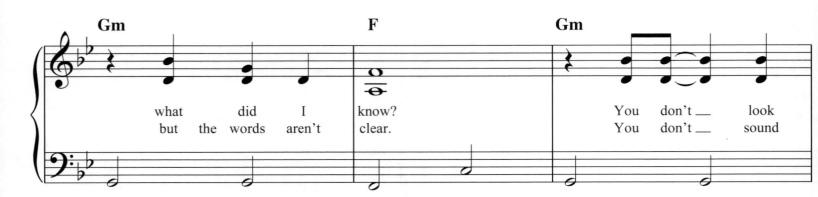

what did I know?
but the words aren't clear.

You don't ____ look
You don't ____ sound

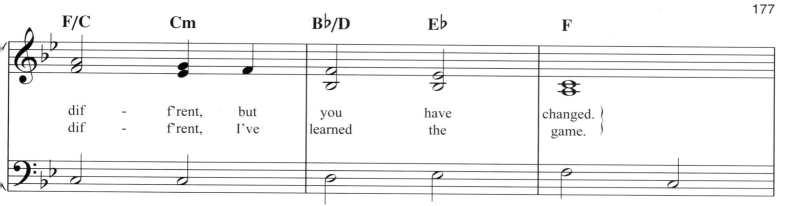

F/C     Cm     Bb/D     Eb     F

dif - f'rent, but    you    have    changed.
dif - f'rent, I've    learned    the    game.

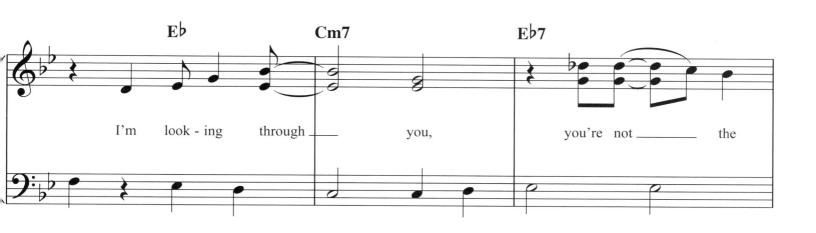

Eb     Cm7     Eb7

I'm look - ing through ___ you,     you're not ___ the

Bb    Eb7     Bb    Eb7     Bb    Eb7

same.

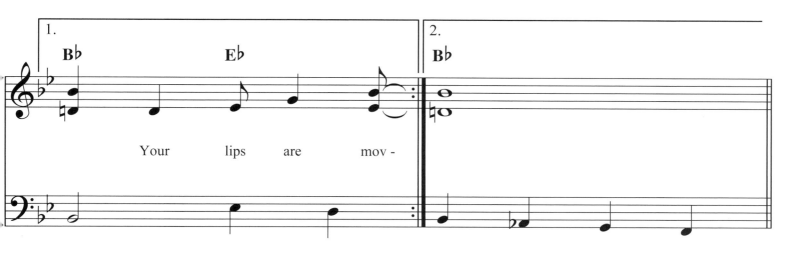

1.
Bb     Eb

Your    lips    are    mov -

2.
Bb

Why, tell me why did you not treat me right? ___

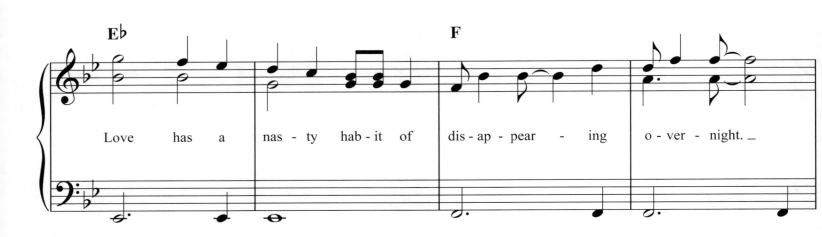

Love has a nas-ty hab-it of dis-ap-pear - ing o-ver-night. _

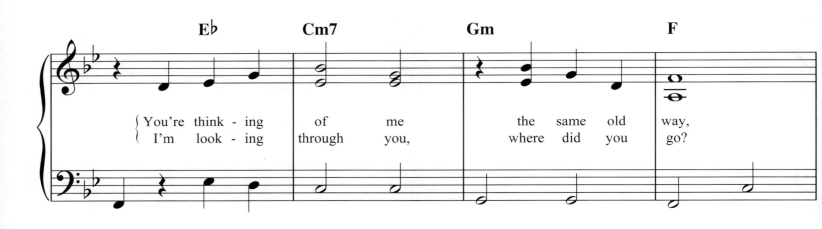

You're think - ing of me the same old way,
I'm look - ing through you, where did you go?

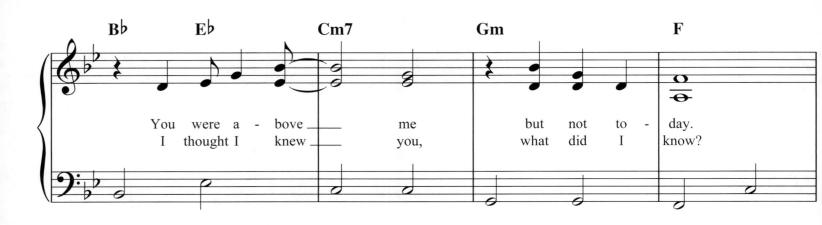

You were a-bove ___ me but not to - day.
I thought I knew ___ you, what did I know?

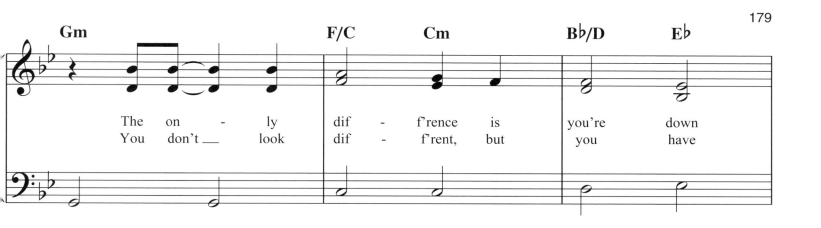

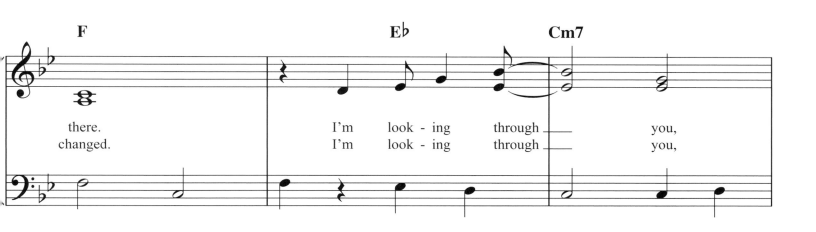

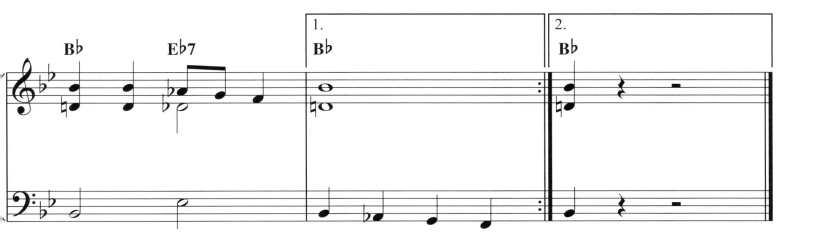

# IF I FELL

Words and Music by JOHN LENNON
and PAUL McCARTNEY

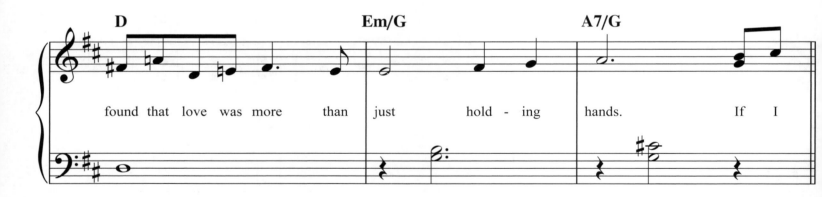

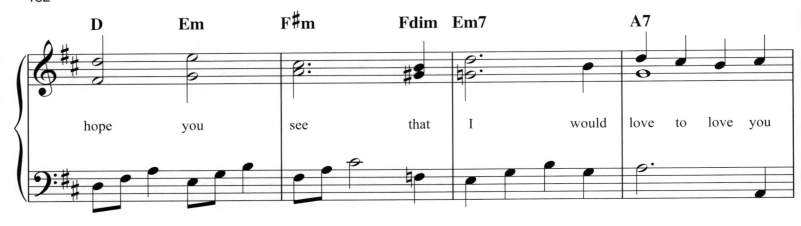

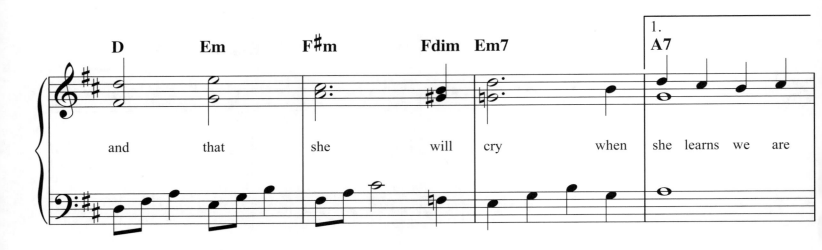

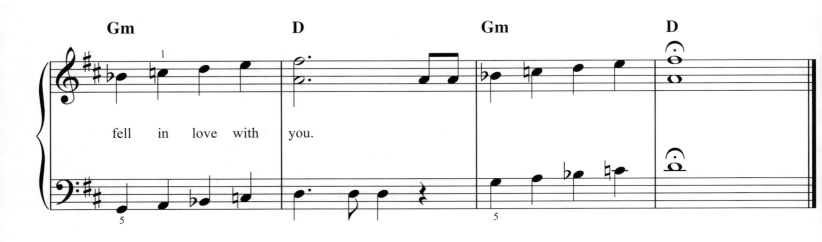

# I'VE JUST SEEN A FACE

Words and Music by JOHN LENNON
and PAUL McCARTNEY

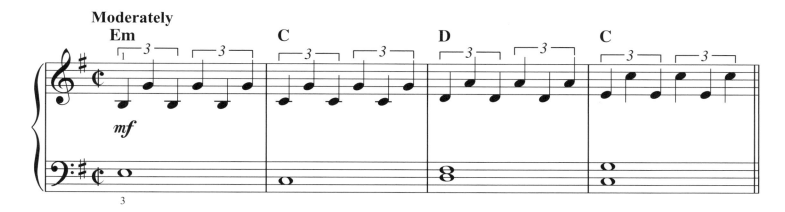

I've just seen a face, I can't for-get the time ___ or place where we just

met. She's just the girl for me, and I want all ___ the world to see we've

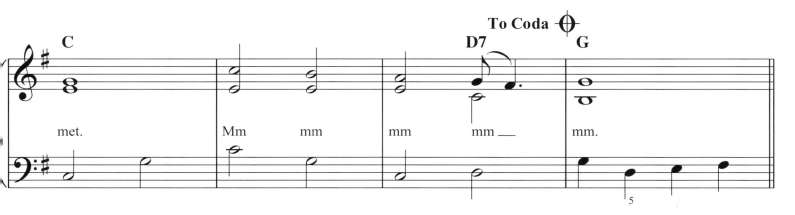

met. Mm mm mm mm ___ mm.

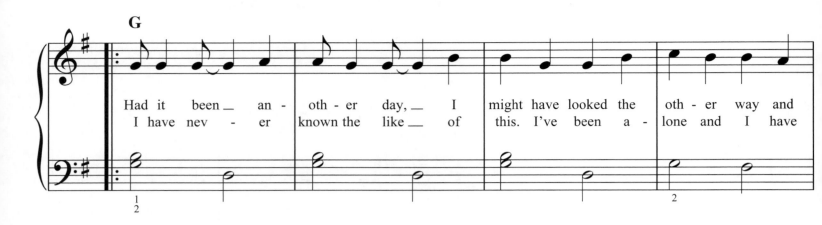

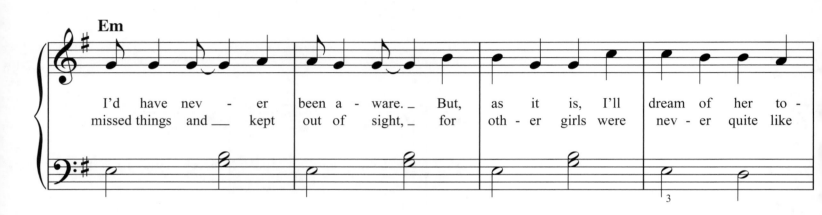

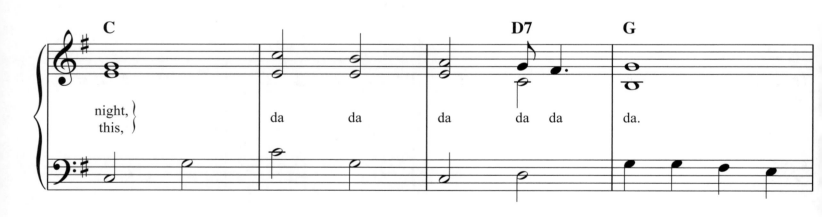

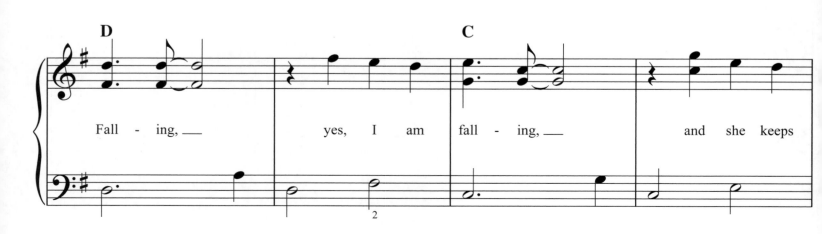

# IN MY LIFE

Words and Music by JOHN LENNON
and PAUL McCARTNEY

There are plac - es I'll re - mem - ber, all my
But of all these friends and lov - ers, there is

life, _____ though some have changed, some for - ev - er, not for
no _____ one com - pares with you, and these mem - 'ries lose their

bet - ter, some have gone, _____ and some re - main. All these
mean - ing when I think of _____ love as some - thing new. Though I

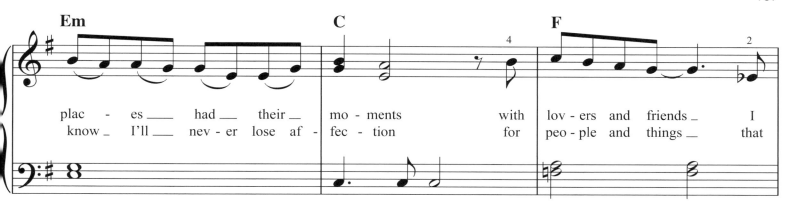

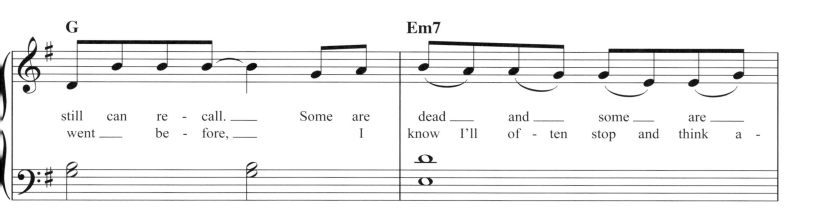

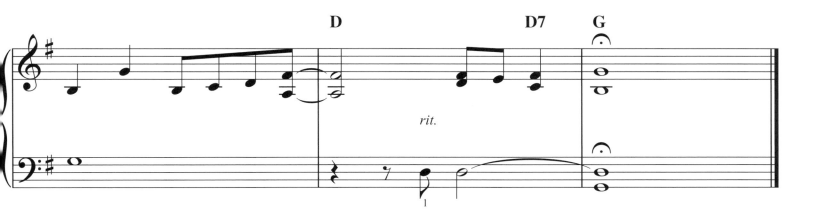

# JULIA

Words and Music by JOHN LENNON
and PAUL McCARTNEY

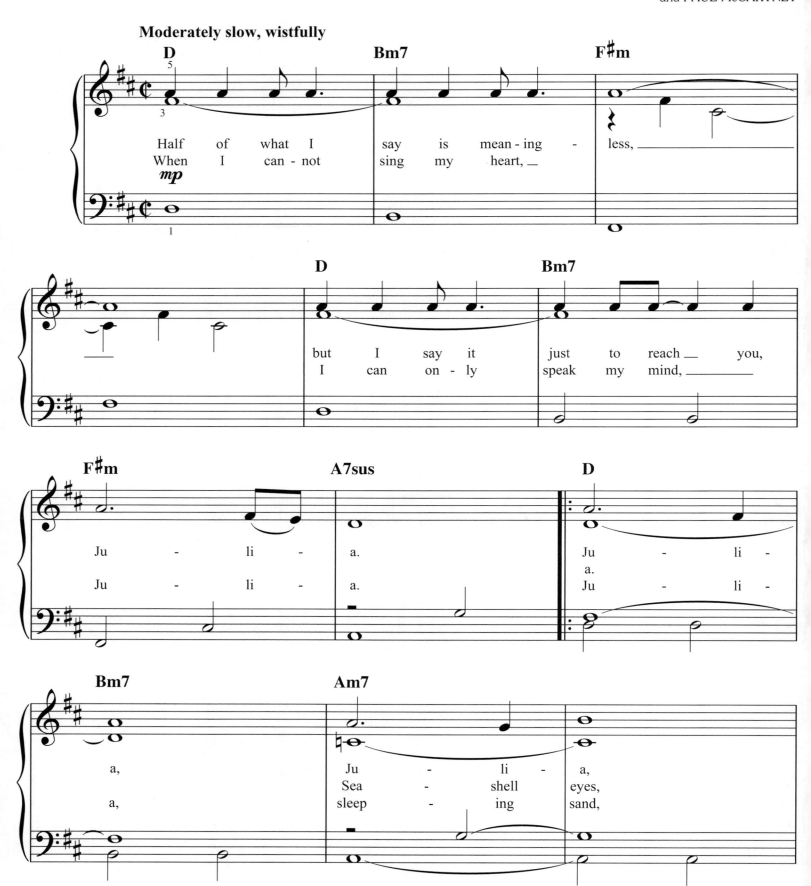

o - cean child, calls
wind - y smile, calls
si - lent cloud, touch

**To Coda**

me.
me.
me.

So I sing a song of love,

Ju - li - a.

Her hair of float - ing sky is

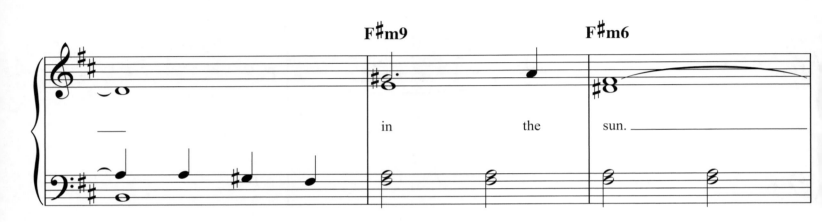

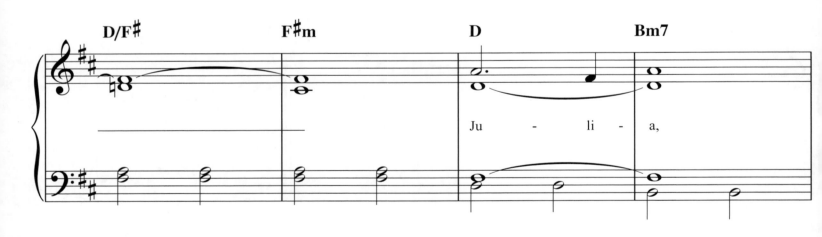

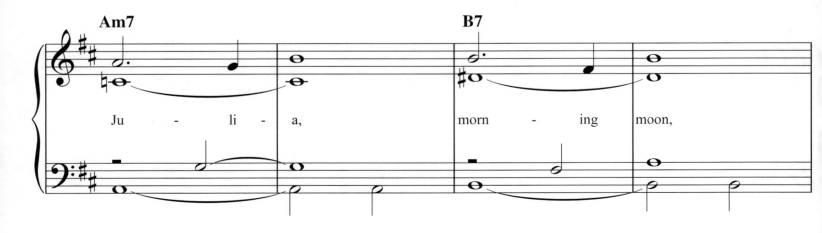

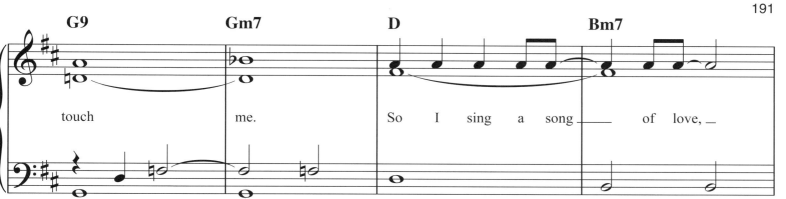

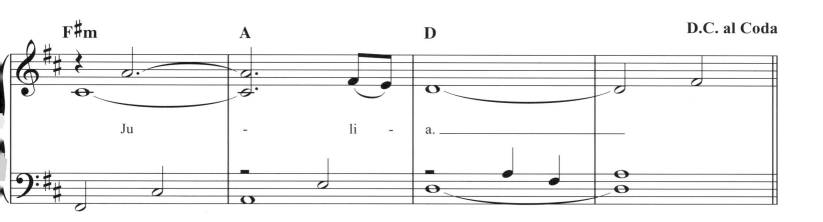

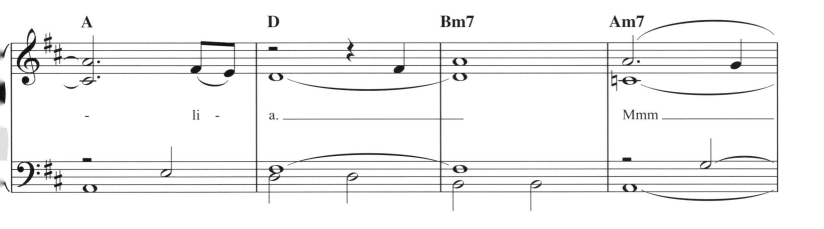

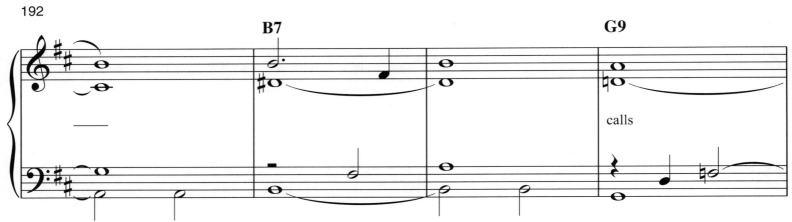

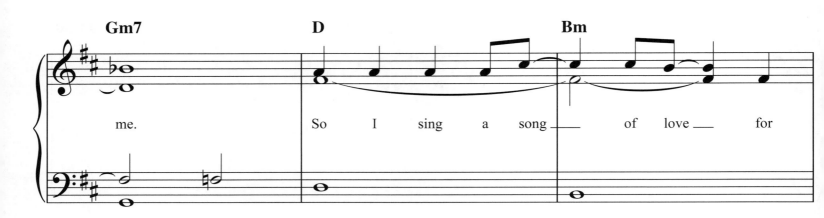

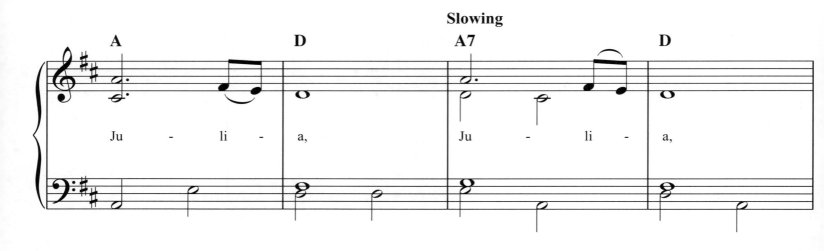

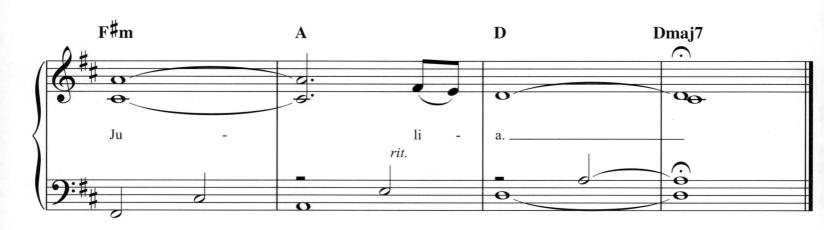

# IT WON'T BE LONG

Words and Music by JOHN LENNON
and PAUL McCARTNEY

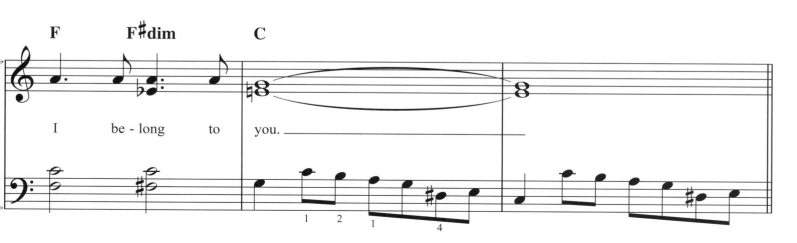

Ev - 'ry night when ev - 'ry - bod - y has fun,
Ev - 'ry night the tears come down __ from my eyes,
ev - 'ry day we'll be hap - py, I know,

here am I, sit - ting all __ on my own.
ev - 'ry day I've done noth - ing but cry.
now I know that you won't leave __ me no more.

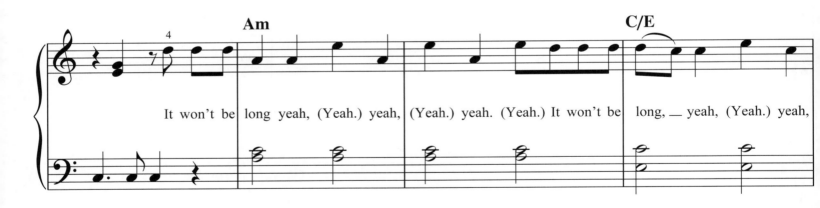

It won't be long yeah, (Yeah.) yeah, (Yeah.) yeah. (Yeah.) It won't be long, __ yeah, (Yeah.) yeah,

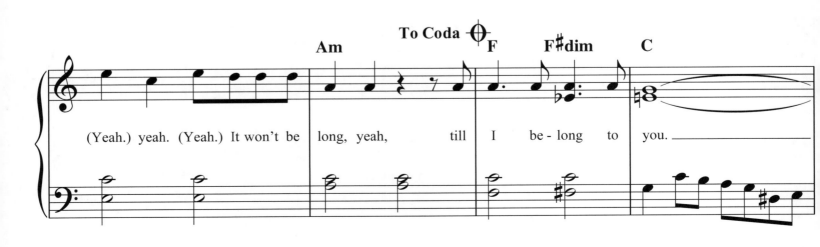

(Yeah.) yeah. (Yeah.) It won't be long, yeah, till I be - long to you. __

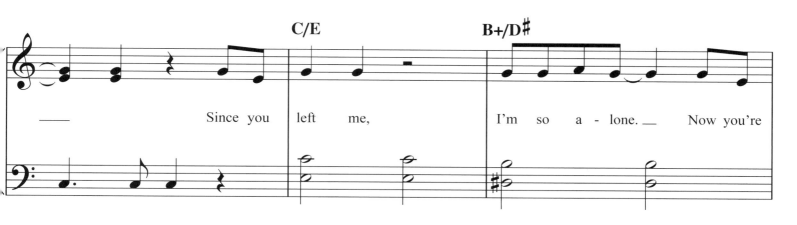

Since you left me, I'm so a - lone.__ Now you're

com - ing, you're com - ing on home.__ I'll be good like I

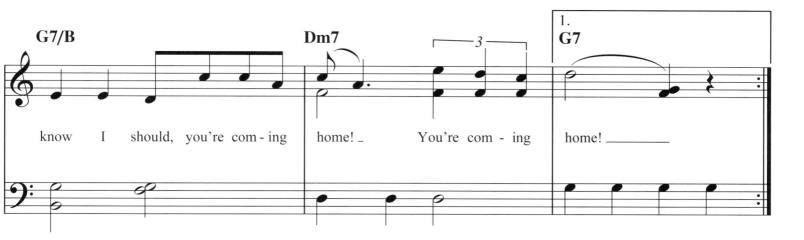

know I should, you're com - ing home! _ You're com - ing home! _____

home! _____ So,

I be - long to __ you.

# IT'S ONLY LOVE

Words and Music by JOHN LENNON
and PAUL McCARTNEY

**Moderately**

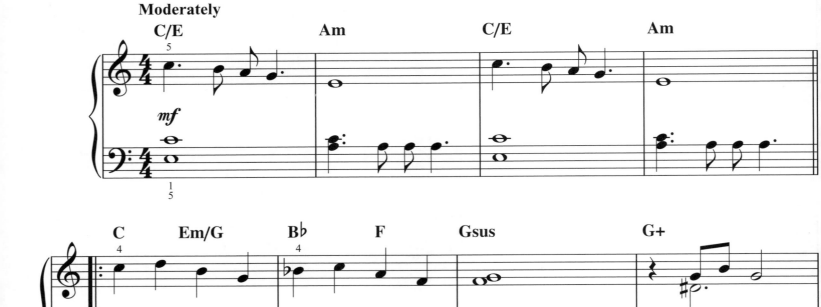

I get high when I see you go by,    my oh my.
Is it right that you and I should fight    ev-'ry night?

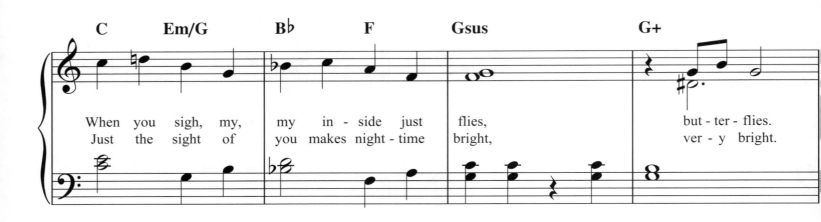

When you sigh, my, my in-side just flies, butter-flies.
Just the sight of you makes night-time bright, ver-y bright.

Why am I so shy when I'm be-side  you?
Have-n't I the right to make it up,  girl?

It's on-ly

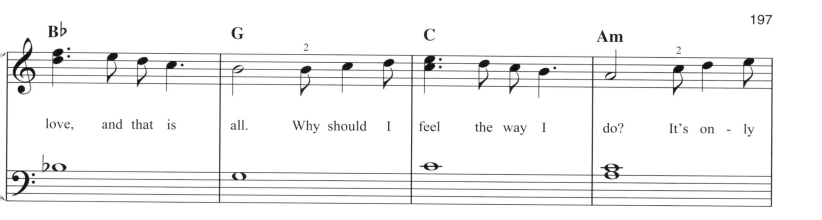

love, and that is all. Why should I feel the way I do? It's on - ly

love, and that is all. But it's so hard lov - ing you.

you, yes, it's so hard ___ lov - ing you, lov - ing you.

# LOVELY RITA

Words and Music by JOHN LENNON
and PAUL McCARTNEY

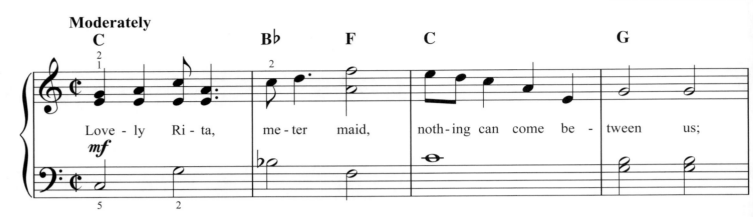

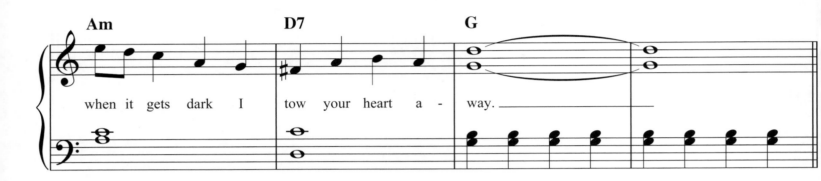

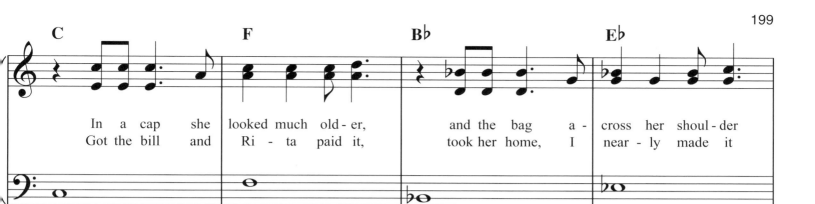

In a cap she | looked much old - er, | and the bag a - | cross her shoul - der
Got the bill and | Ri - ta paid it, | took her home, I | near - ly made it

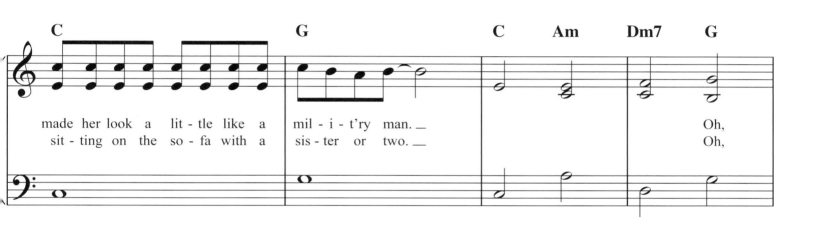

made her look a lit - tle like a | mil - i - t'ry man. __ | | Oh,
sit - ting on the so - fa with a | sis - ter or two. __ | | Oh,

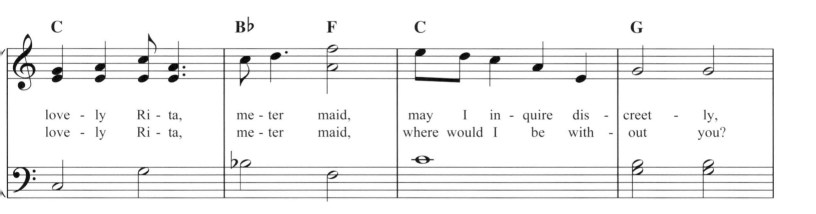

love - ly Ri - ta, | me - ter maid, | may I in - quire dis - creet - ly,
love - ly Ri - ta, | me - ter maid, | where would I be with - out you?

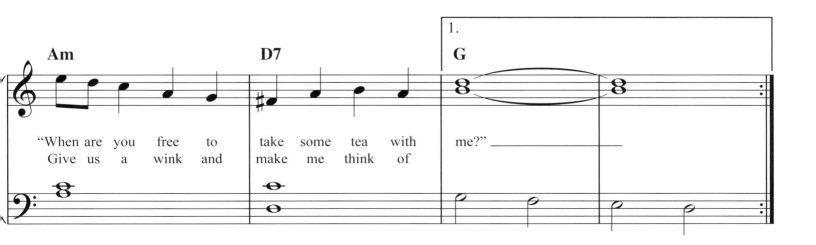

"When are you free to | take some tea with | me?" ____
Give us a wink and | make me think of

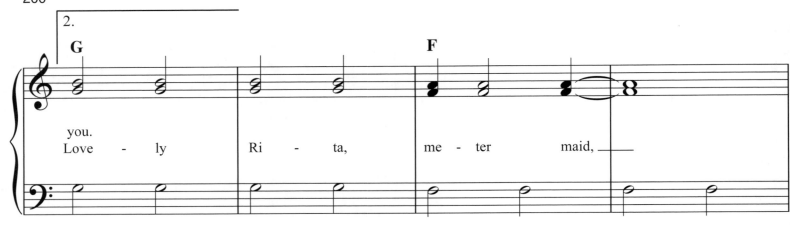

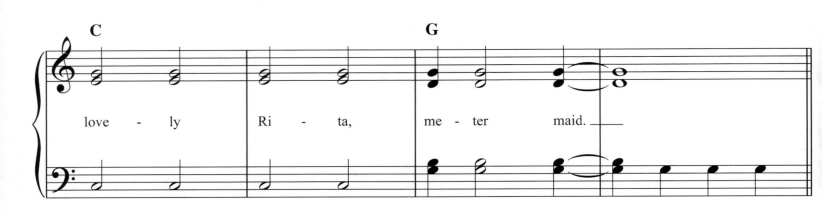

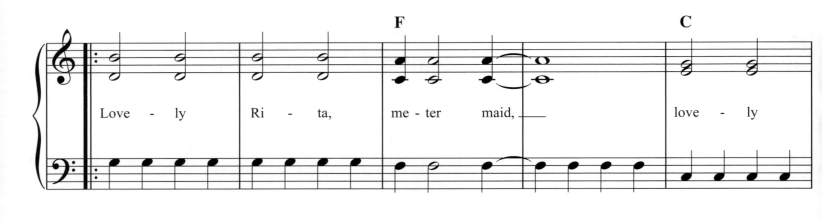

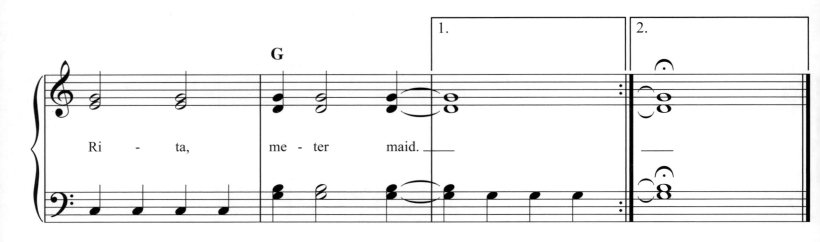

# LADY MADONNA

Words and Music by JOHN LENNON
and PAUL McCARTNEY

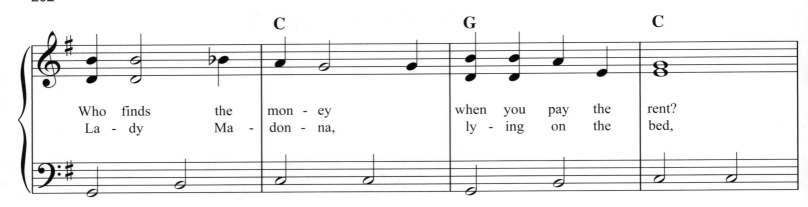

Who finds the mon - ey when you pay the rent?
La - dy Ma - don - na, ly - ing on the bed,

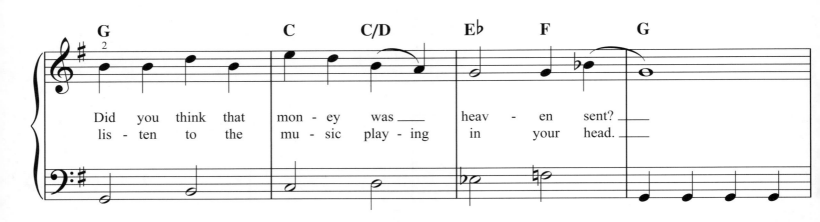

Did you think that mon - ey was heav - en sent?
lis - ten to the mu - sic play - ing in your head.

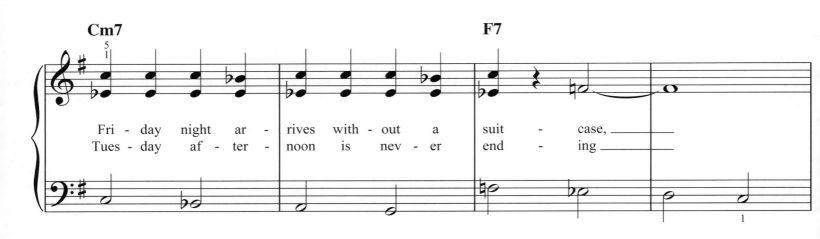

Fri - day night ar - rives with - out a suit - case,
Tues - day af - ter - noon is nev - er end - ing

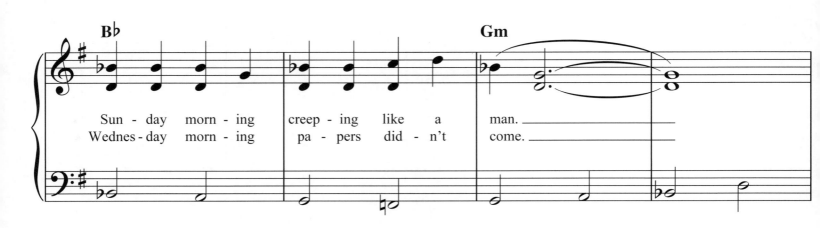

Sun - day morn - ing creep - ing like a man.
Wednes - day morn - ing pa - pers did - n't come.

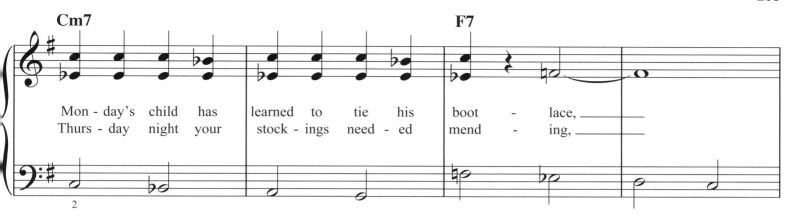

Mon - day's child has learned to tie his boot - lace, _____
Thurs - day night your stock - ings need - ed mend - ing, _____

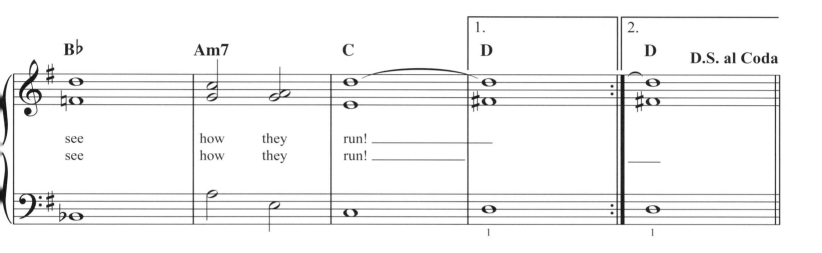

see how they run!
see how they run!

D.S. al Coda

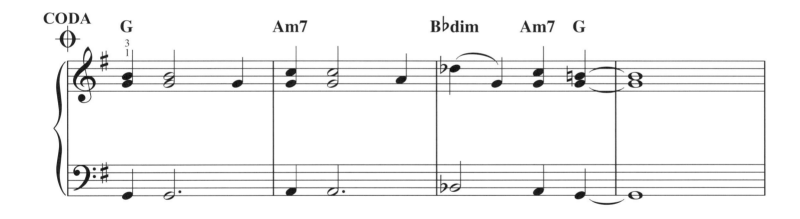

CODA

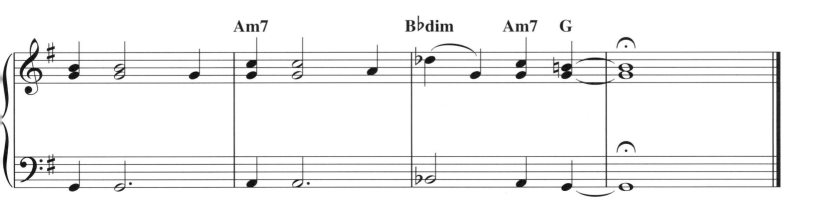

# LET IT BE

Words and Music by JOHN LENNON
and PAUL McCARTNEY

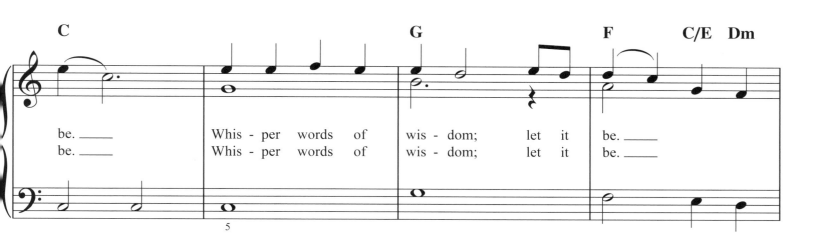

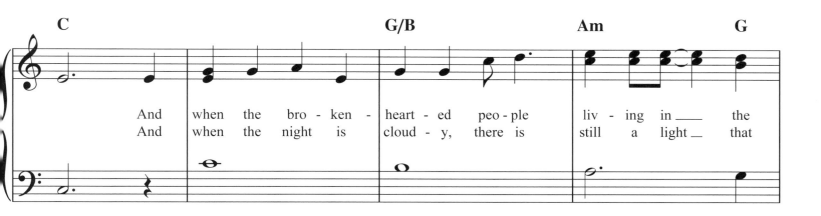

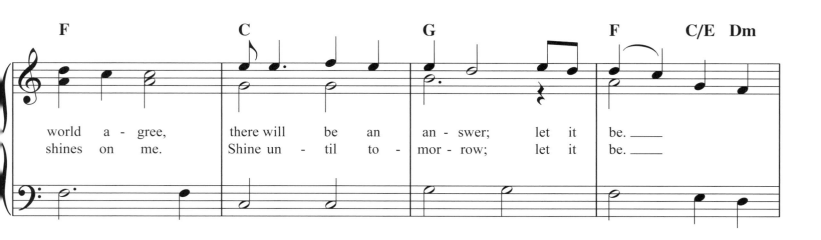

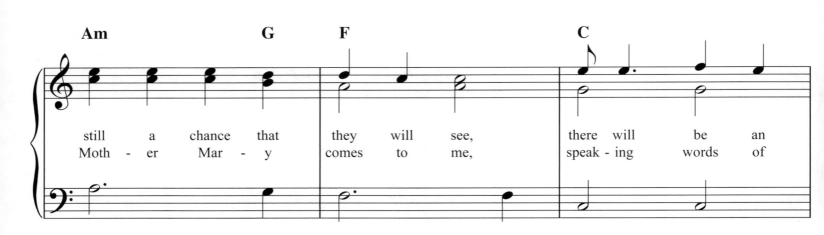

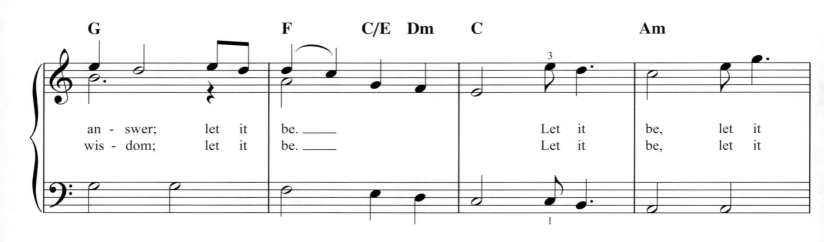

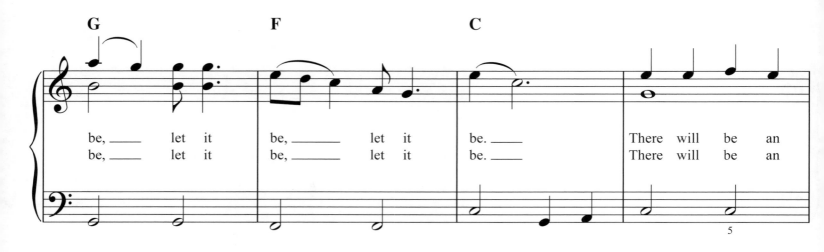

# THE LONG AND WINDING ROAD

Words and Music by JOHN LENNON
and PAUL McCARTNEY

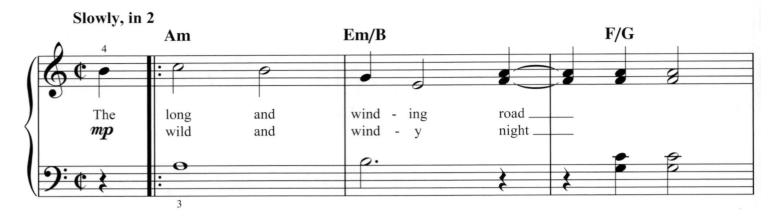

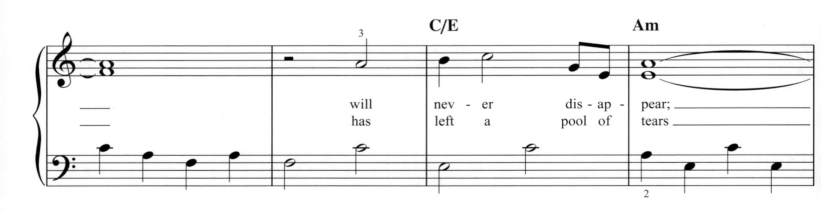

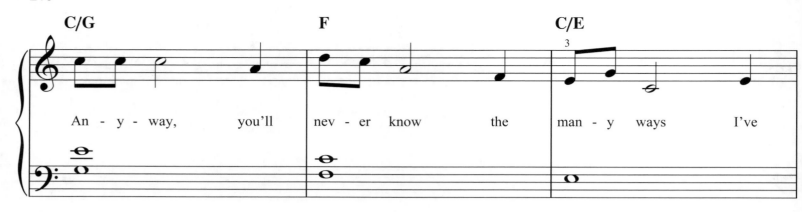

**C/G**      **F**      **C/E**

An - y - way,    you'll   nev - er   know    the    man - y   ways    I've

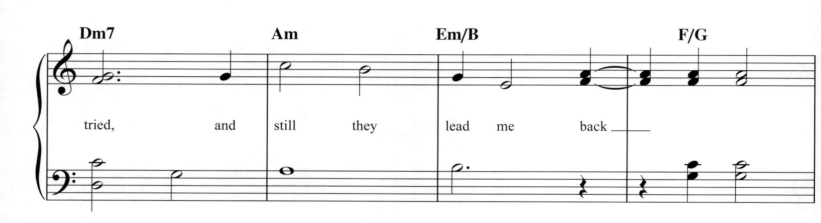

**Dm7**      **Am**      **Em/B**      **F/G**

tried,      and     still    they     lead    me     back

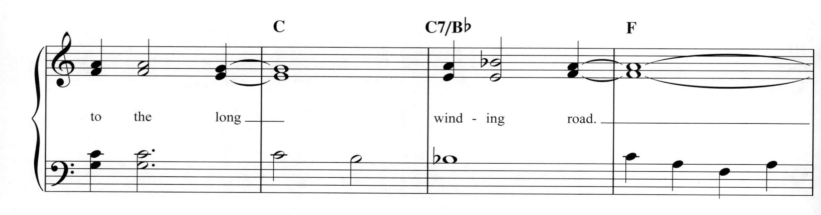

**C**      **C7/B♭**      **F**

to    the     long       wind - ing    road.

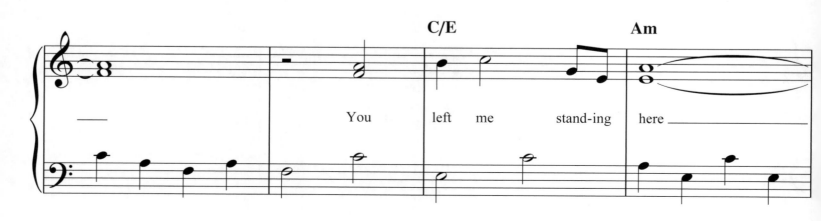

**C/E**      **Am**

You    left    me   stand-ing    here

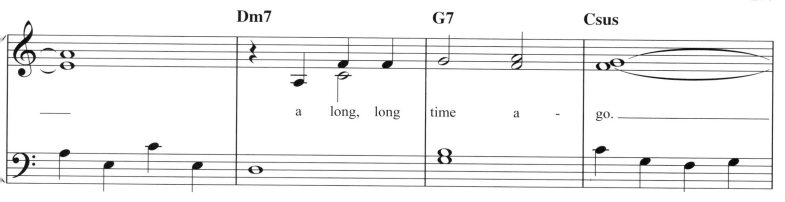

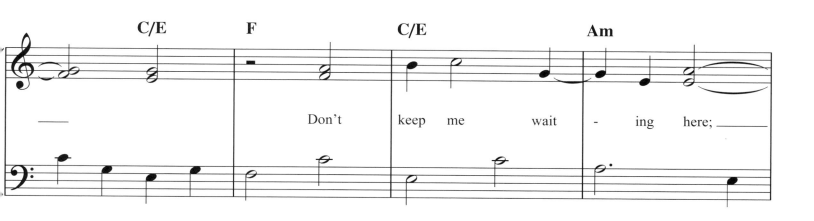

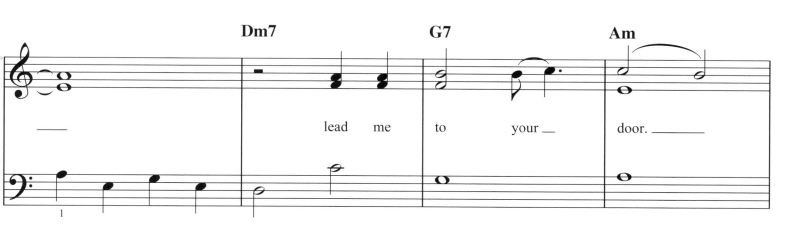

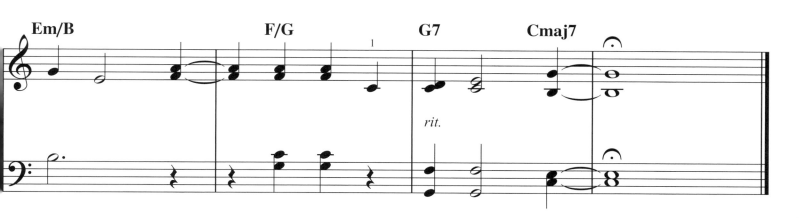

# LOVE ME DO

Words and Music by JOHN LENNON
and PAUL McCARTNEY

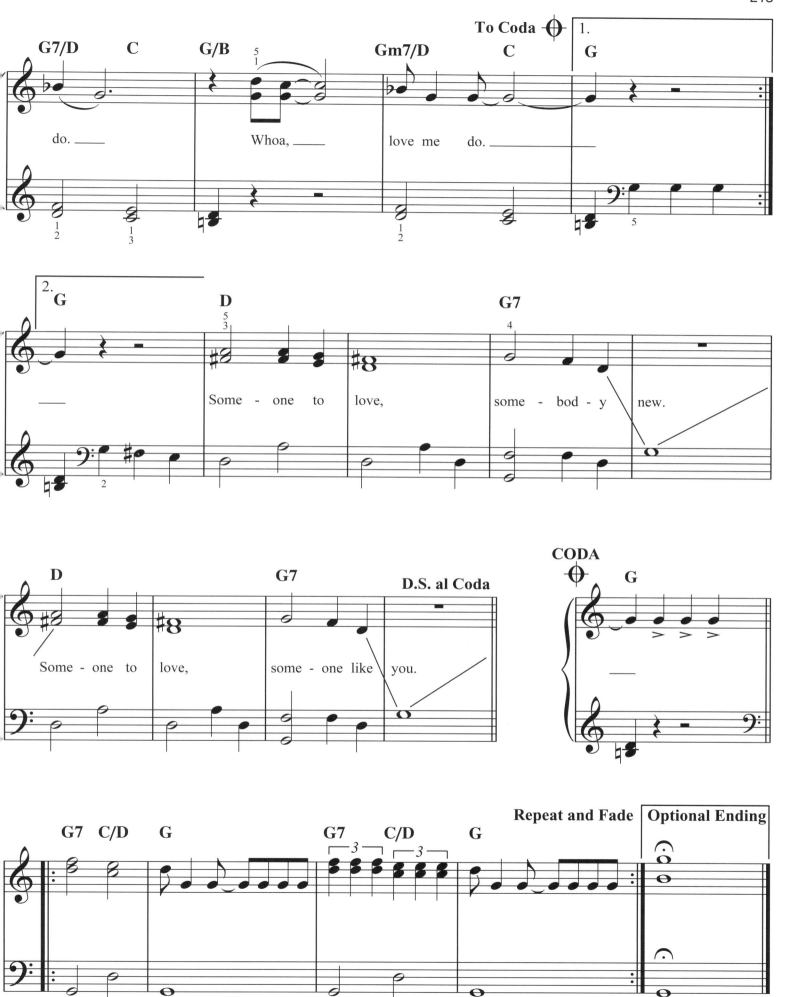

# LUCY IN THE SKY WITH DIAMONDS

Words and Music by JOHN LENNON
and PAUL McCARTNEY

**Moderately flowing**

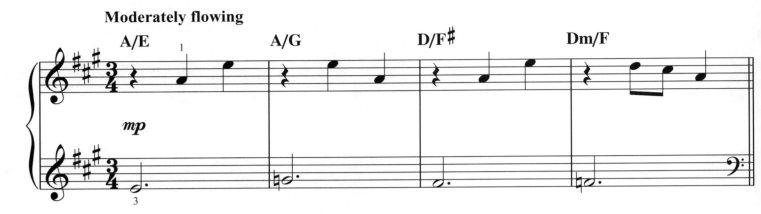

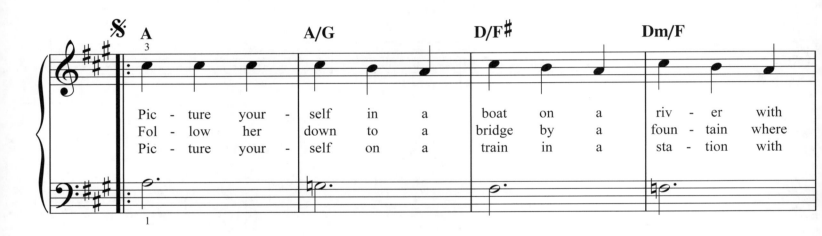

Pic - ture your - self in a boat on a riv - er with
Fol - low her down to a bridge by a foun - tain where
Pic - ture your - self on a train in a sta - tion with

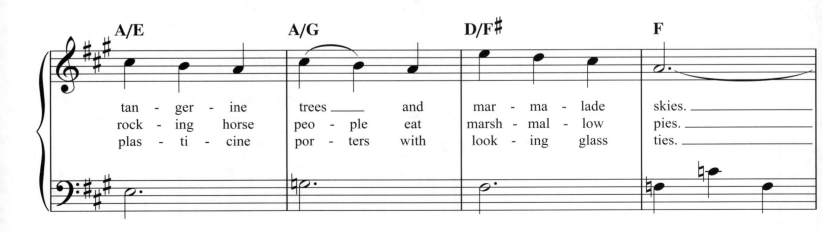

tan - ger - ine trees ____ and mar - ma - lade skies. ____
rock - ing horse peo - ple eat marsh - mal - low pies. ____
plas - ti - cine por - ters with look - ing glass ties. ____

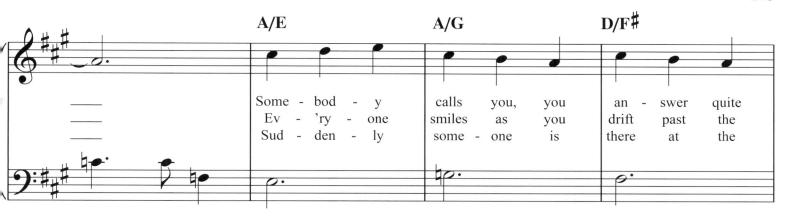

A/E     A/G     D/F♯

Some - bod - y    calls   you,   you    an - swer quite
Ev - 'ry - one    smiles   as   you    drift   past   the
Sud - den - ly    some - one   is    there   at   the

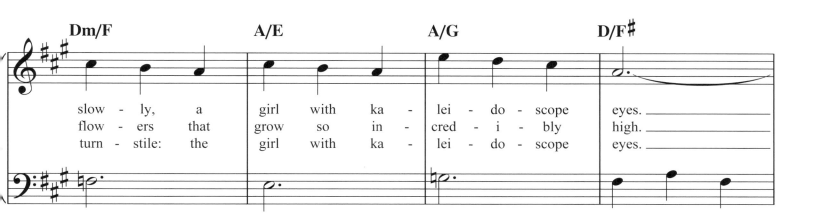

Dm/F     A/E     A/G     D/F♯

slow - ly,   a    girl   with   ka -   lei - do - scope   eyes. _____
flow - ers   that    grow   so   in -   cred - i - bly   high. _____
turn - stile:   the    girl   with   ka -   lei - do - scope   eyes. _____

**To Coda** ⊕

Dm     Dm/C     B♭

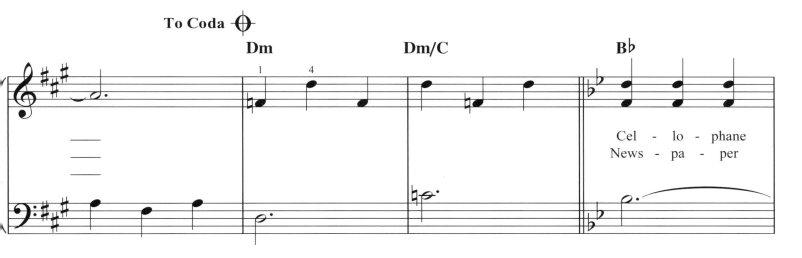

Cel - lo - phane
News - pa - per

C7/G     Dm/F

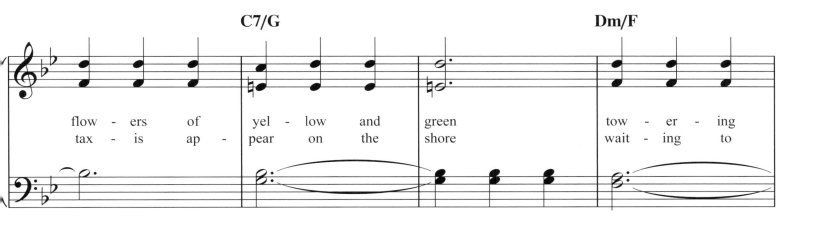

flow - ers   of    yel - low   and    green    tow - er - ing
tax - is   ap -   pear   on   the    shore    wait - ing   to

216

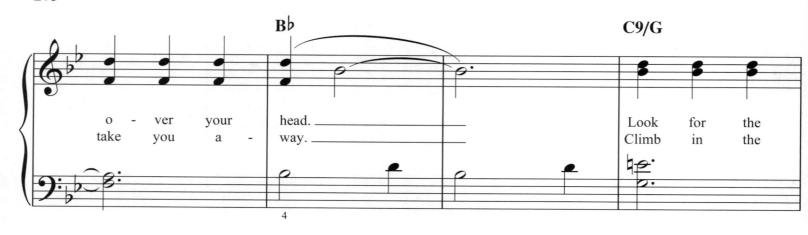

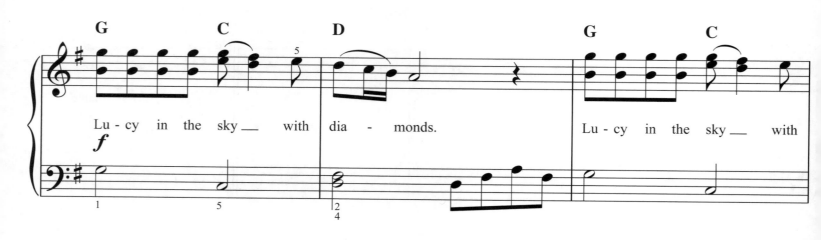

# MAGICAL MYSTERY TOUR

Words and Music by JOHN LENNON
and PAUL McCARTNEY

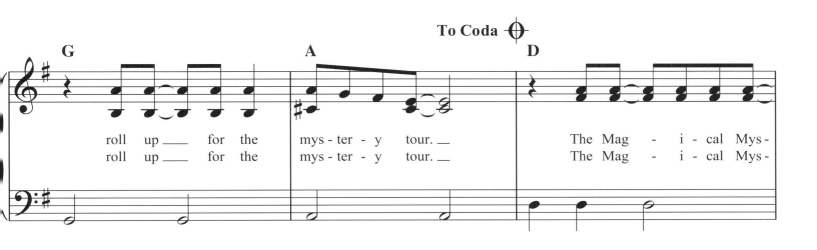

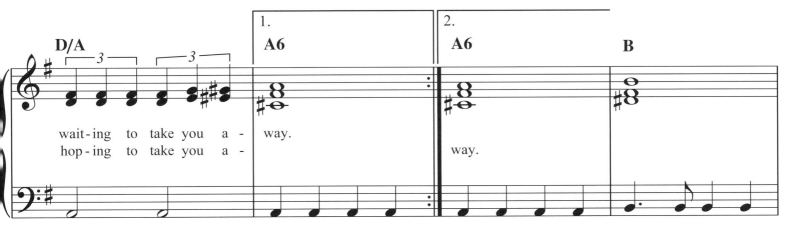

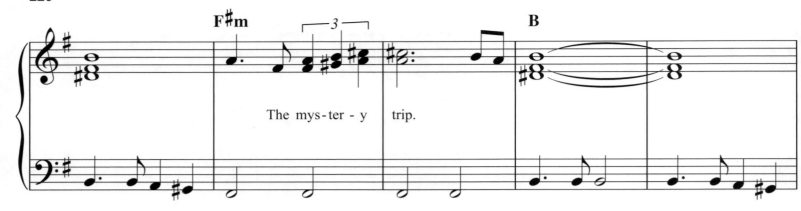

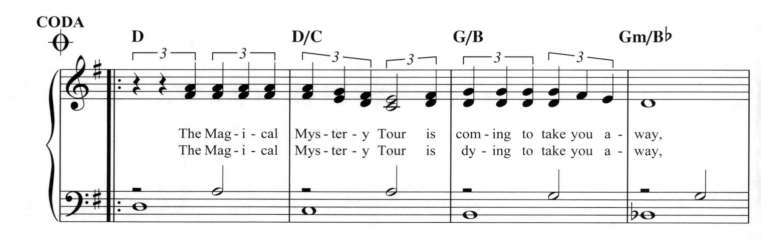

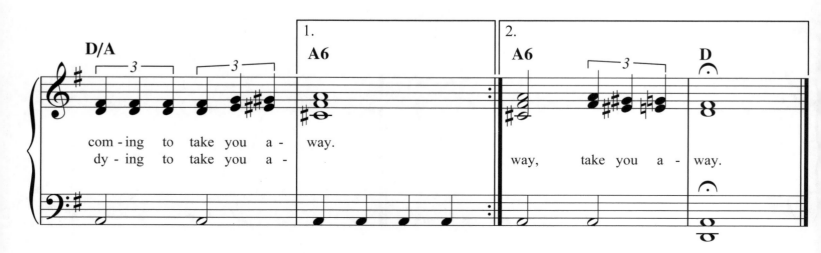

# MAXWELL'S SILVER HAMMER

Words and Music by JOHN LENNON
and PAUL McCARTNEY

phone:
hind,
free.                The

"Can    I    take    you
writ  -  ing    fif  -  ty
judge    does    not    a  -

out    to    the    pic  -    tures,
times,    "I    must    not ___    be
gree    and    he    tells ___    them

**G7/B**

**C**                                    **G**                        **D7/F#**

Jo  -    o  -  o  -  oan?" ___
so  -    o  -  o  -  o." ___
so  -    o  -  o  -  o. ___

But    as    she's    get  -    ting
But    when    she    turns    her
But    as    the    words    are

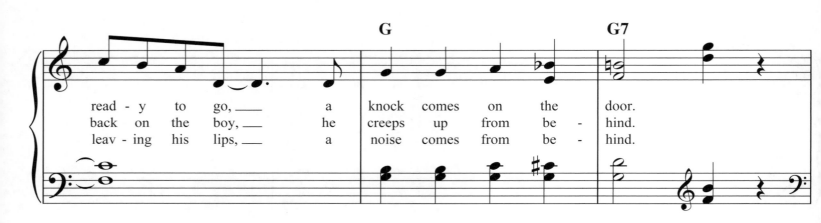

                                    **G**                        **G7**

read  -  y    to    go, ___        a
back    on    the    boy, ___    he
leav  -  ing    his    lips, ___    a

knock    comes    on    the    door.
creeps    up    from    be  -    hind.
noise    comes    from    be  -    hind.

**C**                                                        **D**

Bang!    Bang!    Max  -  well's
Bang!    Bang!    Max  -  well's
Bang!    Bang!    Max  -  well's

sil  -  ver    ham  -    mer    came
sil  -  ver    ham  -    mer    came
sil  -  ver    ham  -    mer    came

down    up  -  on    her
down    up  -  on    her
down    up  -  on    his

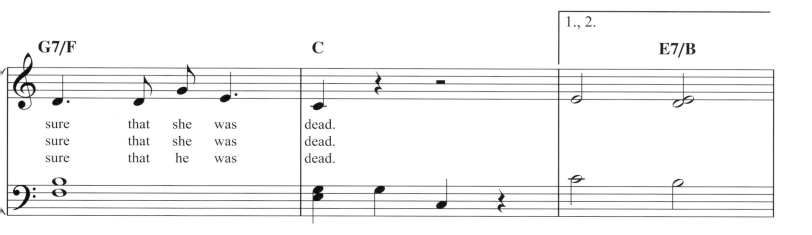

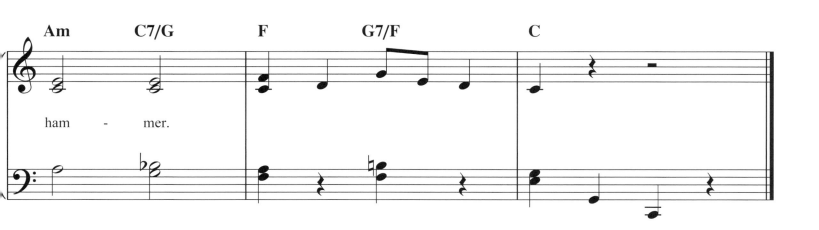

# MARTHA MY DEAR

Words and Music by JOHN LENNON
and PAUL McCARTNEY

Hold your head ___ up, you sil - ly girl; ___
Hold your hand ___ out you sil - ly girl; ___

look what you've done. ___
see what you've done. ___

When ___ you find ___

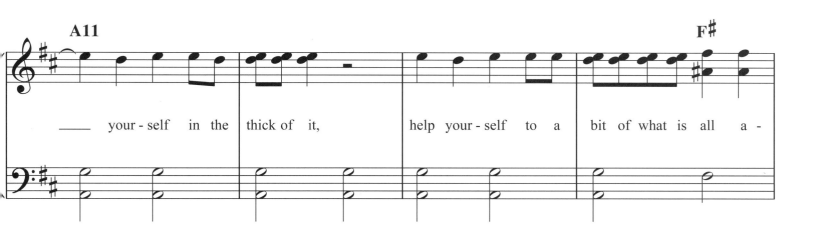

___ your-self in the thick of it, help your-self to a bit of what is all a-

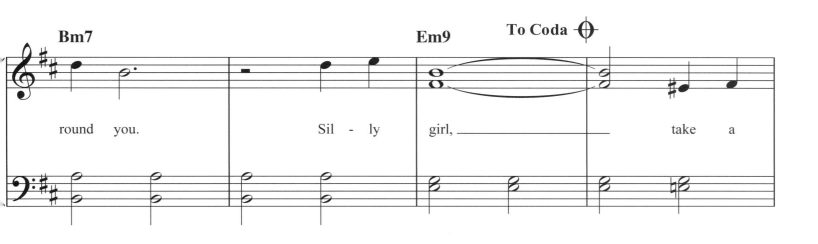

round you. Sil - ly girl, ___ take a

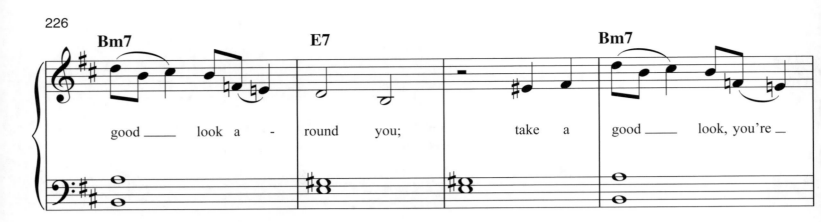

good ___ look a - round you; take a good ___ look, you're ___

bound to see ___ that you and me ___ were

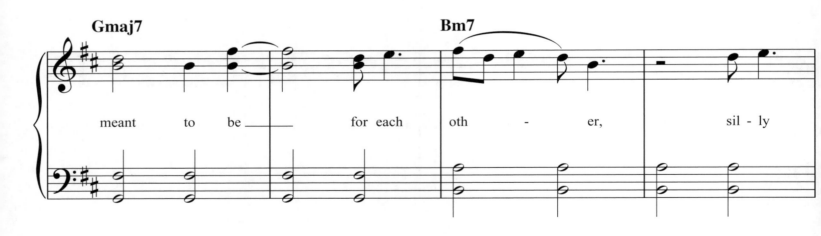

meant to be ___ for each oth - er, sil - ly

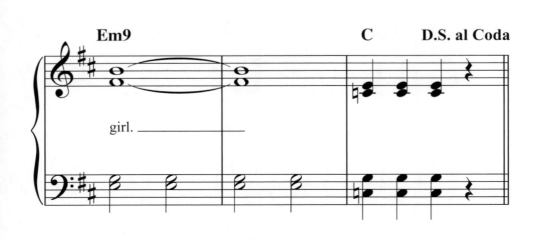

girl. ___

D.S. al Coda

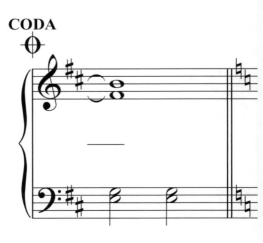

CODA

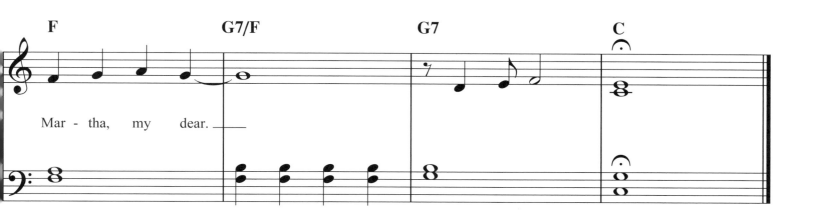

# MEAN MR. MUSTARD

Words and Music by JOHN LENNON
and PAUL McCARTNEY

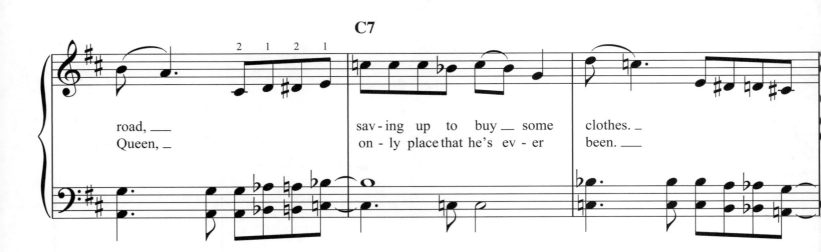

# MICHELLE

Words and Music by JOHN LENNON
and PAUL McCARTNEY

**Gentle Ballad (but not too slow)**

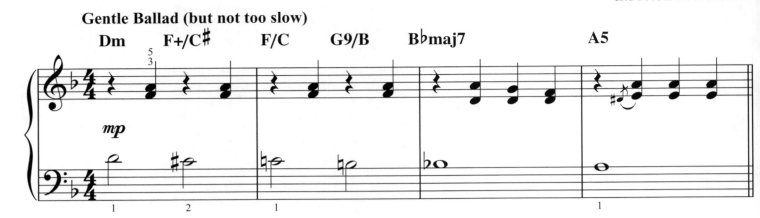

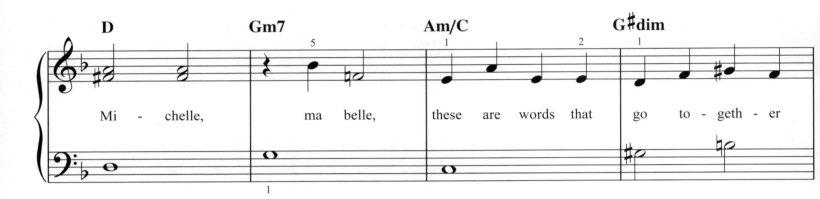

Mi - chelle, ma belle, these are words that go to - geth - er

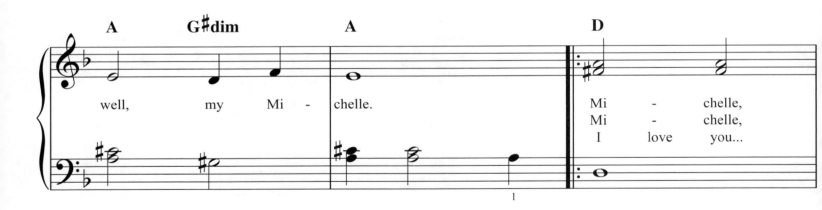

well, my Mi - chelle.

Mi - chelle,
Mi - chelle,
I love you...

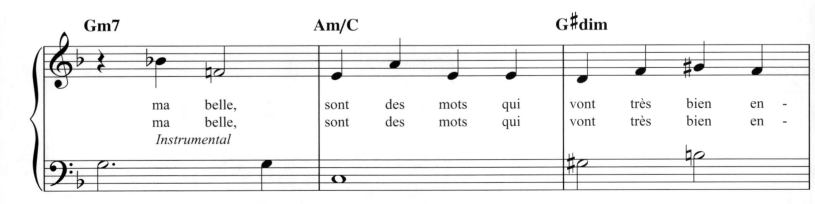

ma belle, sont des mots qui vont très bien en -
ma belle, sont des mots qui vont très bien en -
*Instrumental*

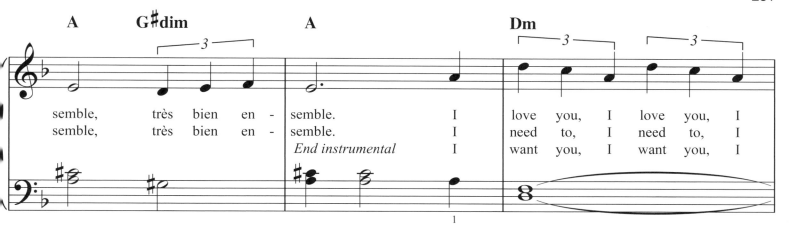

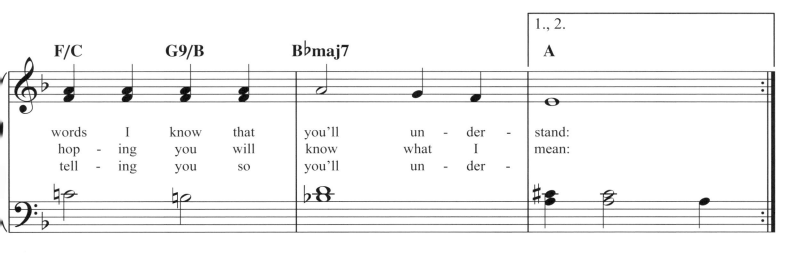

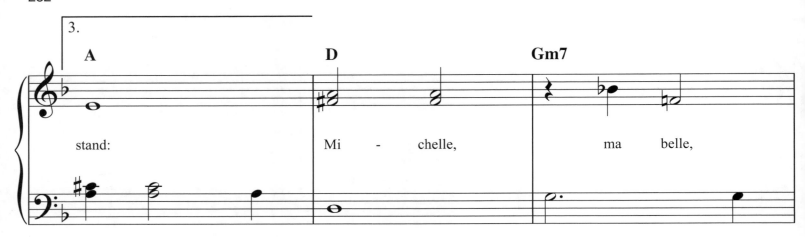

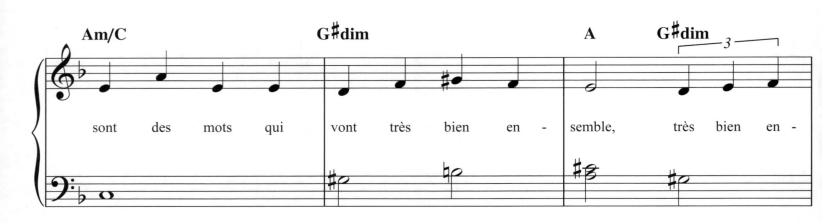

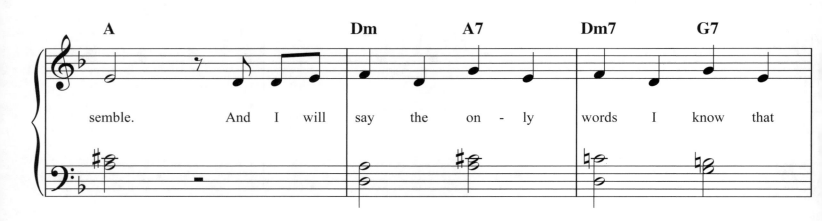

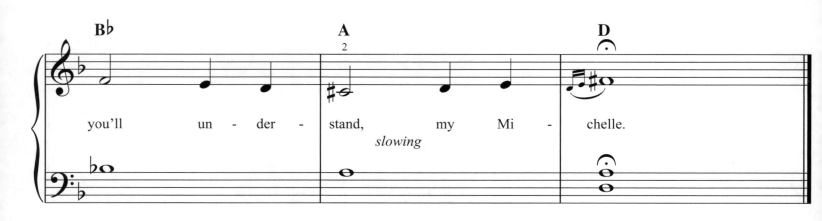

# NORWEGIAN WOOD
## (This Bird Has Flown)

Words and Music by JOHN LENNON
and PAUL McCARTNEY

**Moderately flowing, in 1**

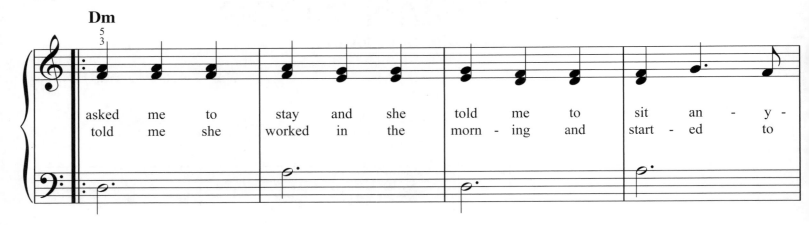

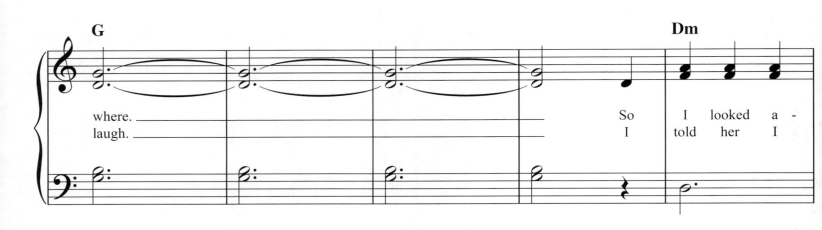

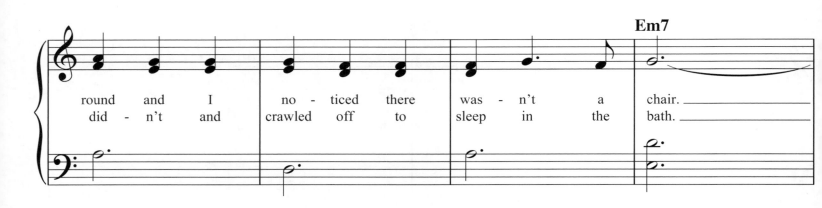

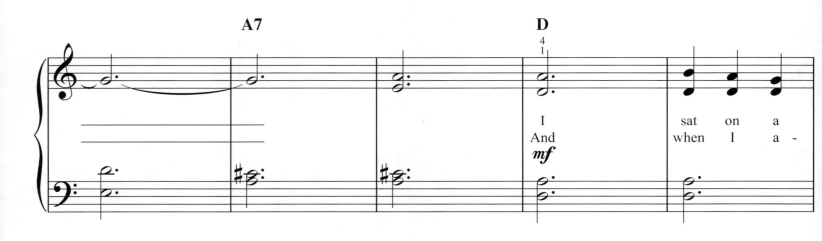

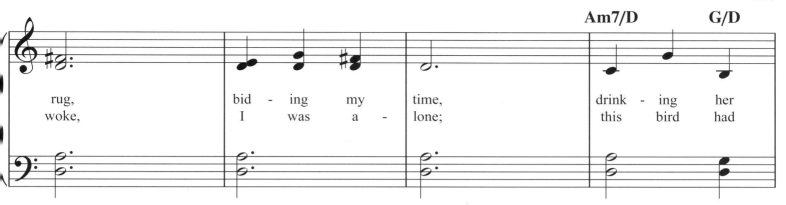

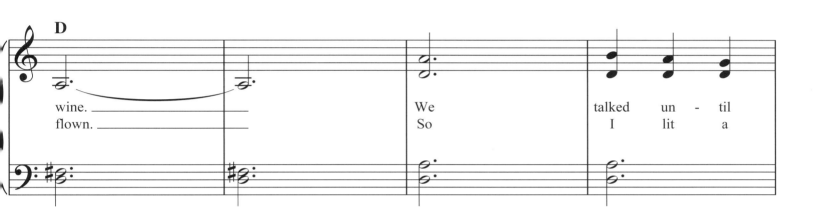

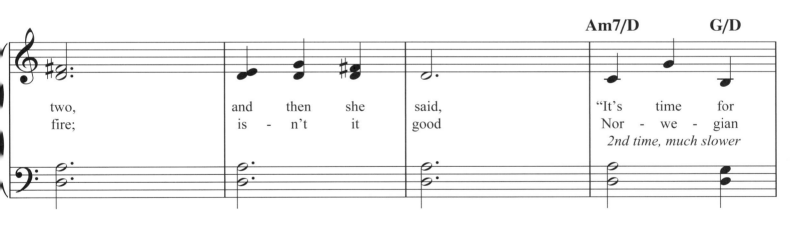

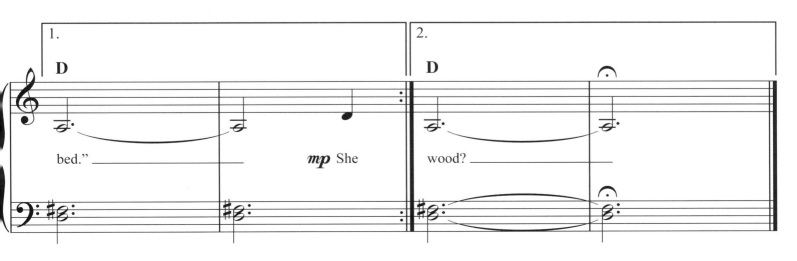

# NO REPLY

Words and Music by JOHN LENNON
and PAUL McCARTNEY

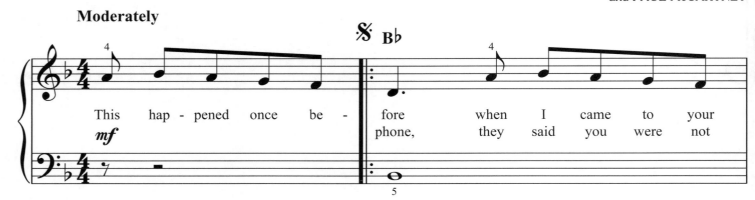

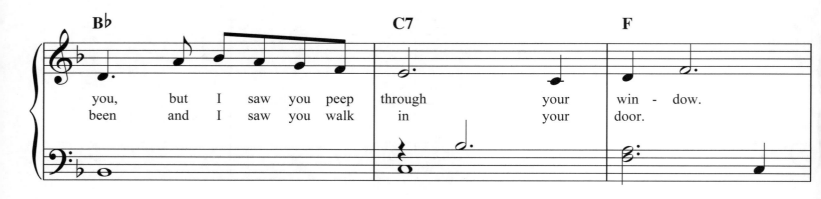

I know that you saw
'cause you walked hand in

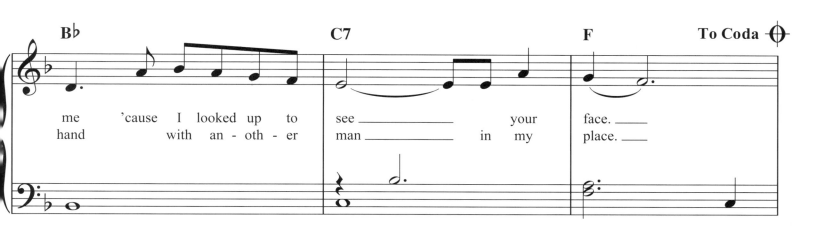

me 'cause I looked up to
hand with an - oth - er

see _____ your
man _____ in my

face. _____
place. _____

1.
I tried to tel - e -

2.
If I were you I'd
give the

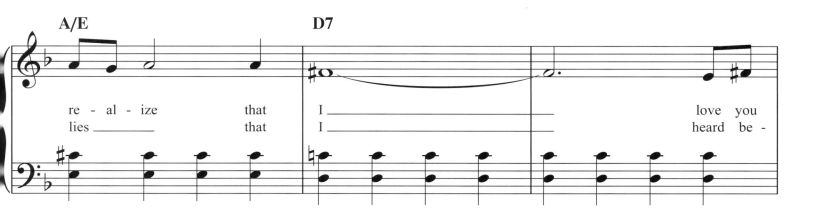

re - al - ize that
lies _____ that

I _____
I _____

love you
heard be -

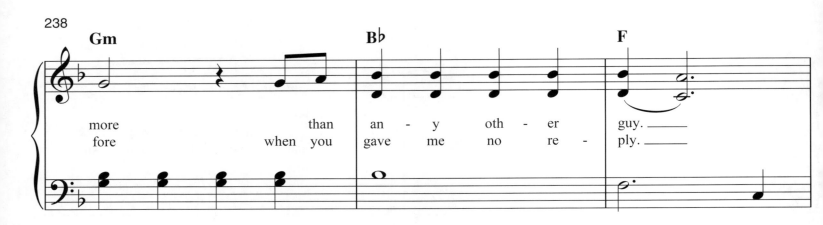

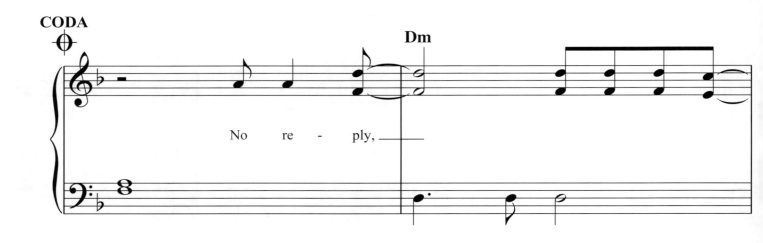

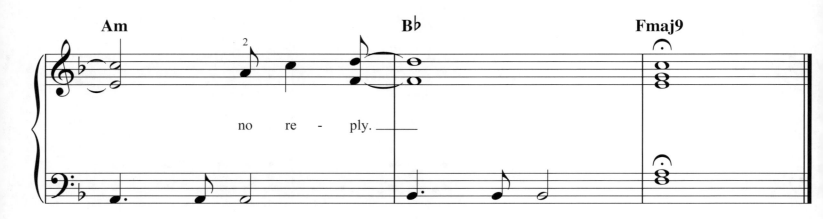

# OCTOPUS'S GARDEN

Words and Music by
RICHARD STARKEY

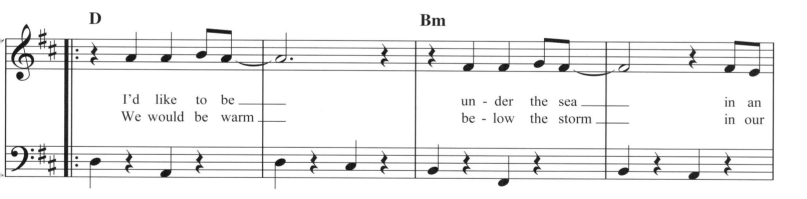

I'd like to be _____ under the sea _____ in an
We would be warm _____ be-low the storm _____ in our

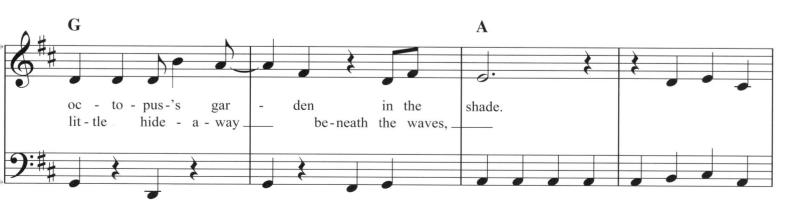

oc - to - pus-'s gar - den in the shade.
lit - tle hide - a - way _____ be-neath the waves,

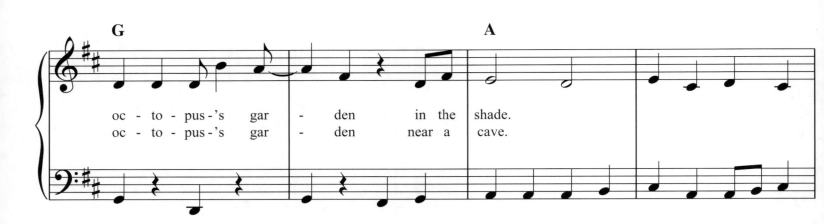

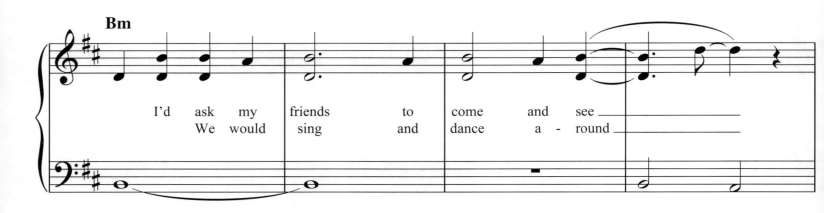

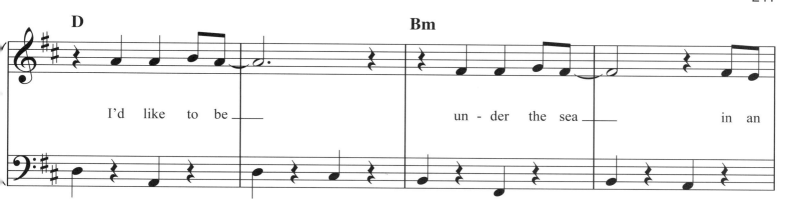

I'd like to be ___ un - der the sea ___ in an

oc - to - pus -'s gar - den in the shade. ___

We would shout ___

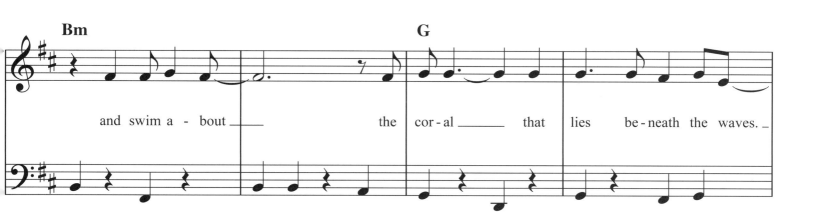

and swim a - bout ___ the cor - al ___ that lies be - neath the waves. ___

Oh, what joy ____ for

ev - 'ry girl and boy ____ know-ing ____ they're hap - py and they're

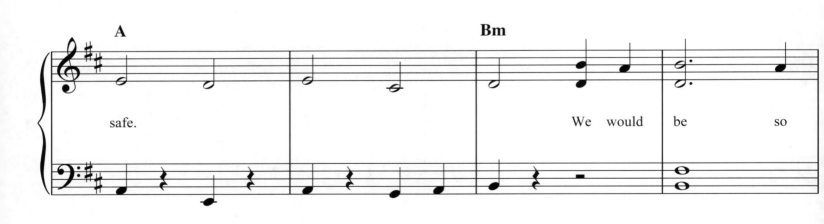

safe. We would be so

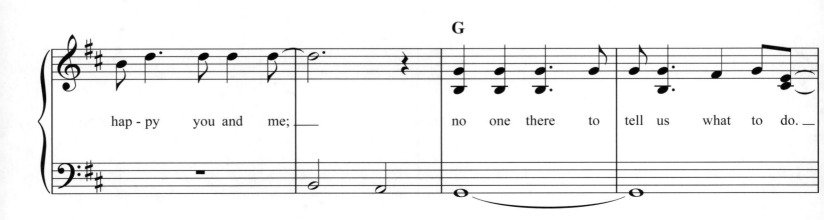

hap - py you and me; ____ no one there to tell us what to do. ____

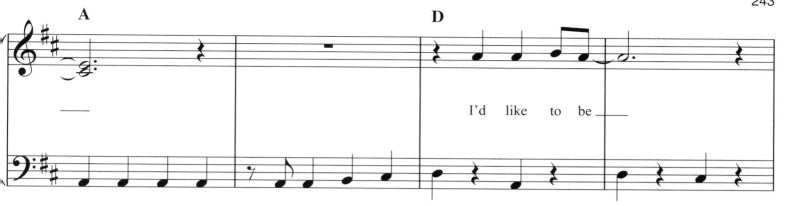

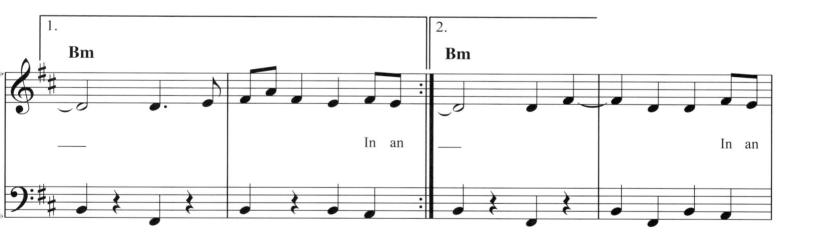

# NOWHERE MAN

Words and Music by JOHN LENNON
and PAUL McCARTNEY

**Moderate Rock Ballad**

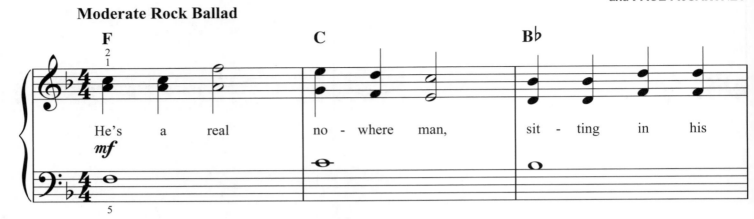

He's a real no-where man, sit-ting in his

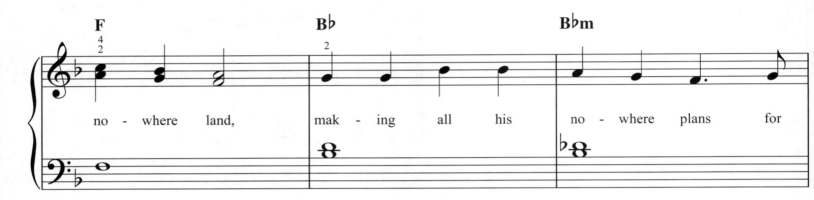

no-where land, mak-ing all his no-where plans for

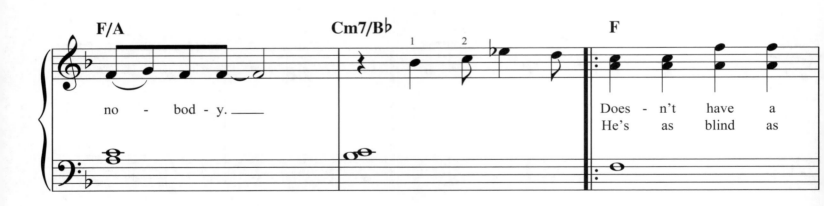

no-bod-y. ___ Does-n't have a
He's as blind as

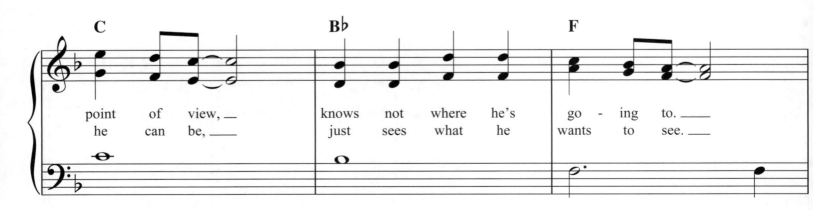

point of view, ___ knows not where he's go-ing to. ___
he can be, ___ just sees what he wants to see. ___

Is - n't he a bit like you and me? ____
No - where man, can you see me at all? ____

No - where man, please lis - ten: You don't
No - where man, don't wor - ry; take your

know what you're miss - ing. No - where man,                    the
time,      don't hur - ry. Leave it all              till

world _____ is at your com - mand.
some - bod - y else lends you a hand.

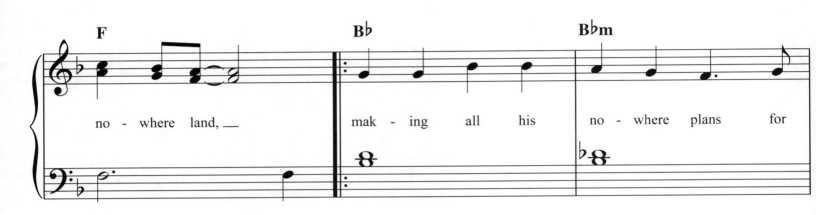

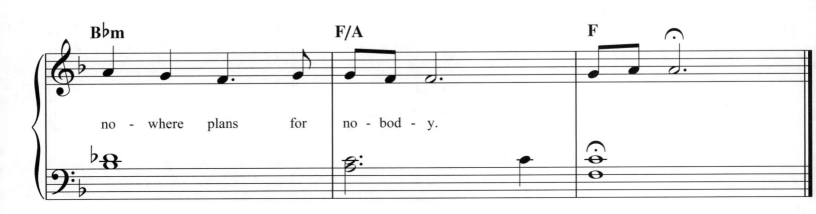

# PAPERBACK WRITER

Words and Music by JOHN LENNON
and PAUL McCARTNEY

**Bright Rock beat**

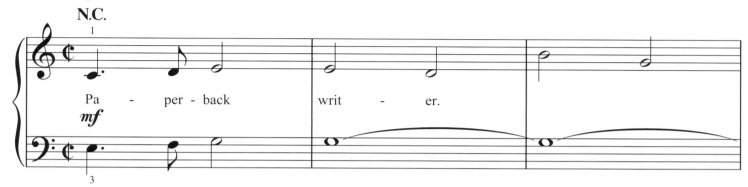

Pa - per-back writ - er.

Dear __ Sir or Mad-am, will you
It's a thou-sand pag-es, give or

read my book? It took me years to write, will you take a look? It's __ I can
take a few, __ I'll be writ - ing more in a week or two.

based on a nov-el by a man named Lear, and I need a job so I
make it ____ long-er if you like the style, I can change it 'round and I

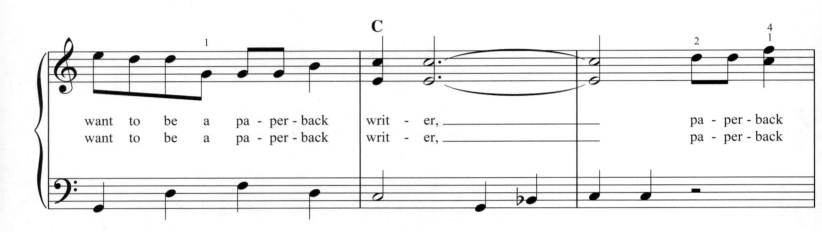

want to be a pa-per-back writ - er, ____ pa-per-back
want to be a pa-per-back writ - er, ____ pa - per - back

writ - er. ____ It's the dirt-y sto-ry of a
writ - er. ____ If you real-ly like it you can

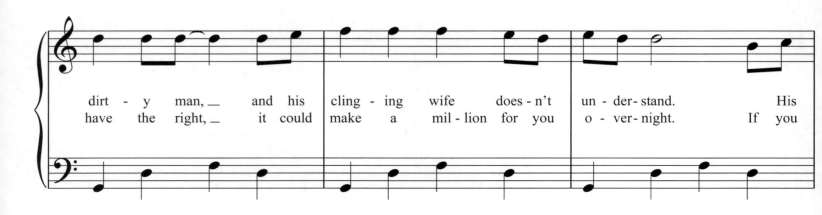

dirt-y man, ___ and his cling-ing wife does-n't un-der-stand. His
have the right, ___ it could make a mil-lion for you o-ver-night. If you

son     is    work-ing  for  the     Dai — ly   Mail; __   it's   a       stead — y  job, __   but  he
must    re — turn it,   you  can     send   it    here, __  but  I       need  a  break __ and  I

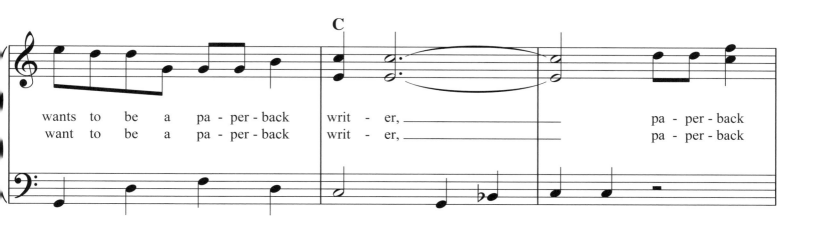

**C**

wants   to   be    a   pa-per-back     writ  —  er, _____      pa - per - back
want    to   be    a   pa-per-back     writ  —  er, _____      pa - per - back

**G7**

writ  —  er. _____      Pa  —  per - back

writ  —  er. _____

# OB-LA-DI, OB-LA-DA

Words and Music by JOHN LENNON
and PAUL McCARTNEY

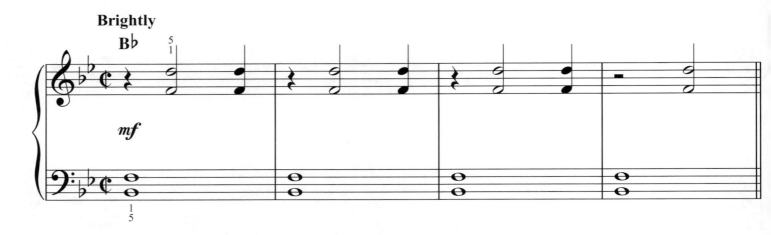

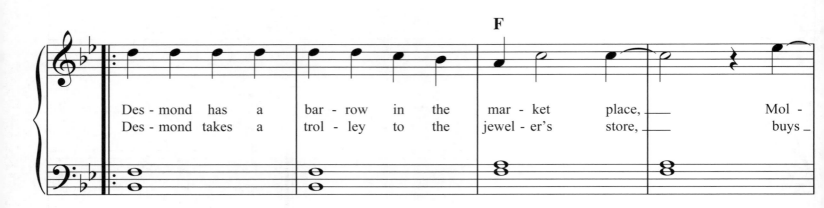

Des - mond has a bar - row in the mar - ket place,___ Mol -
Des - mond takes a trol - ley to the jewel - er's store,___ buys

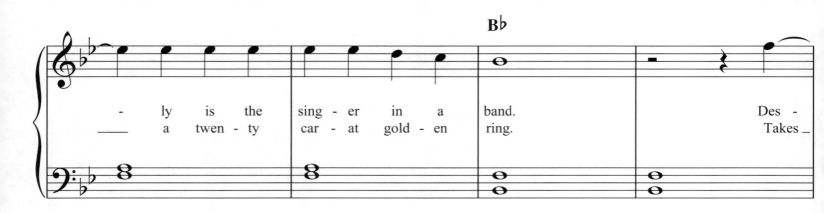

- ly is the sing - er in a band.
___ a twen - ty car - at gold - en ring.

Des -
Takes ___

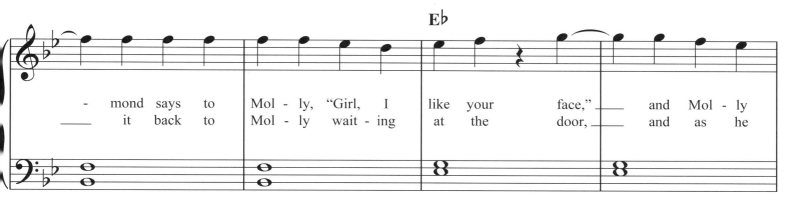

- mond says to Mol - ly, "Girl, I like your face," ___ and Mol - ly
___ it back to Mol - ly wait - ing at the door, ___ and as he

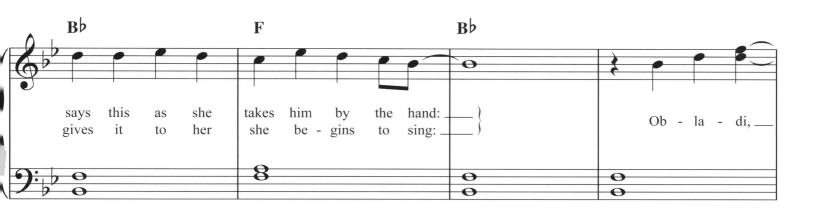

says this as she takes him by the hand: ___
gives it to her she be - gins to sing: ___

Ob - la - di, ___

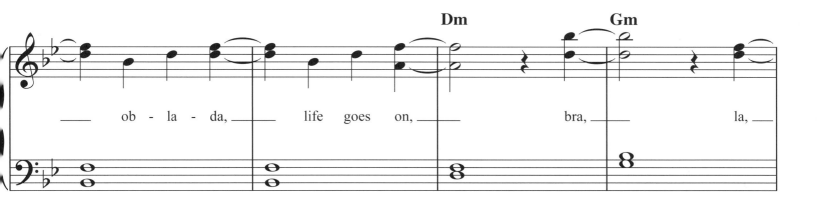

___ ob - la - da, ___ life goes on, ___ bra, ___ la,

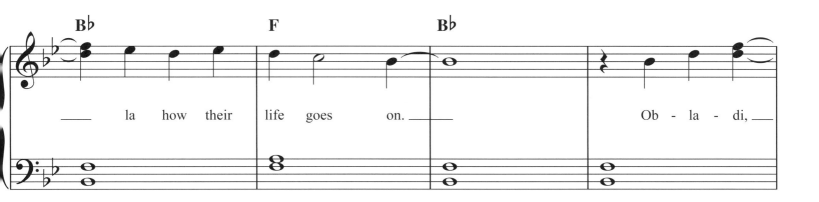

___ la how their life goes on. ___

Ob - la - di, ___

ob - la - da, _____ life goes on, _____ bra, _____ la, _____

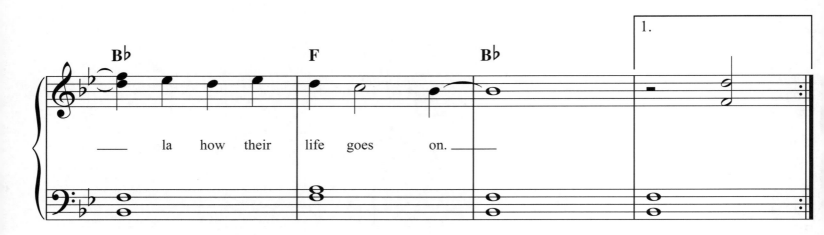

_____ la how their life goes on. _____

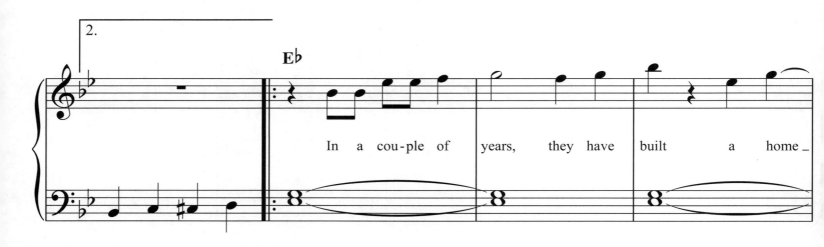

In a cou-ple of years, they have built a home _____

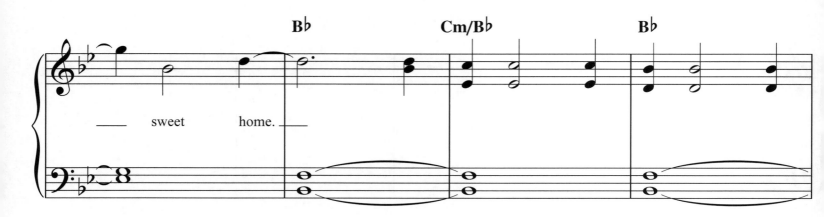

_____ sweet home. _____

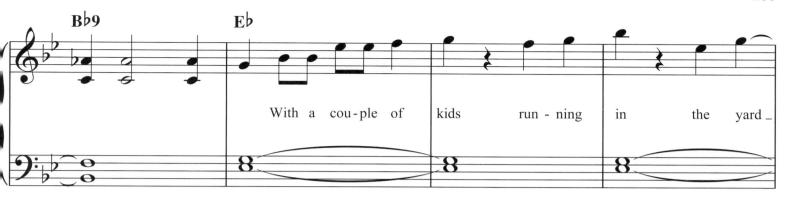

With a cou-ple of kids run - ning in the yard _

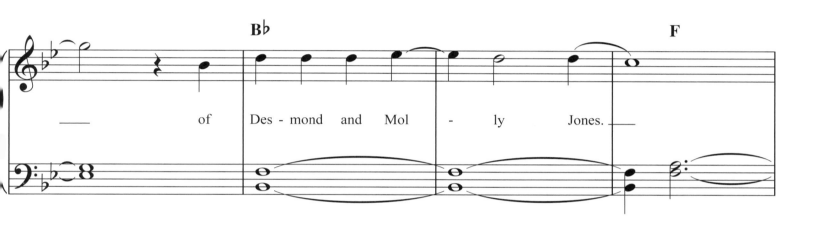

_ of Des - mond and Mol - ly Jones. _

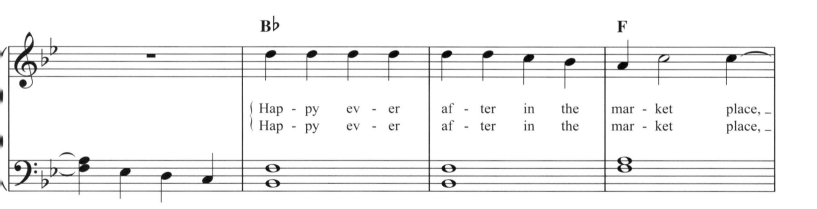

Hap - py ev - er af - ter in the mar - ket place, _
Hap - py ev - er af - ter in the mar - ket place, _

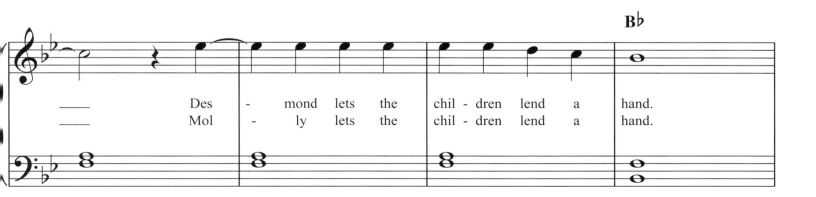

_ Des - mond lets the chil - dren lend a hand.
_ Mol - ly lets the chil - dren lend a hand.

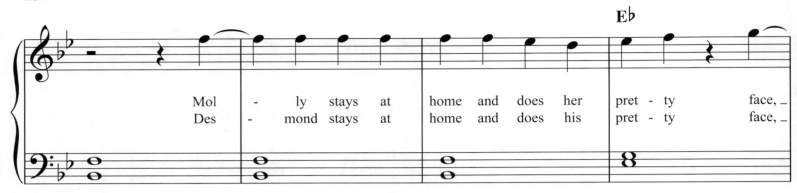

Mol - ly stays at home and does her pret - ty face, ___
Des - mond stays at home and does his pret - ty face, ___

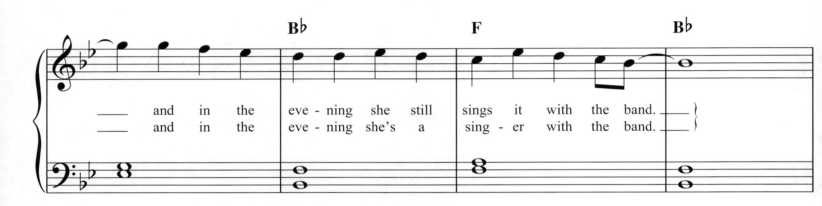

___ and in the eve - ning she still sings it with the band. ___
___ and in the eve - ning she's a sing - er with the band. ___

Ob - la - di, ___ ob - la - da, ___ life goes on, ___ bra, ___

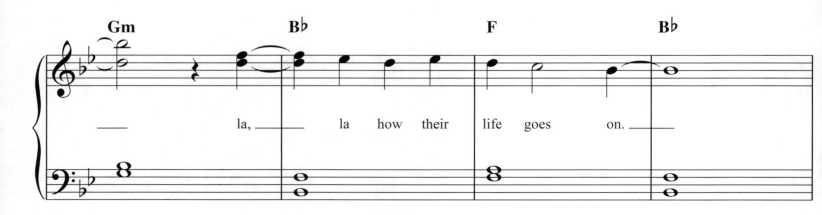

___ la, ___ la how their life goes on. ___

Ob - la - di, \_\_\_ ob - la - da, \_\_\_ life goes on, \_\_\_ bra, \_\_\_

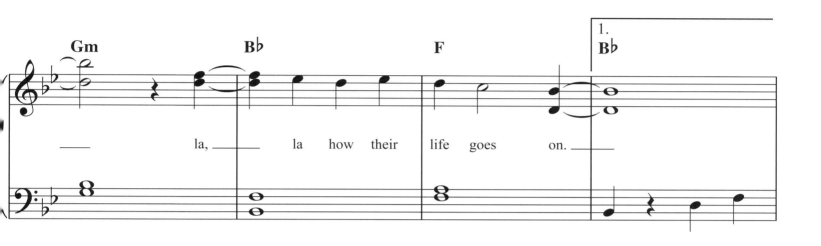

\_\_\_ la, \_\_\_ la how their life goes on. \_\_\_

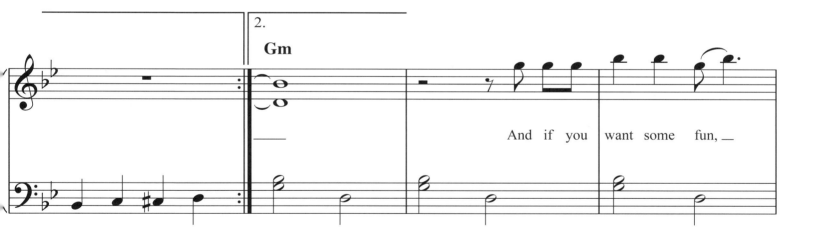

And if you want some fun, \_\_

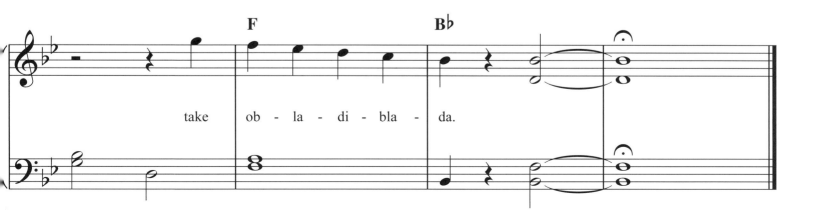

take ob - la - di - bla - da.

# OH! DARLING

Words and Music by JOHN LENNON
and PAUL McCARTNEY

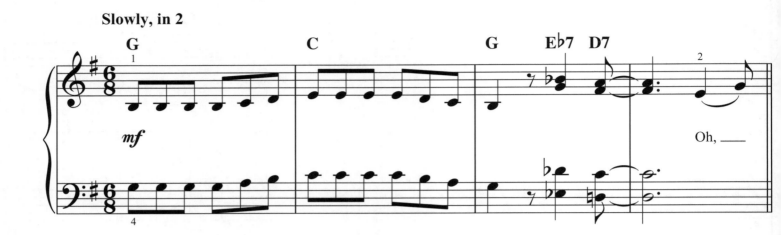

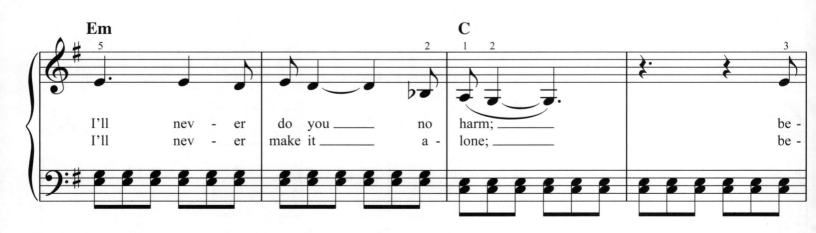

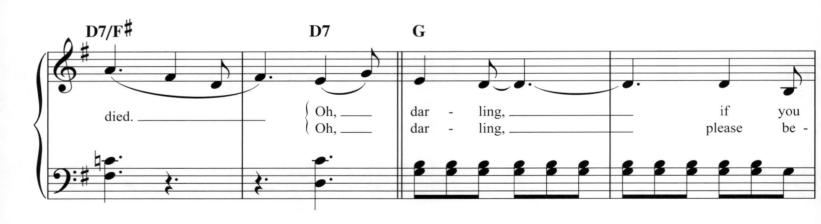

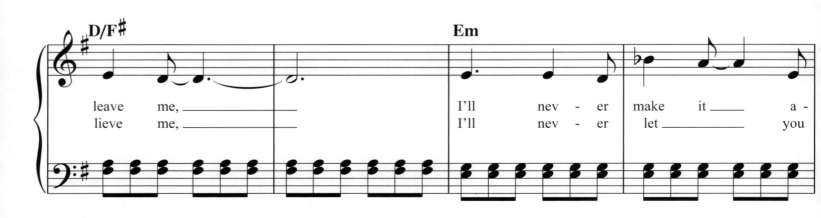

# PENNY LANE

Words and Music by JOHN LENNON<br/>and PAUL McCARTNEY

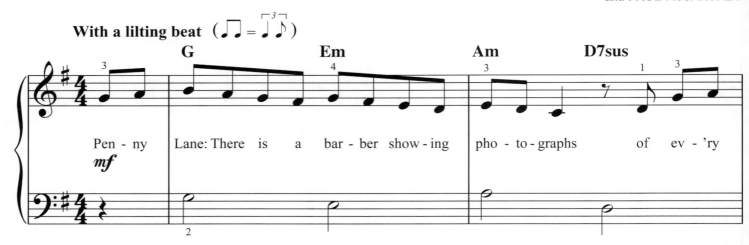

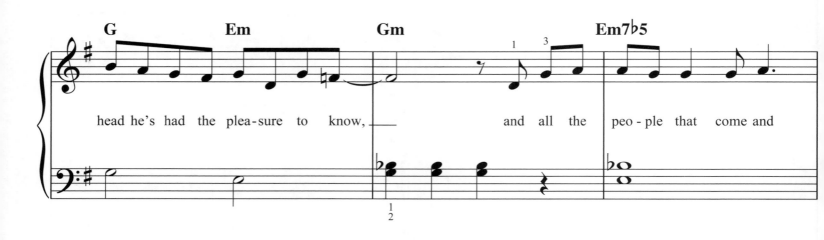

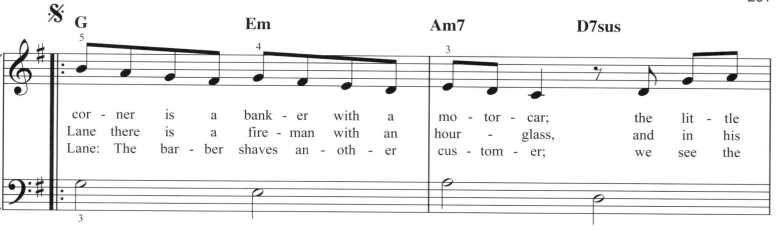

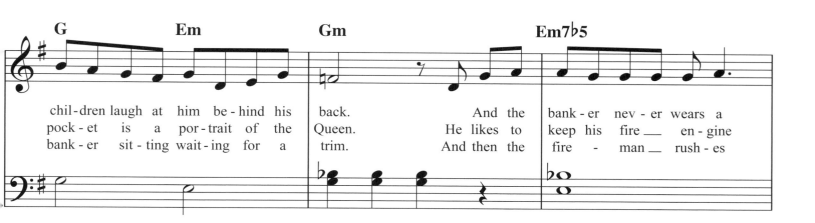

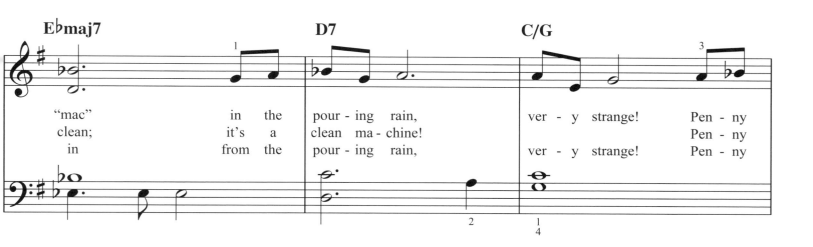

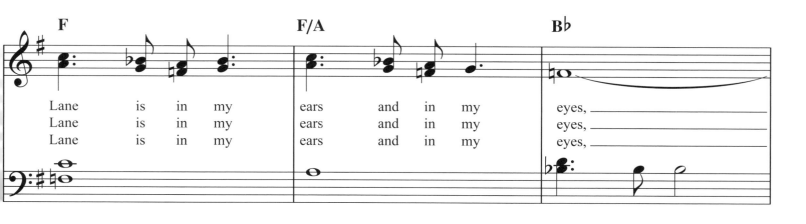

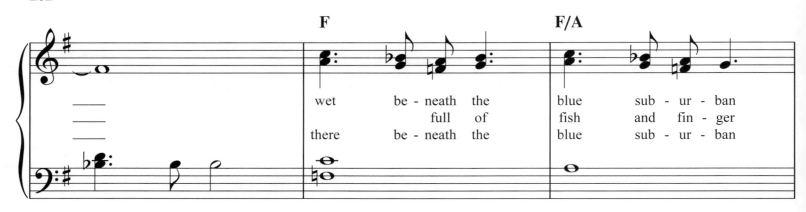

**F** · **F/A**

wet    be - neath   the      blue    sub - ur - ban
full   of       fish    and  fin - ger
there    be - neath   the      blue    sub - ur - ban

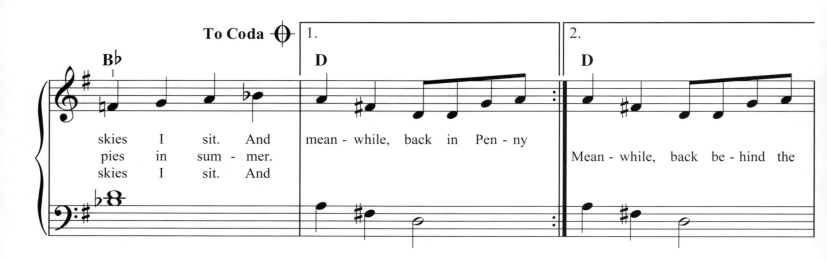

**To Coda**   **1.** **Bb** **D** **2.** **D**

skies    I   sit.   And   mean - while,  back  in  Pen - ny
pies   in  sum - mer.
skies    I   sit.   And           Mean - while,  back  be - hind  the

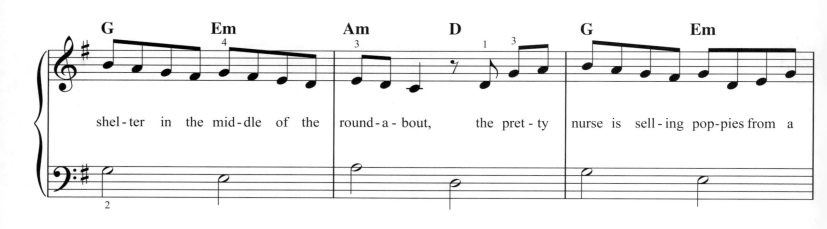

**G** **Em** **Am** **D** **G** **Em**

shel - ter  in the mid - dle of the   round - a - bout,   the pret - ty   nurse is sell - ing pop - pies from a

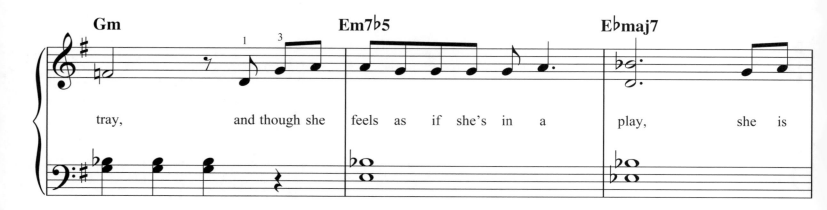

**Gm** **Em7b5** **Ebmaj7**

tray,    and though she   feels  as  if  she's  in  a   play,      she is

# PLEASE PLEASE ME

Words and Music by JOHN LENNON
and PAUL McCARTNEY

Last night I said these words to my girl,
You don't I need said me to show to the my way, girl,
love,

I know { you } { I } nev - er e - ven
why do I al - ways have to

try, girl.
say, girl, love,

Come on, (come on,) come
come on, (come on,) come

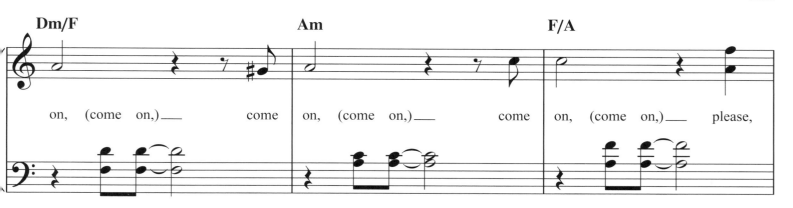

on, (come on,)___ come on, (come on,)___ come on, (come on,)___ please,

please me, whoa, yeah, like I please you.

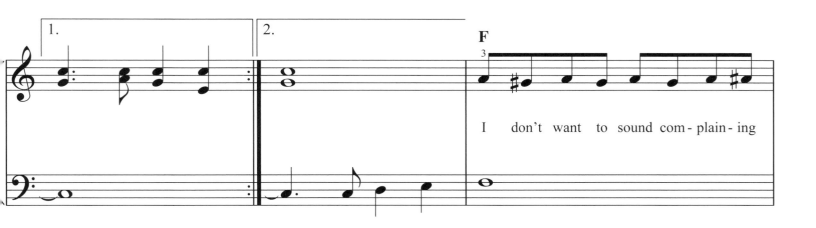

I don't want to sound com-plain-ing

but you know there's al-ways rain in my_____ heart. (In___ my heart.)

I do all the pleas-ing with you, it's so hard to rea-son with you, whoa,

**D.S. al Coda**
**(Verse 1)**

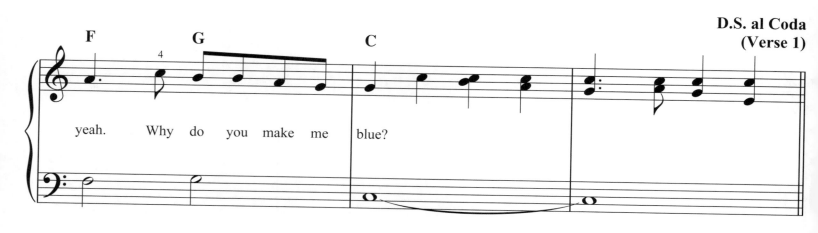

yeah. Why do you make me blue?

**CODA**

yeah, like I please you, whoa, yeah, like I please

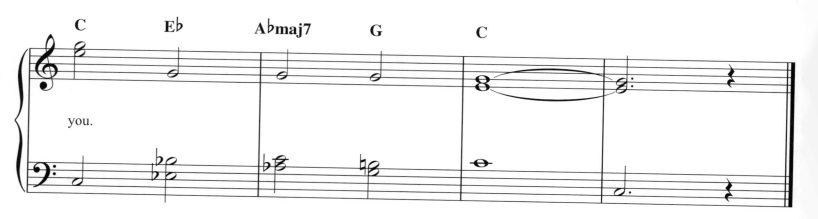

you.

# P.S. I LOVE YOU

Words and Music by JOHN LENNON
and PAUL McCARTNEY

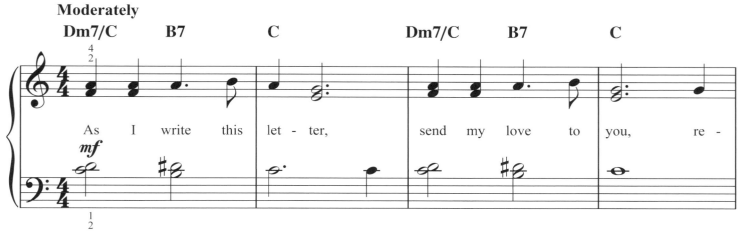

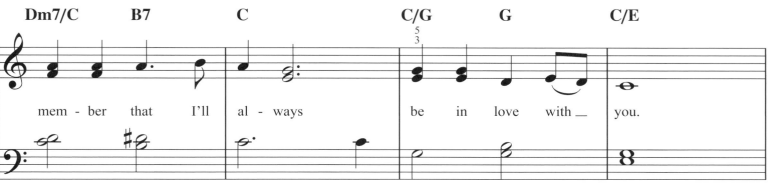

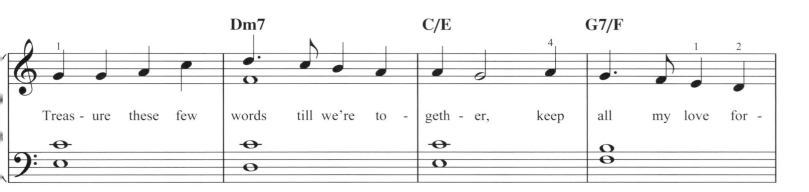

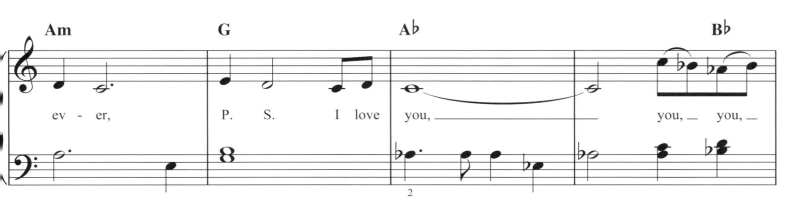

you.

**C/E**  **Dm7**

I'll be com - ing home a - gain to
Treas - ure these few words till we're to -

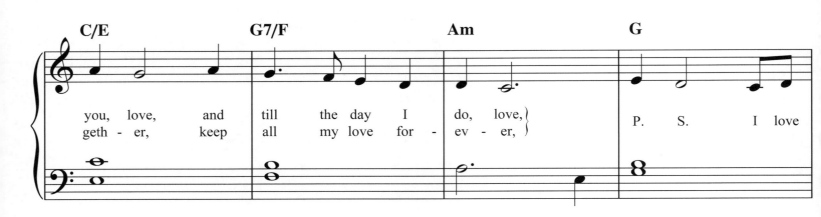

**C/E**  **G7/F**  **Am**  **G**

you, love, and till the day I do, love,
geth - er, and keep all my love for - ev - er,

P. S. I love

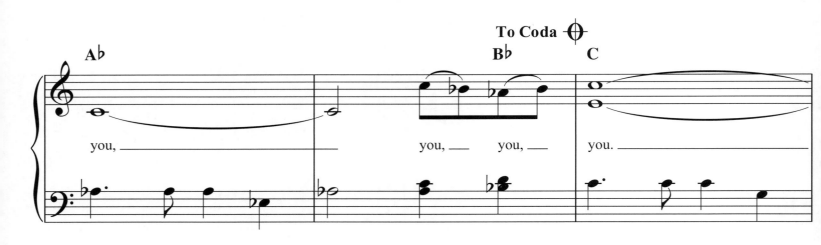

**Ab**  **Bb**  **To Coda**  **C**

you, you, you, you.

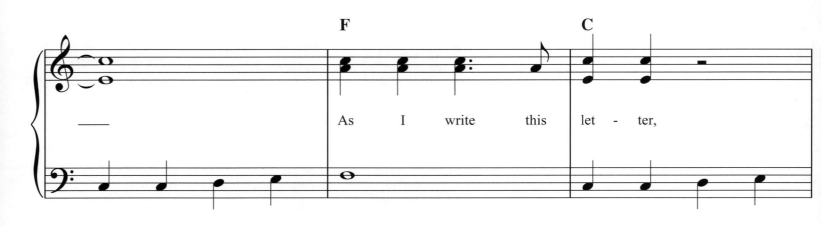

**F**  **C**

As I write this let - ter,

send my love to you, re - mem - ber that I'll

al - ways be in love with \_\_\_ you.

**2.**
C/E
**D.S. al Coda**
**(verse 1)**

you.

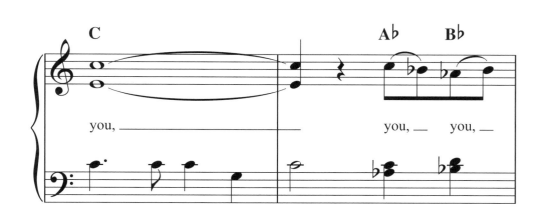

you, _____ you, \_\_\_ you, \_\_\_

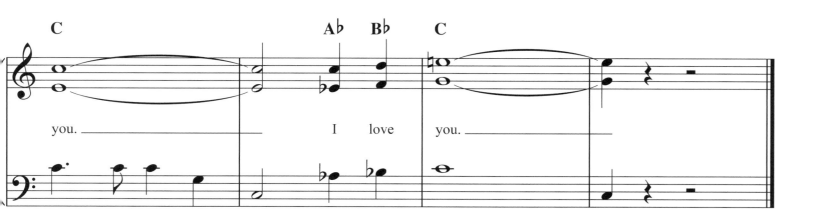

you. _____ I love you. _____

# POLYTHENE PAM

Words and Music by JOHN LENNON
and PAUL McCARTNEY

Yeah,     yeah,     yeah.

Get a

*rit.*

*Additional Lyrics*

2. Get a dose of her in jackboots and kilt.
   She's killer diller when she's dressed to the hilt.
   She's the kind of a girl that makes the news of the world.
   Yes, you could say she was attractively built.
   Yeah, yeah, yeah.

# REVOLUTION

Words and Music by JOHN LENNON
and PAUL McCARTNEY

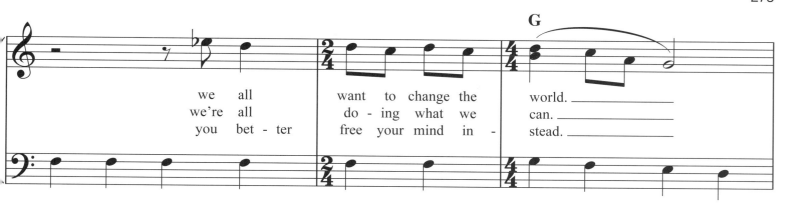

we all    want to change the    world. _____
we're all    do - ing what we    can. _____
you bet - ter    free your mind in -    stead. _____

But when you talk a - bout de -
But if you want mon-ey for peo - ple with
But if you go car - ry-ing pic-tures of

struc - tion, _____    don't you know that you can
minds that hate, _____    all I can tell you is, broth - er, you
Chair - man Mao, _____    you ain't going to make it with an - y - one

count me out? _____
have to wait. _____
an - y - how. _____

Don't you know it's gon - na be al -

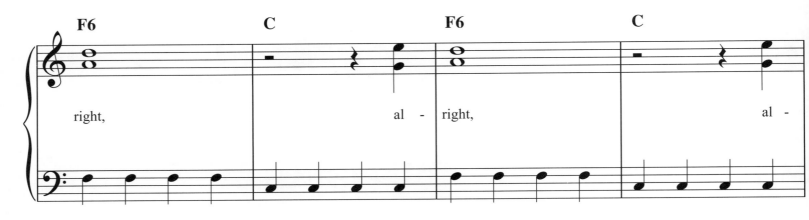

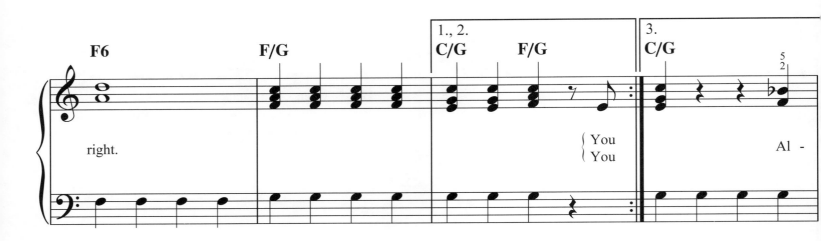

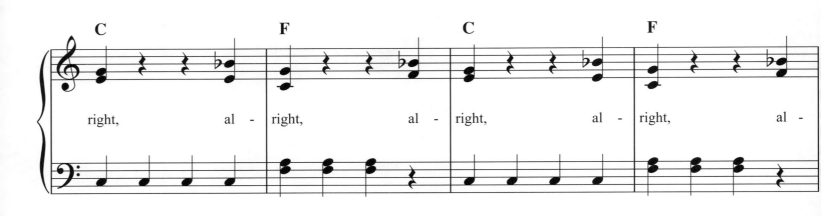

# RAIN

Words and Music by JOHN LENNON
and PAUL McCARTNEY

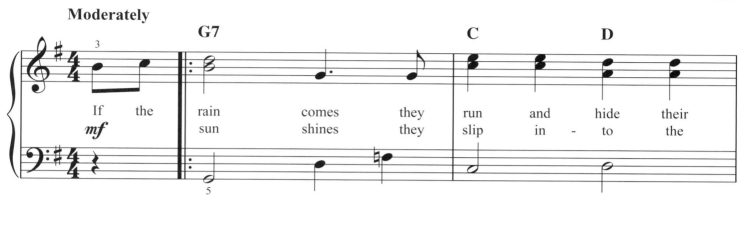

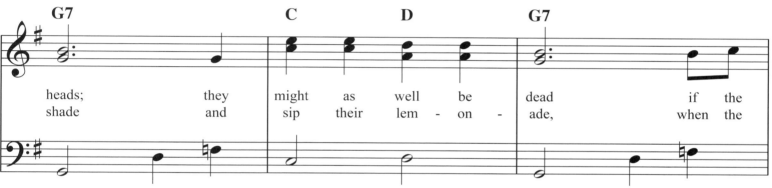

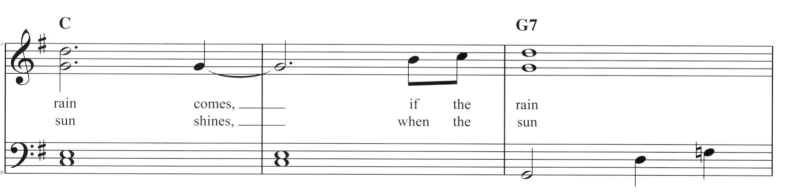

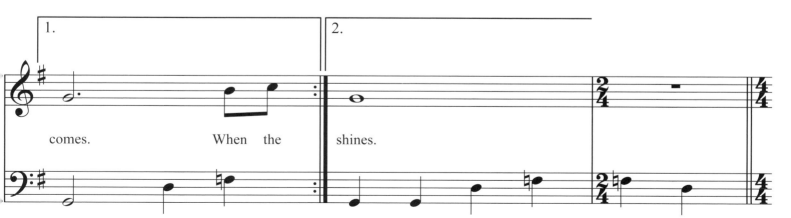

show      you       that      when      it      starts      to
hear      me       that      when      it      rains      and

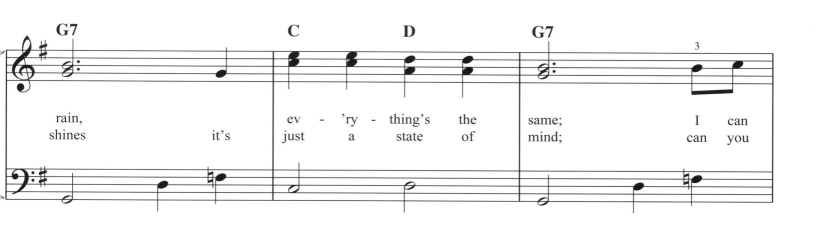

rain,              ev - 'ry - thing's   the      same;      I   can
shines      it's      just    a    state    of      mind;      can   you

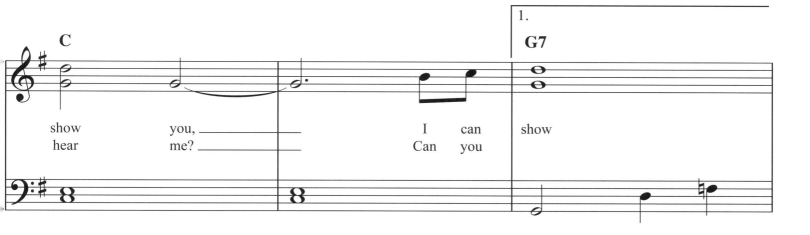

show      you,                I   can    show
hear      me?               Can  you

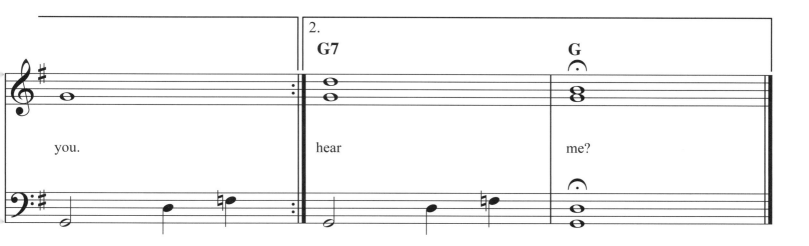

you.                hear            me?

# ROCKY RACCOON

Words and Music by JOHN LENNON
and PAUL McCARTNEY

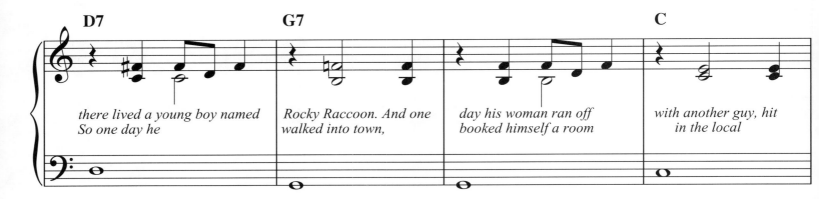

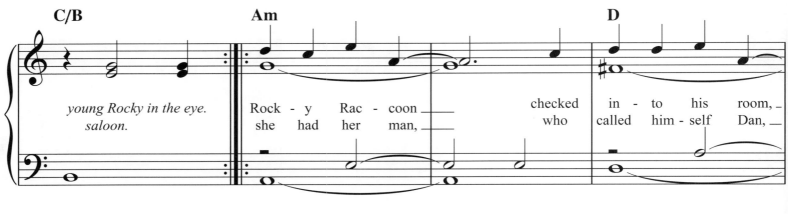

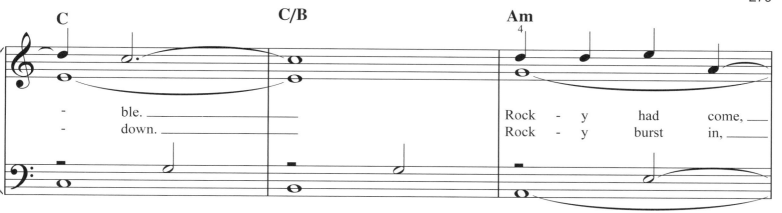

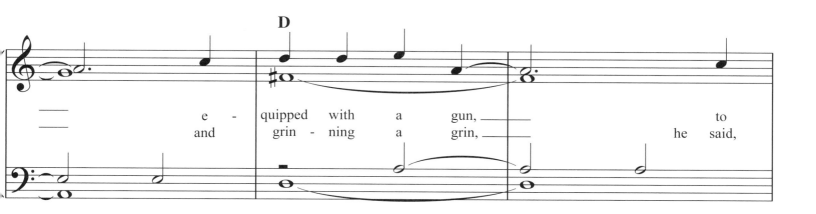

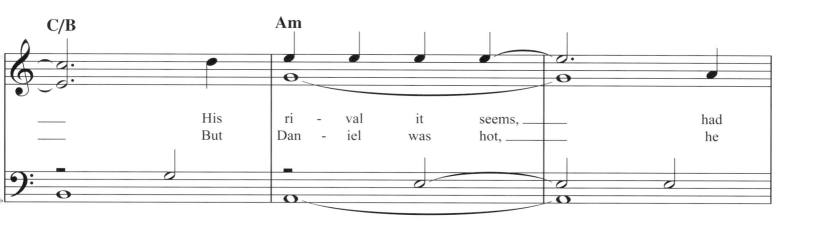

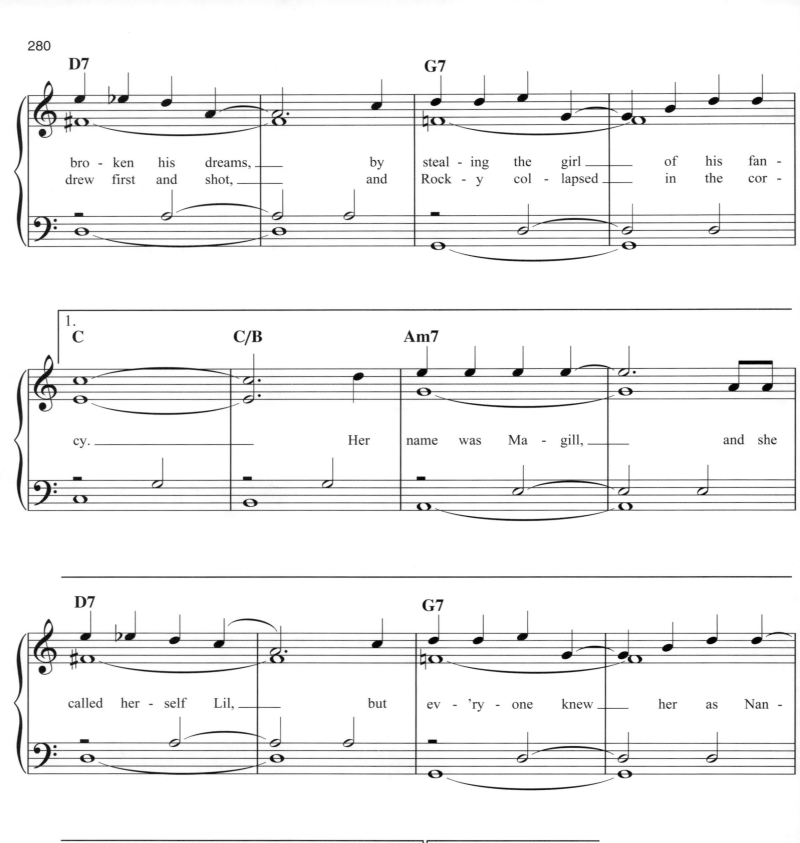

bro - ken his dreams, ____ by steal - ing the girl ____ of his fan -
drew first and shot, ____ and Rock - y col - lapsed ____ in the cor -

**1.**

cy. ____ Her name was Ma - gill, ____ and she

called her - self Lil, ____ but ev - 'ry - one knew ____ her as Nan -

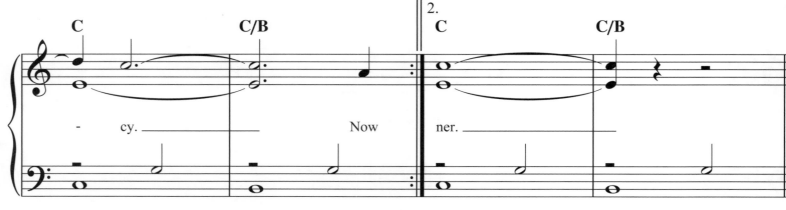

- cy. ____ Now ner. ____

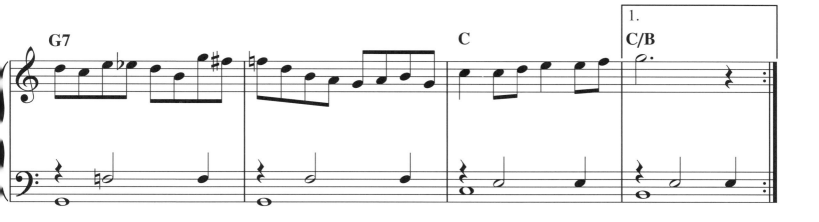

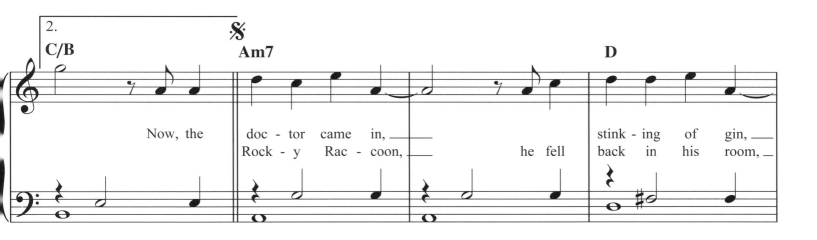

Now, the doc - tor came in, _____ stink - ing of gin, _____
Rock - y Rac - coon, _____ he fell back in his room, _____

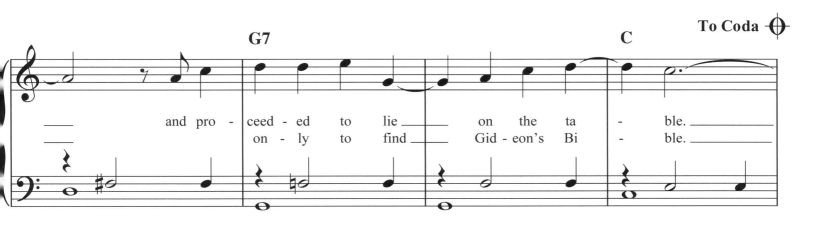

_____ and pro - ceed - ed to lie _____ on the ta - ble. _____
_____ on - ly to find _____ Gid - eon's Bi - ble. _____

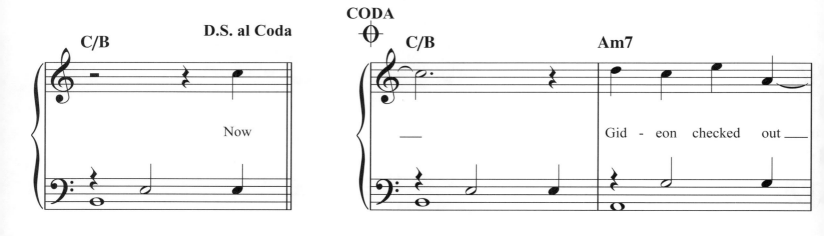

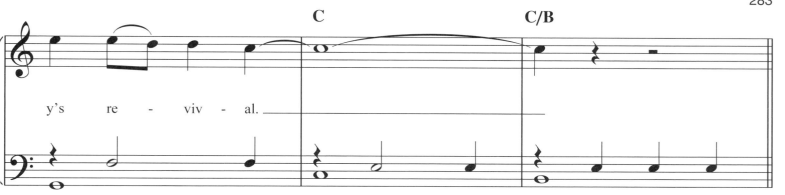

y's re - viv - al.

# RUN FOR YOUR LIFE

Words and Music by JOHN LENNON
and PAUL McCARTNEY

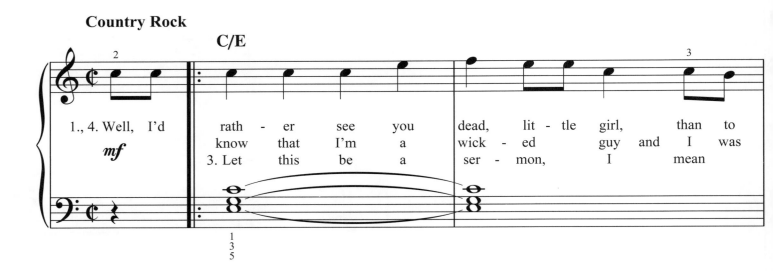

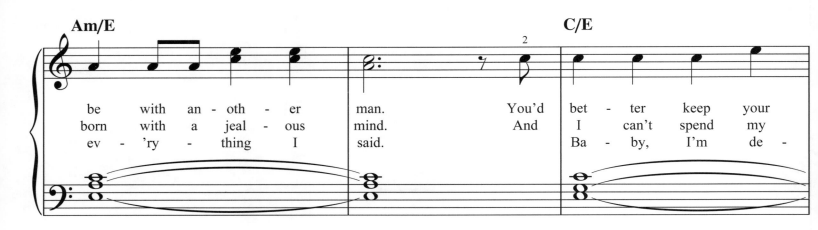

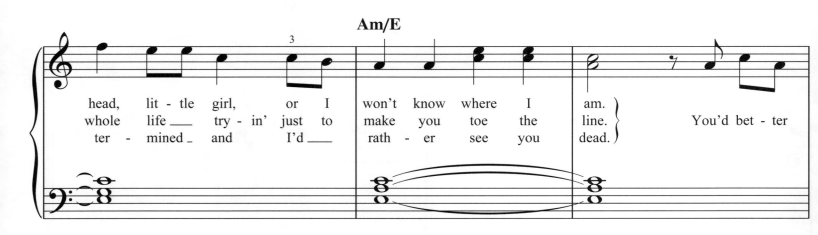

run for your life if you can, lit - tle girl, ___ Hide your head ___ in the

sand, lit - tle girl, ___ catch you with an - oth - er man, that's the

end - a, lit - tle girl!

2. Well, you
4. Well, I'd

# SGT. PEPPER'S LONELY HEARTS CLUB BAND

Words and Music by JOHN LENNON
and PAUL McCARTNEY

**Slowly, with a beat**

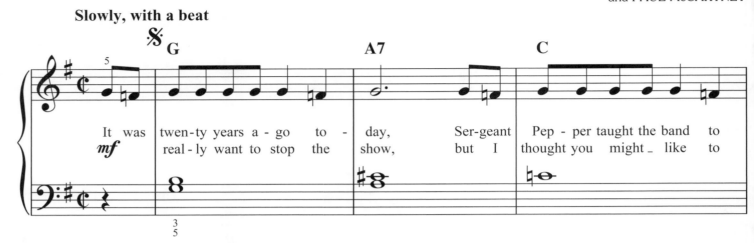

It was twen-ty years a - go to - day,  Ser-geant Pep - per taught the band to
real - ly want to stop the  show,  but I  thought you might _ like to

play.  They've been  go - ing in and out of  style,  but they're
know  that the  sing - er's gon - na sing a  song,  and he

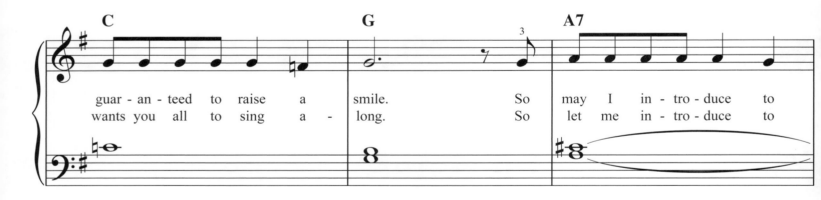

guar - an - teed to raise a  smile.  So may I in - tro - duce to
wants you all to sing a - long.  So let me in - tro - duce to

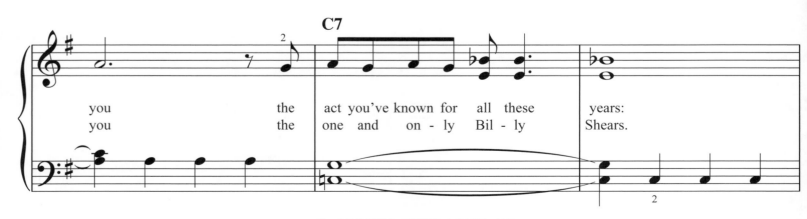

you  the  act you've known for all these  years:
you  the  one and on - ly Bil - ly  Shears.

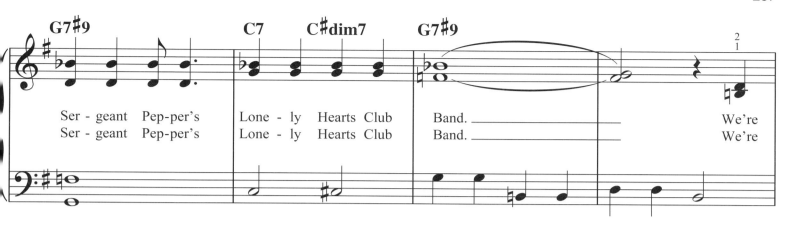

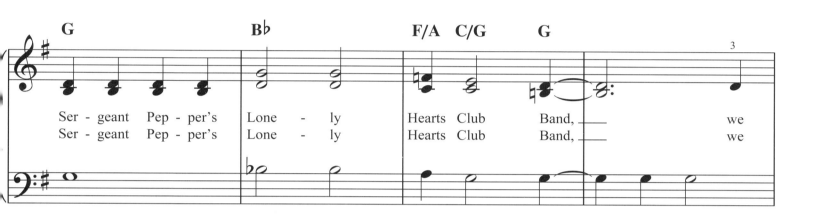

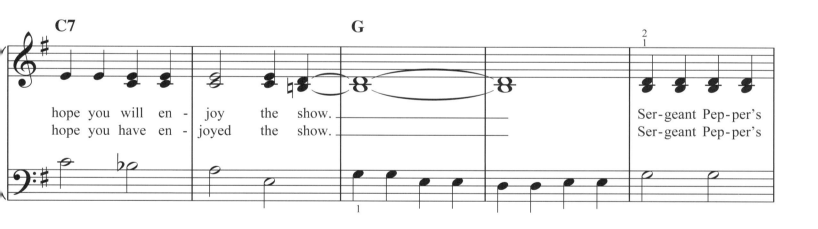

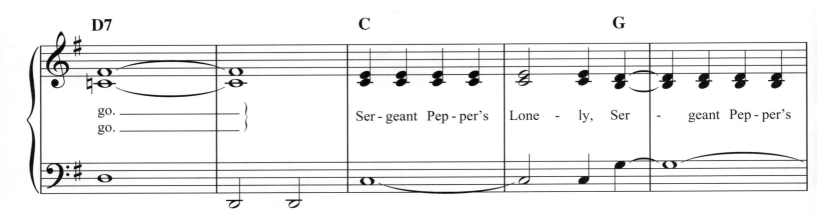

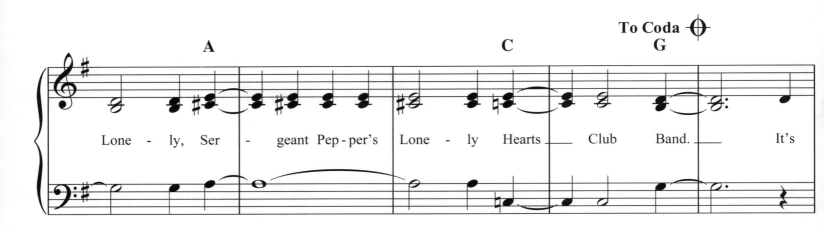

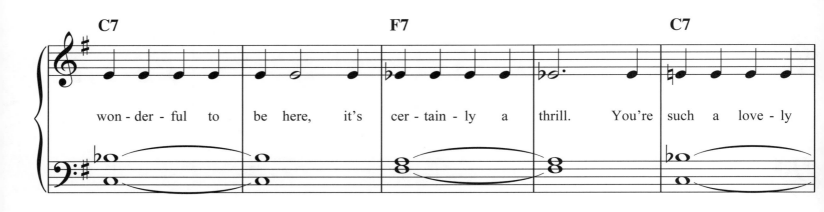

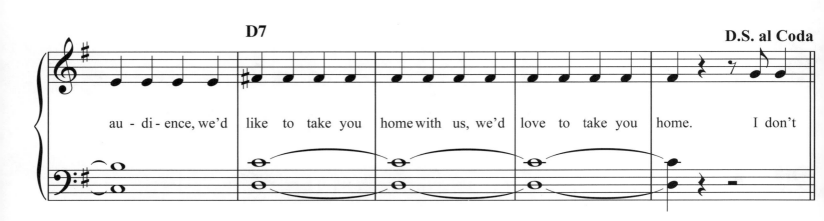

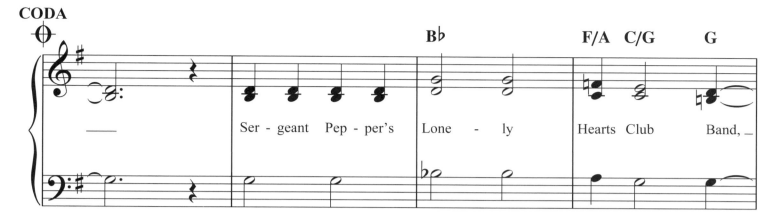

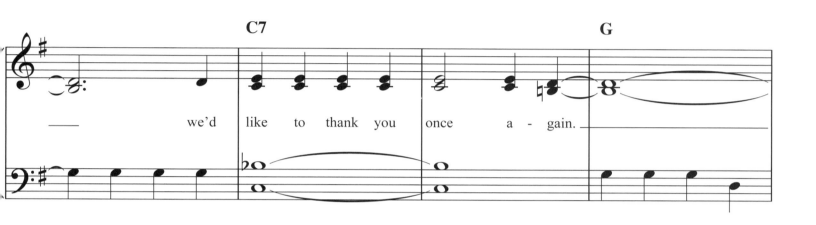

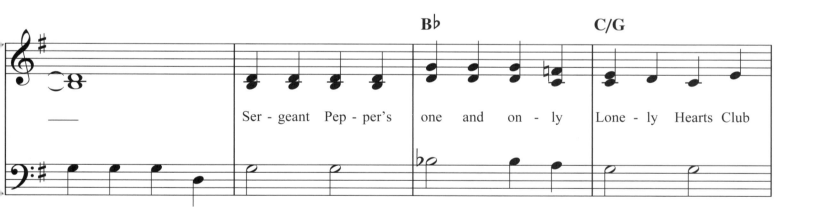

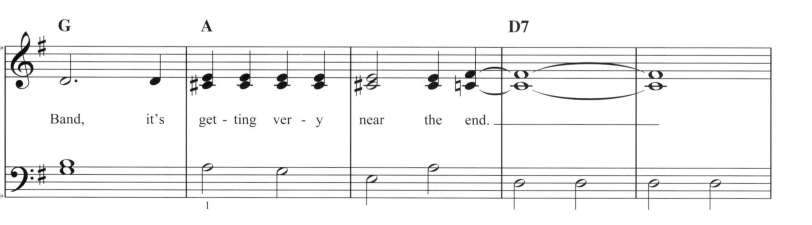

290

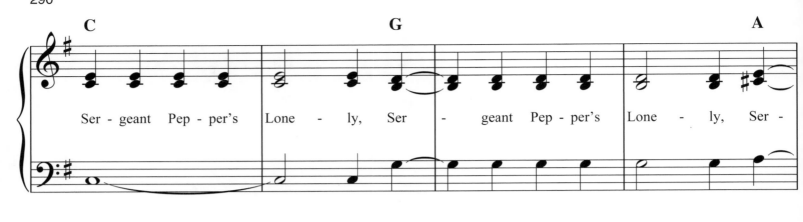

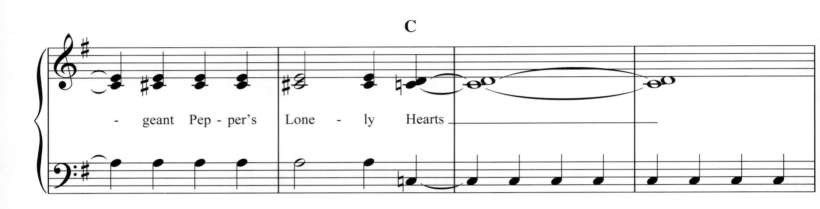

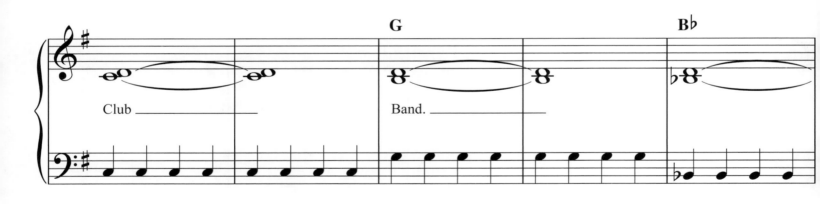

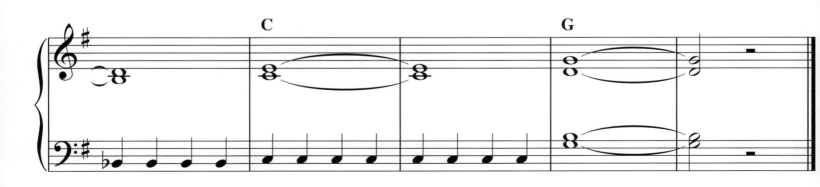

# SHE CAME IN THROUGH THE BATHROOM WINDOW

Words and Music by JOHN LENNON
and PAUL McCARTNEY

**Moderately slow**

She came in through the bath-room
And so I quit the p'lice de-

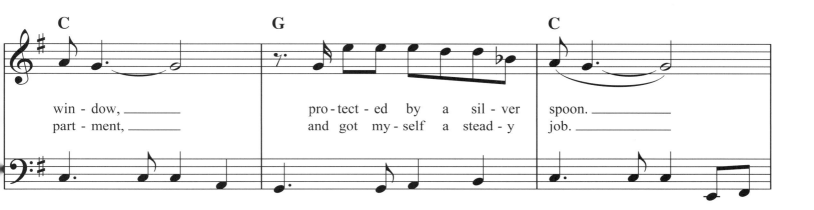

win - dow, _____ pro - tect - ed by a sil - ver spoon. _____
part - ment, _____ and got my - self a stead - y job. _____

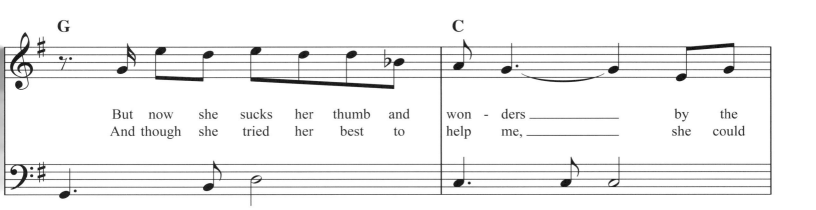

But now she sucks her thumb and won - ders _____ by the
And though she tried her best to help me, _____ she could

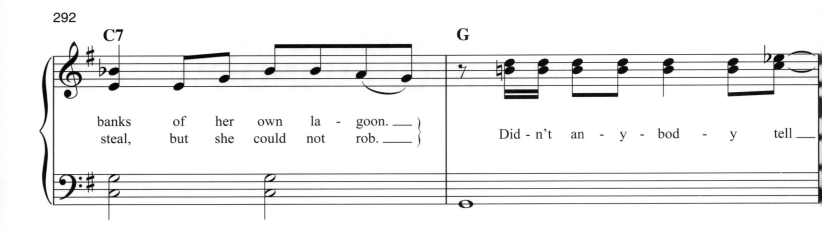

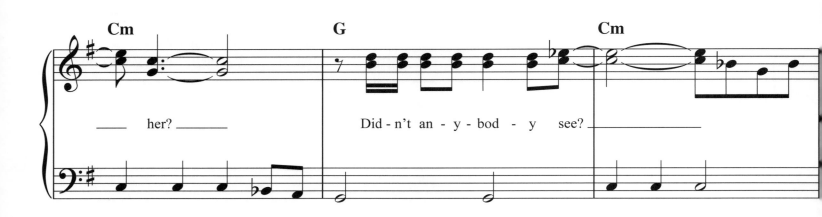

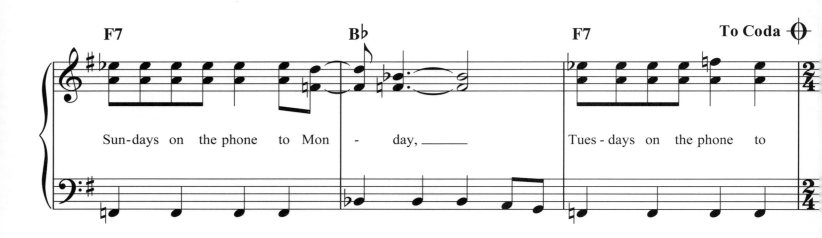

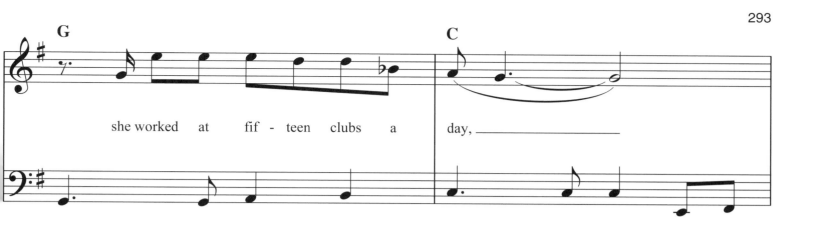

she worked at fif - teen clubs a day, _____

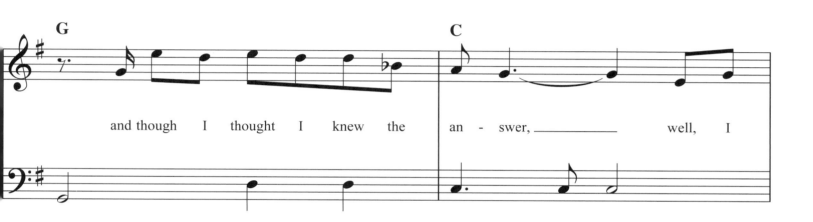

and though I thought I knew the an - swer, _____ well, I

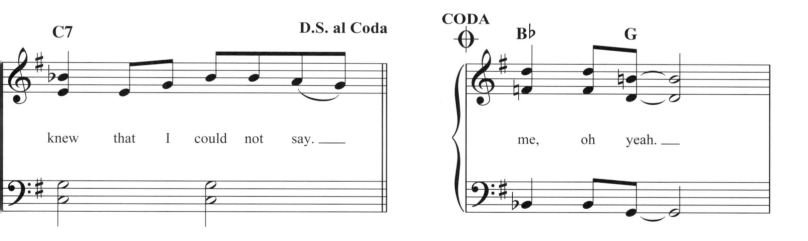

knew that I could not say. ___    me, oh yeah. ___

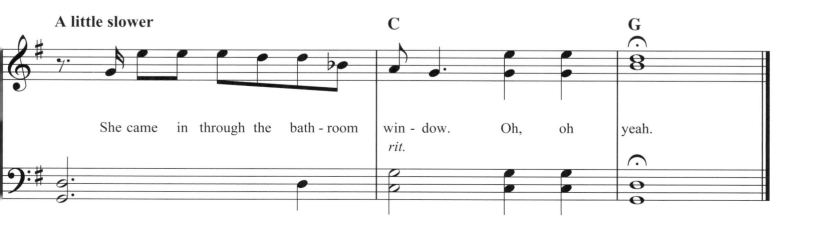

She came in through the bath - room win - dow. Oh, oh yeah.

# SEXY SADIE

Words and Music by JOHN LENNON
and PAUL McCARTNEY

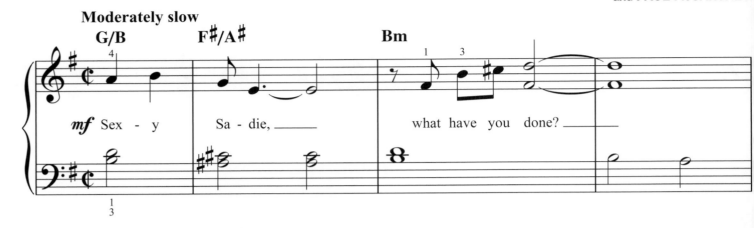

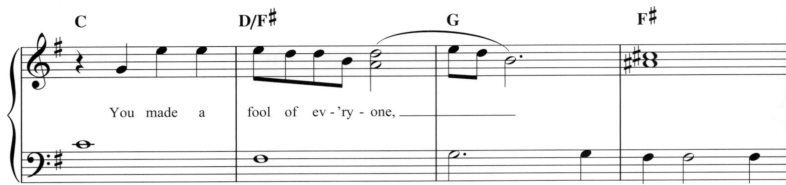

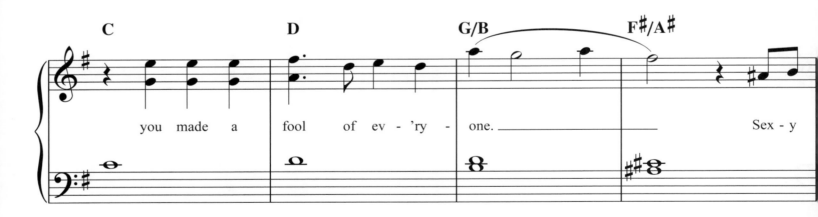

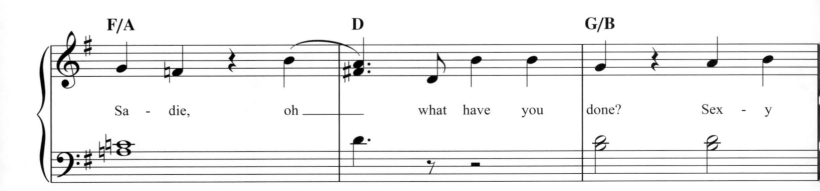

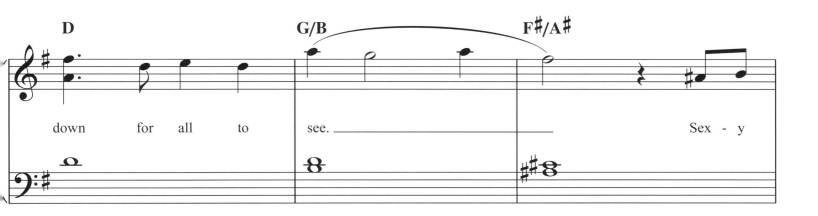

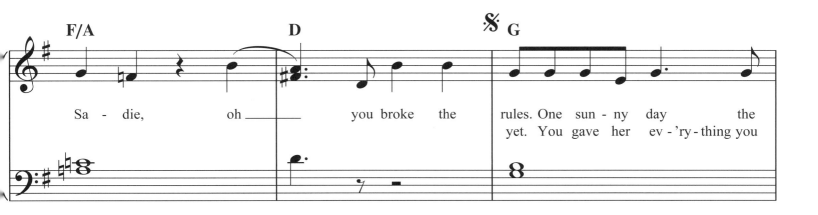

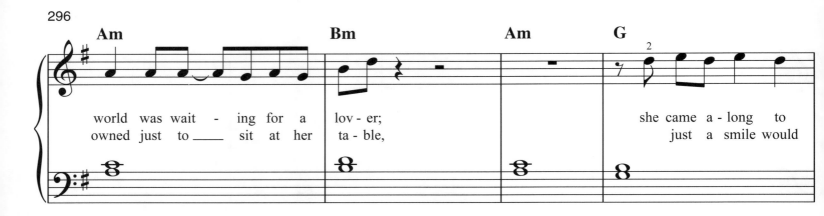

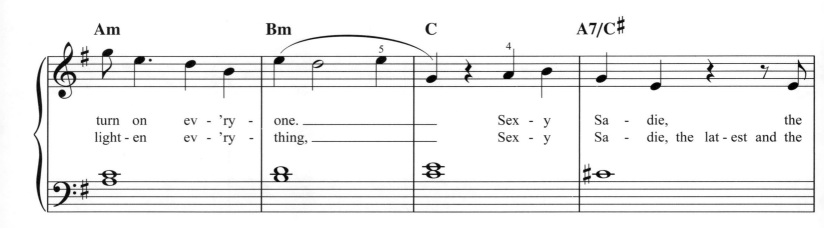

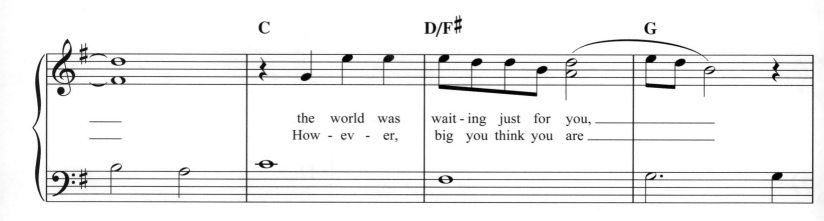

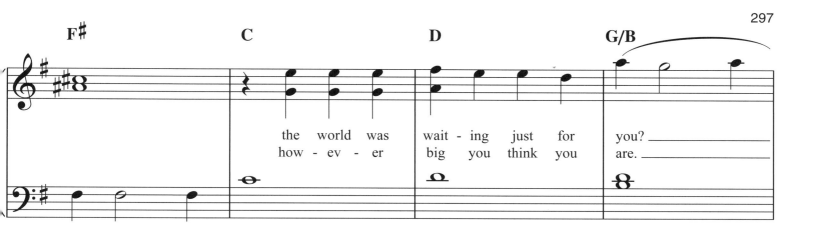

the world was waiting just for you? _____
how - ev - er big you think you are. _____

_____ Sex - y Sa - die, oh, how did you
_____ Sex - y

**2.** Sa - die, oh,

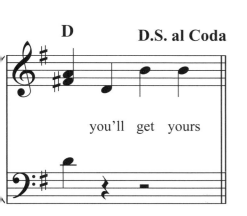

**D.S. al Coda**

you'll get yours

**CODA**

all. Sex - y Sa - die, she's the great - est of them all.

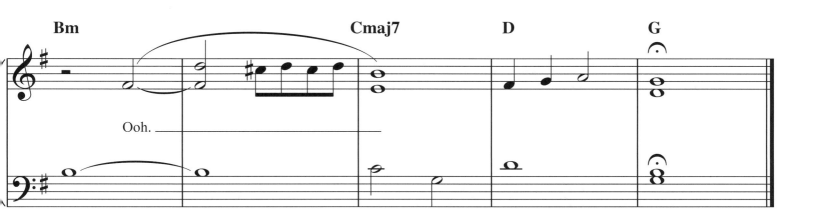

Ooh. _____

# SHE LOVES YOU

Words and Music by JOHN LENNON
and PAUL McCARTNEY

**Brisk Rock tempo**

She loves you yeah, yeah, yeah, she loves you, yeah,

yeah, yeah, she loves you, yeah, yeah, yeah, yeah. ____

____ You think you've lost your love? Well, I saw her yes-ter-

day. ____ It's you she's think-ing of and she told me what to

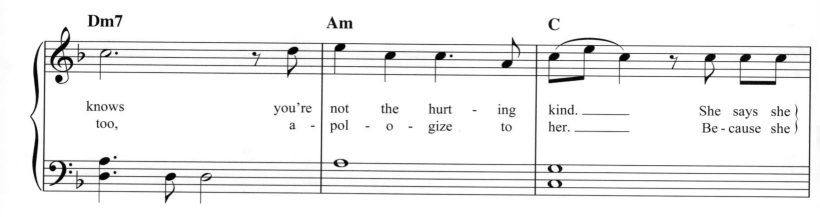

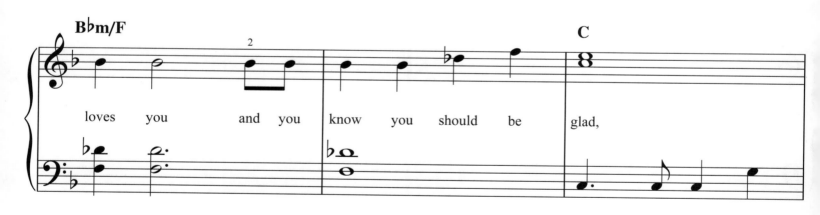

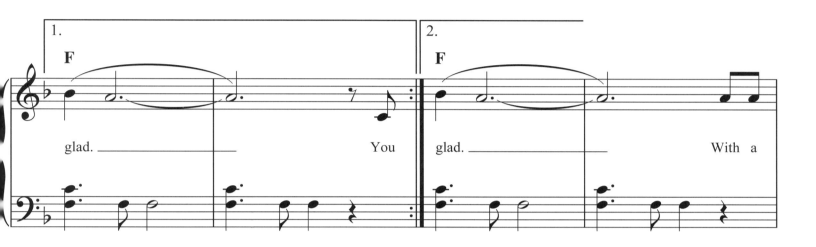

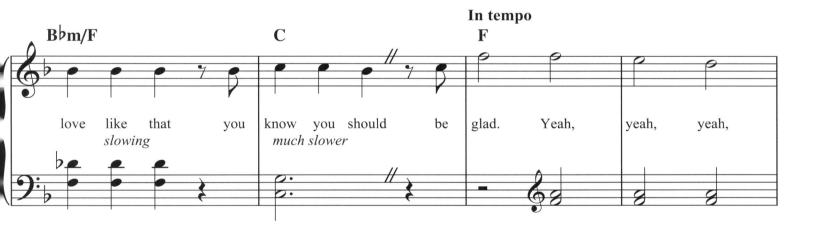

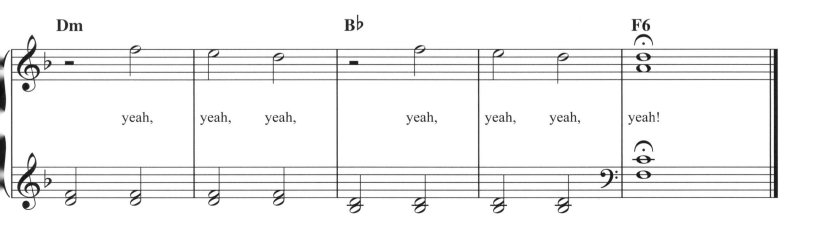

# SHE'S A WOMAN

Words and Music by JOHN LENNON
and PAUL McCARTNEY

**Moderately, with a strong back beat**

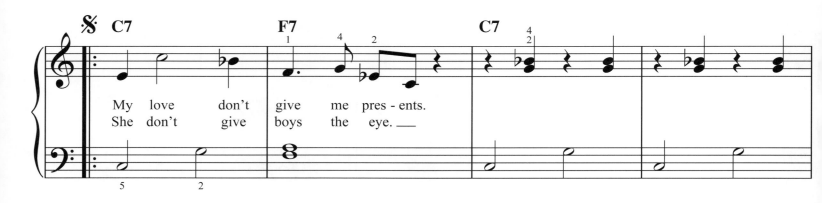

My love don't give me pres-ents.
She don't give boys the eye. __

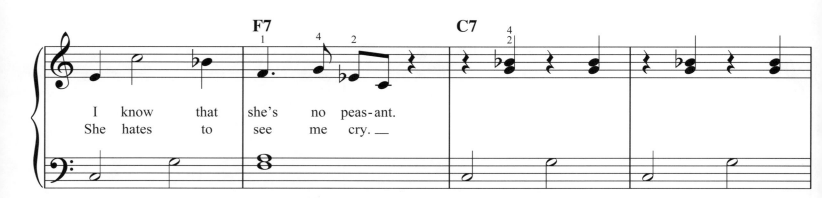

I know that she's no peas-ant.
She hates to see me cry. __

Only ever has to give me love for - ev - er
She is hap - py just to hear me say that I will

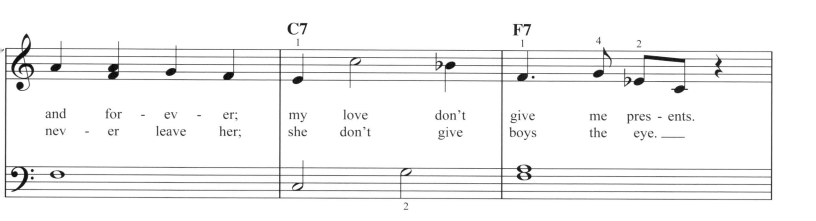

and for - ev - er; my love don't give me pres - ents.
nev - er leave her; she don't give boys the eye. ___

Turn me on when
She will nev - er

I get lone - ly, peo - ple tell me that she's on - ly
make me jeal - ous, gives me all her time as well as

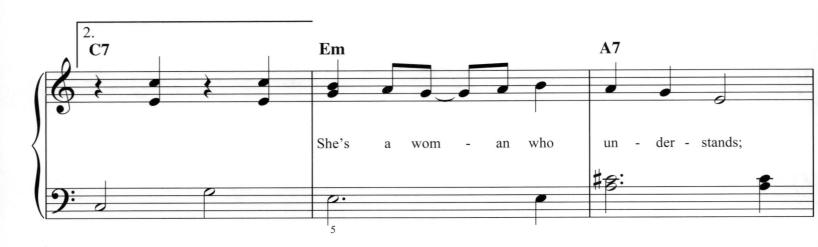

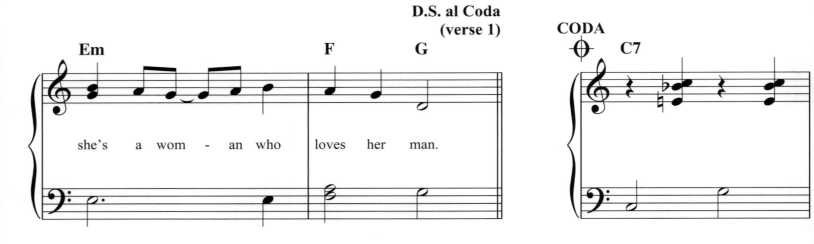

# SOMETHING

Words and Music by
GEORGE HARRISON

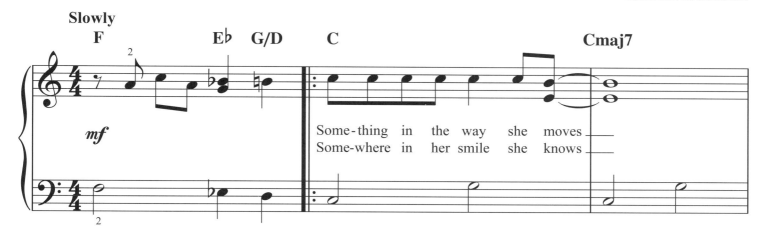

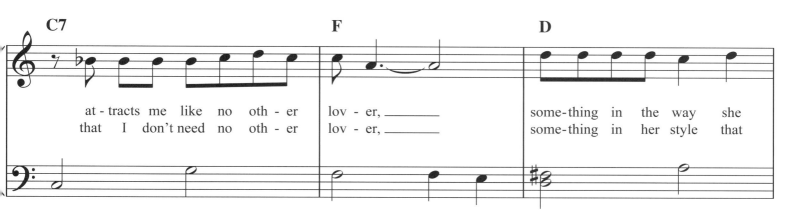

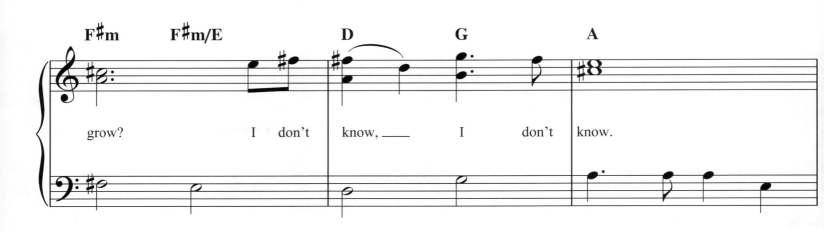

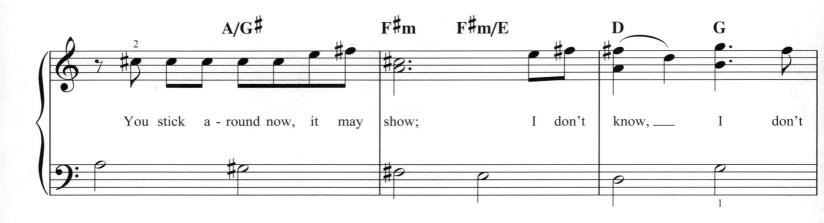

and all I have to do is think of her, some-thing in the things she

shows ___ me. I don't want to leave ___ her now, you

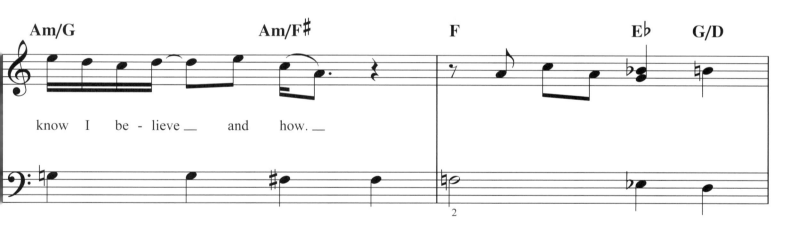

know I be - lieve ___ and how. ___

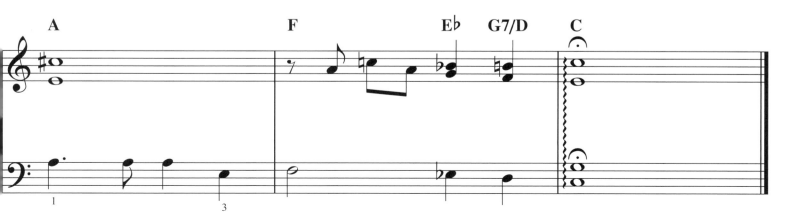

# TICKET TO RIDE

Words and Music by JOHN LENNON
and PAUL McCARTNEY

**Moderate Rock**

I think I'm gon - na be sad, \_\_\_ I think it's to - day, \_\_\_
said that liv - ing with me \_\_\_ is bring - in' her down, \_\_\_

\_\_\_ yeah! The girl that's driv - ing me mad \_\_\_
\_\_\_ yeah! For she would nev - er be free \_\_\_

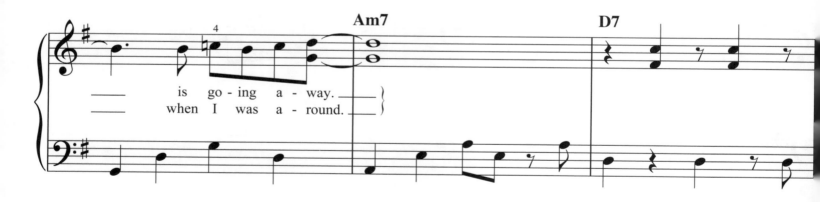

**Am7** **D7**

\_\_\_ is go - ing a - way. \_\_\_
\_\_\_ when I was a - round.

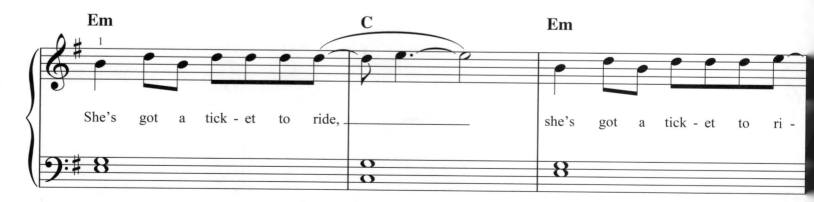

**Em** **C** **Em**

She's got a tick - et to ride, \_\_\_ she's got a tick - et to ri -

me. Be - fore she gets to say - in' good - bye, ___

___ she ought - a think twice, she ought - a do right by

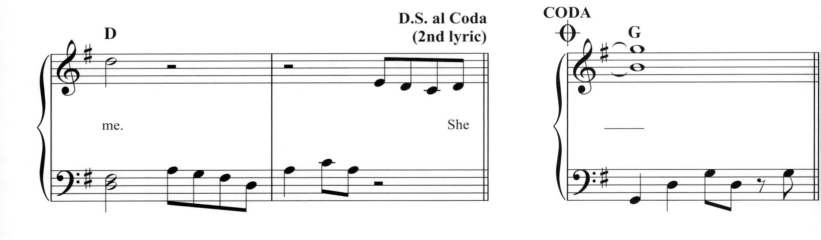

**D.S. al Coda**
**(2nd lyric)**

**CODA**

me. She

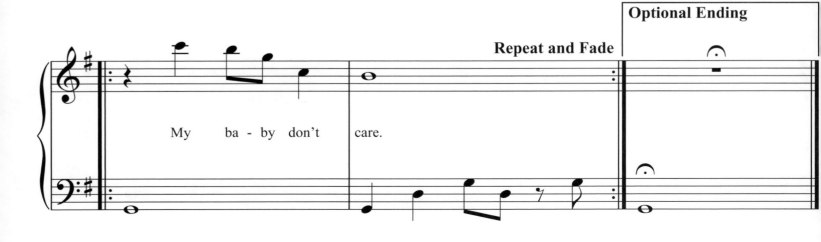

**Optional Ending**

**Repeat and Fade**

My ba - by don't care.

# STRAWBERRY FIELDS FOREVER

Words and Music by JOHN LENNON
and PAUL McCARTNEY

**Slowly, but not dragging**

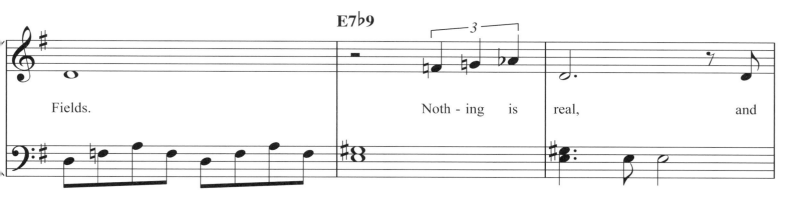

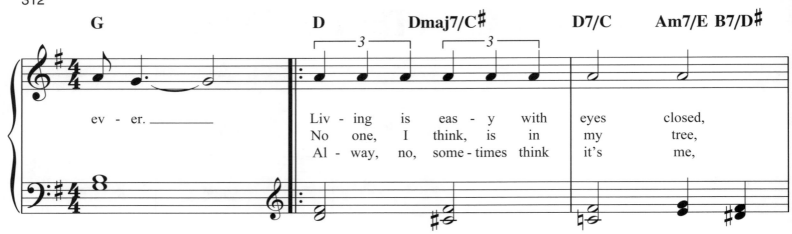

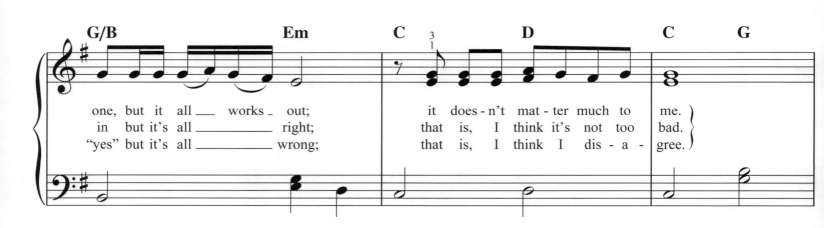

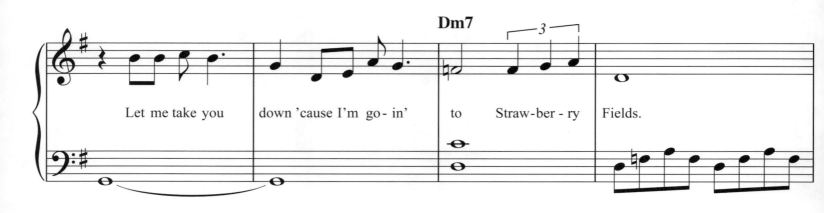

# SUN KING

Words and Music by JOHN LENNON
and PAUL McCARTNEY

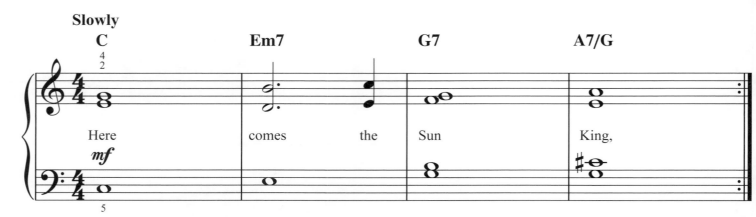

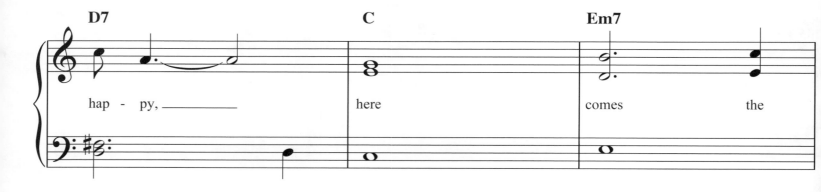

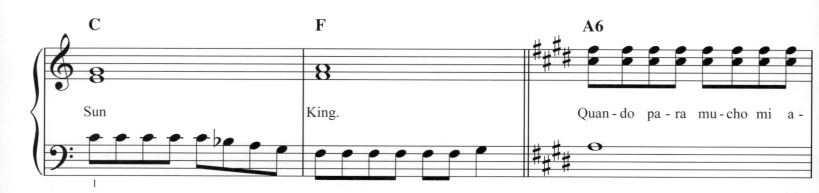

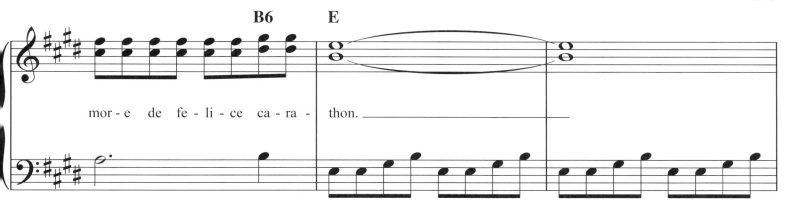

mor - e de fe - li - ce ca - ra - thon. _____

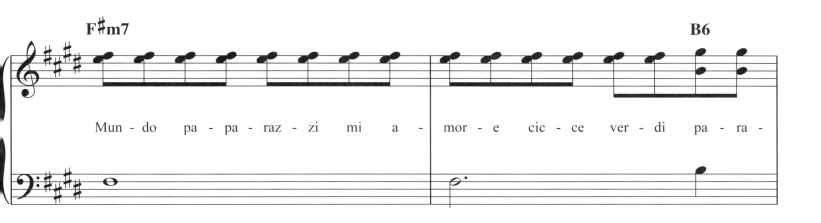

Mun - do pa - pa - raz - zi mi a - mor - e cic - ce ver - di pa - ra -

sol. _____ Que - sto a - bri - ga - do tan - ta

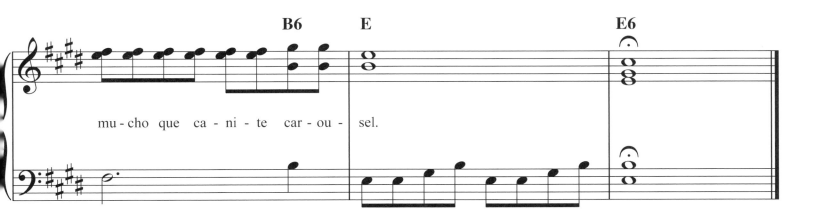

mu - cho que ca - ni - te car - ou - sel.

# TWIST AND SHOUT

Words and Music by BERT RUSSELL
and PHIL MEDLEY

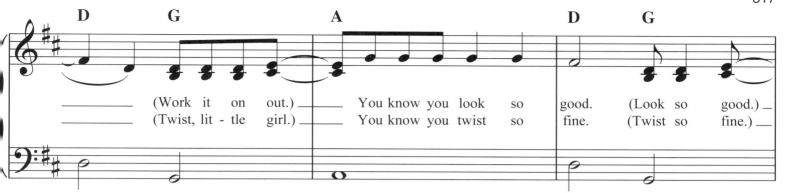

(Work it on out.) ___ You know you look so good. (Look so good.) ___
(Twist, lit-tle girl.) ___ You know you twist so fine. (Twist so fine.) ___

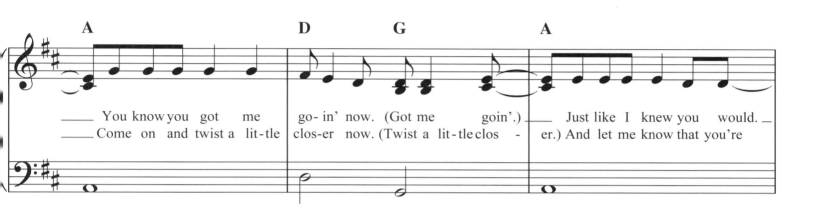

___ You know you got me go-in' now. (Got me goin'.) ___ Just like I knew you would. ___
___ Come on and twist a lit-tle clos-er now. (Twist a lit-tle clos - er.) And let me know that you're

To Coda

1.

2.

___ (Like I knew you would.) Well, shake it up, ba -
mine. (Let me know you're mine.)

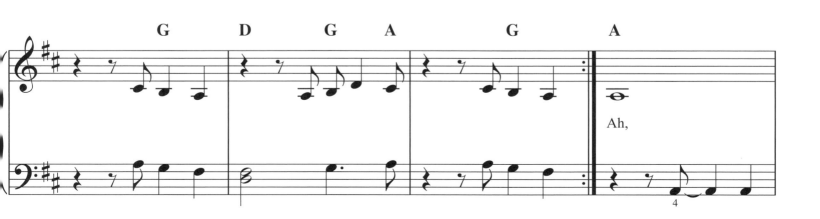

Ah,

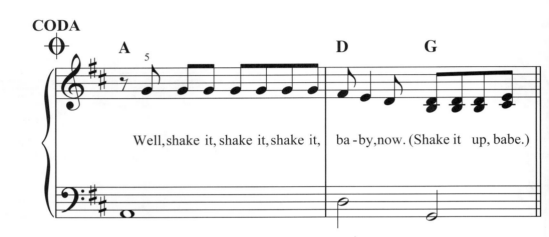

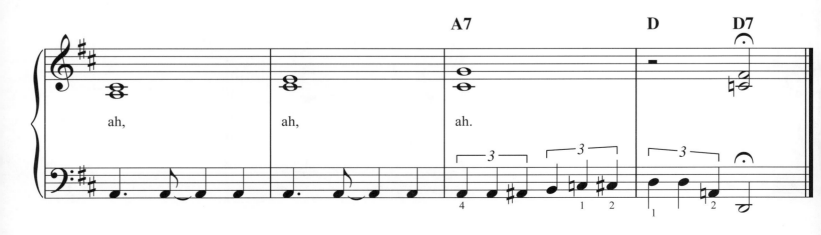

# TAXMAN

Words and Music by
GEORGE HARRISON

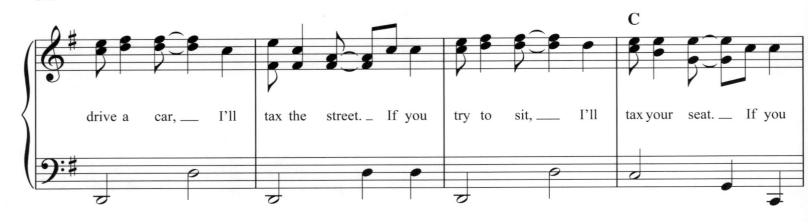

drive a car, __ I'll tax the street. __ If you try to sit, ___ I'll tax your seat. __ If you

get too cold, __ I'll tax the heat. __ If you take a walk, __ I'll tax your feet. _____

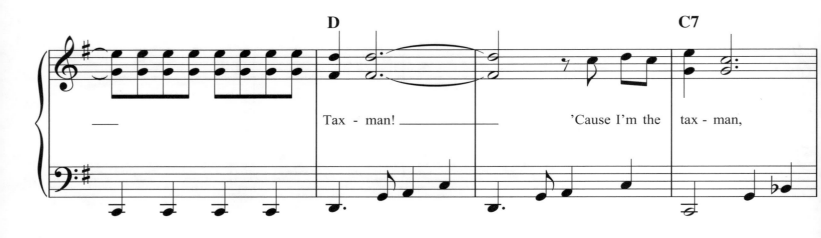

Tax - man! _____ 'Cause I'm the tax - man,

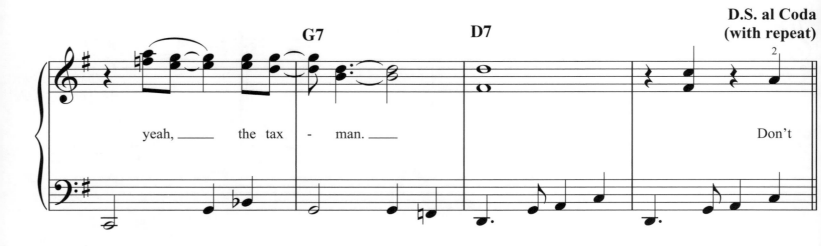

yeah, ___ the tax - man. ___

**D.S. al Coda (with repeat)**

Don't

**CODA**

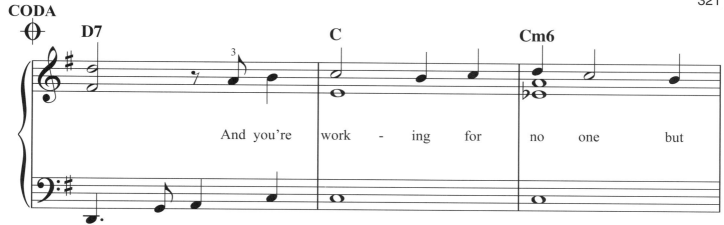

And you're work - ing for no one but

me.

*Additional Lyrics*

2. Should five percent appear too small,
   Be thankful I don't take it all.
   'Cause I'm the taxman, yeah,
   I'm the taxman.

3. Don't ask me what I want it for,
   If you don't want to pay some more.
   'Cause I'm the taxman, yeah,
   I'm the taxman.

4. Now my advice for those who die;
   Declare the pennies on your eyes.
   'Cause I'm the taxman, yeah,
   I'm the taxman.

# TELL ME WHY

Words and Music by JOHN LENNON
and PAUL McCARTNEY

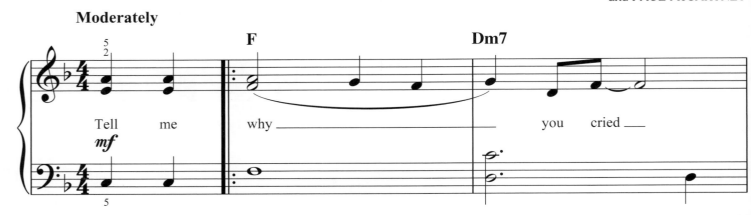

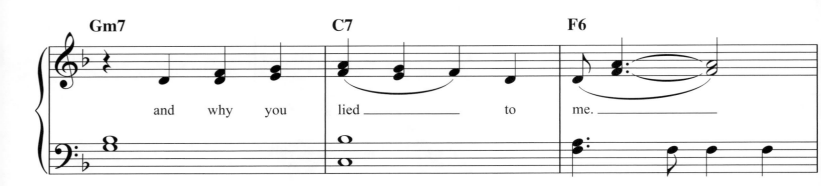

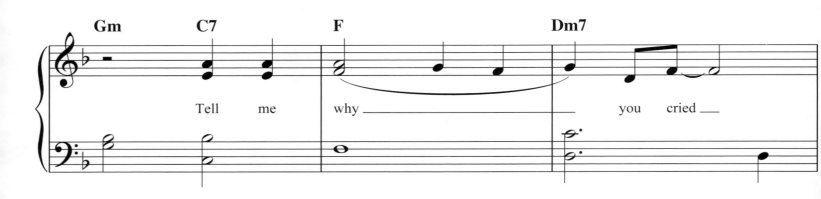

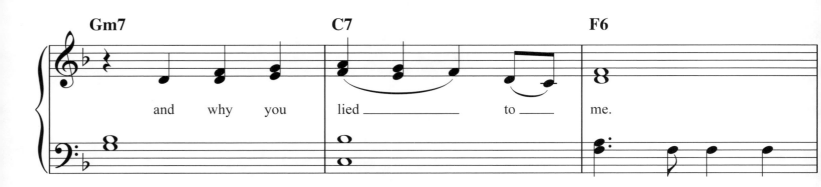

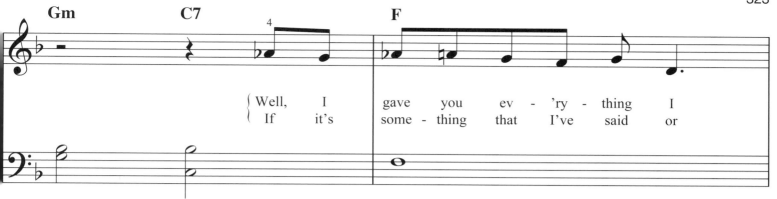

Well, I gave you ev - 'ry - thing I
If it's some - thing that I've said or

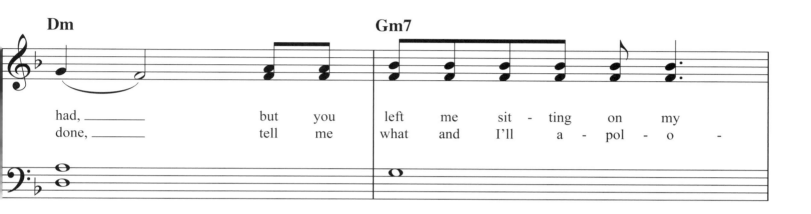

had, _____ but you left me sit - ting on my
done, _____ tell me what and I'll a - pol - o -

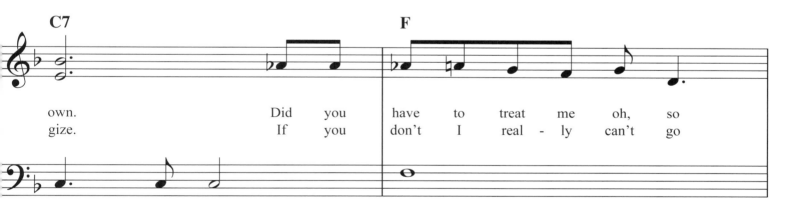

own. Did you have to treat me oh, so
gize. If you don't I real - ly can't go

bad? ____ All I do is hang my head and moan. Tell me
on ____ hold - ing back __ these __ tears in my eyes. Tell me

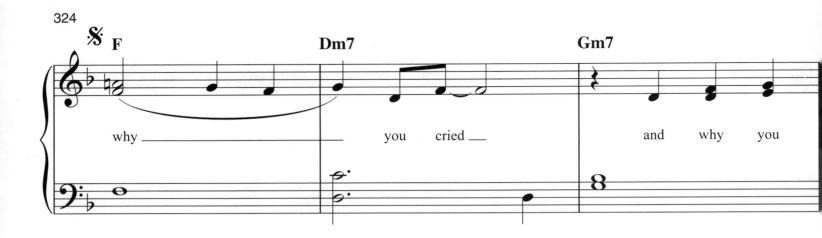

why ___ you cried ___ and why you

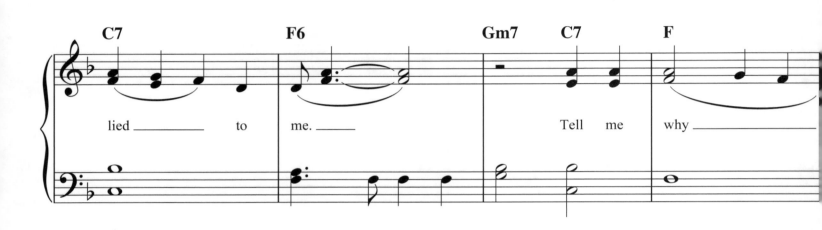

lied ___ to me. ___ Tell me why ___

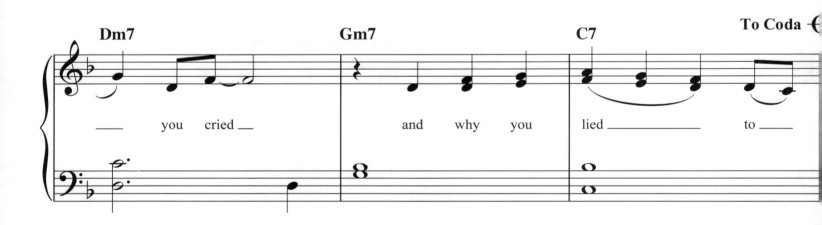

___ you cried ___ and why you lied ___ to ___

me. Well, I beg you on my bend - ed

knees _____ if you'll on-ly lis-ten to my pleas. Is there

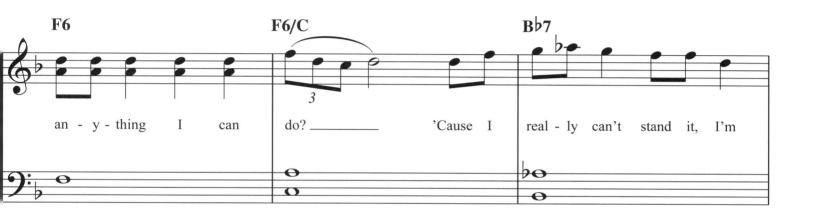

an-y-thing I can do? _____ 'Cause I real-ly can't stand it, I'm

so in love with _____ you! Tell me

me.

# THANK YOU GIRL

Words and Music by JOHN LENNON
and PAUL McCARTNEY

thank you, girl. __ Thank you, girl, for lov - in' me the way that you do;

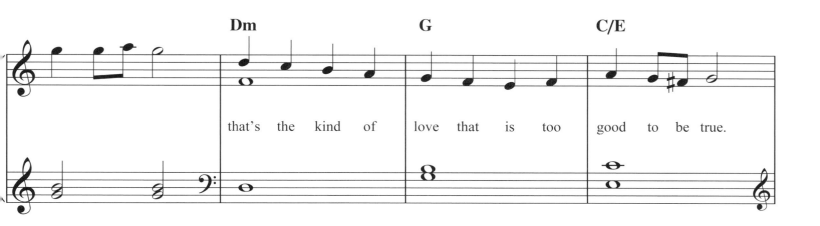

that's the kind of love that is too good to be true.

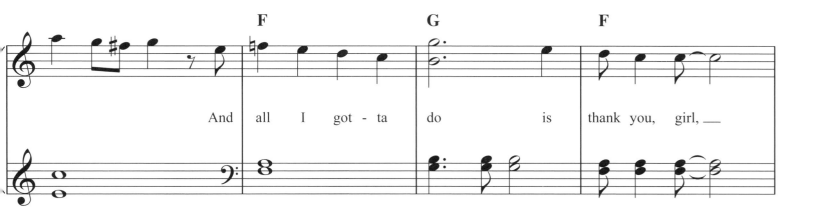

And all I got - ta do is thank you, girl, __

thank you, girl. __

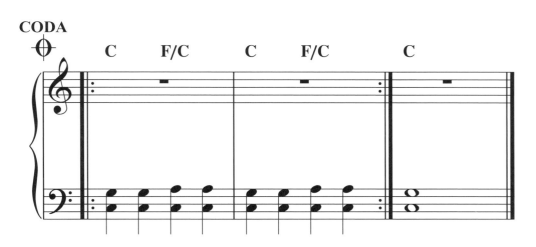

# TWO OF US

Words and Music by JOHN LENNON
and PAUL McCARTNEY

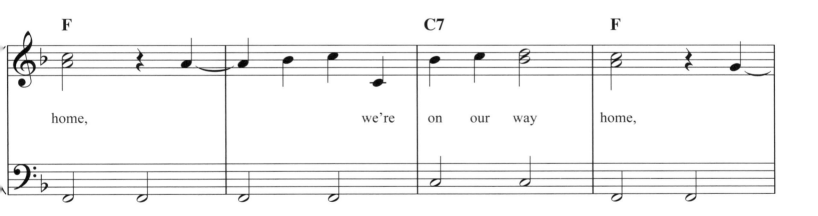

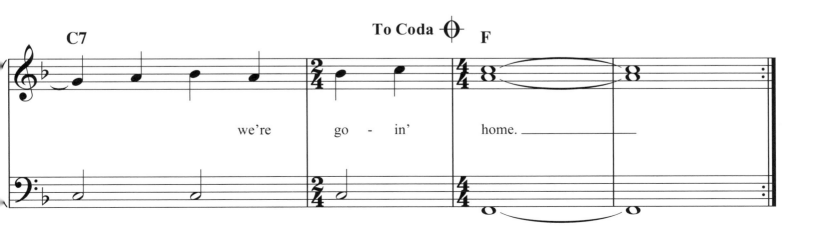

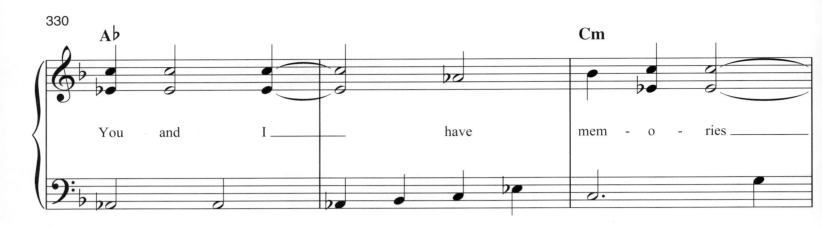

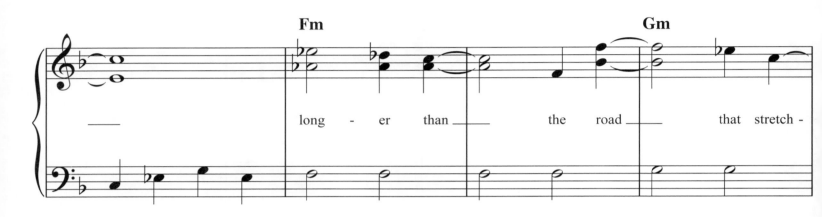

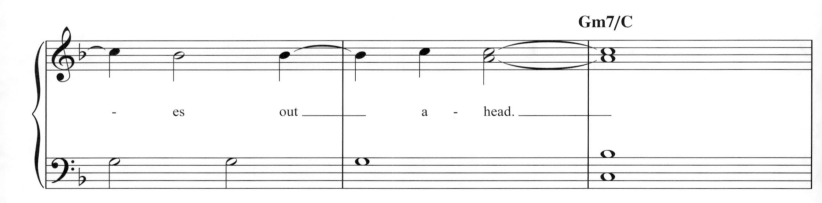

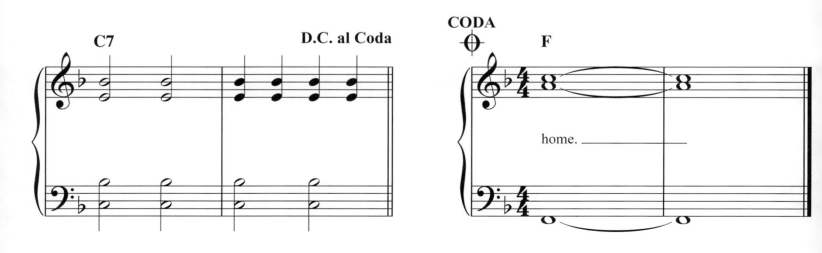

# THERE'S A PLACE

Words and Music by JOHN LENNON
and PAUL McCARTNEY

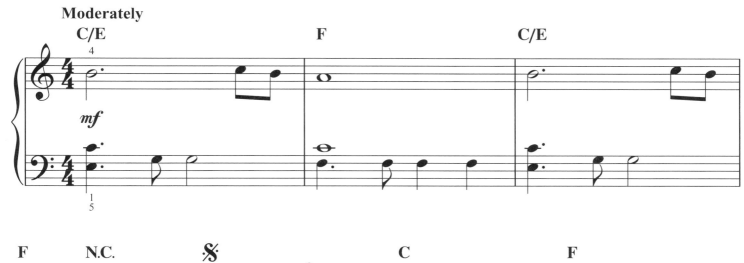

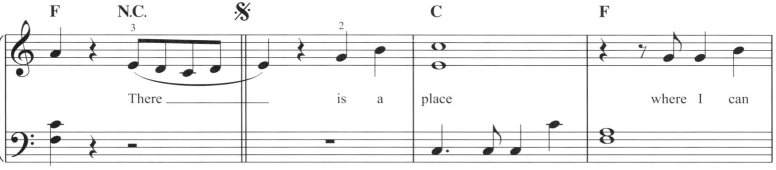

There _____ is a place where I can

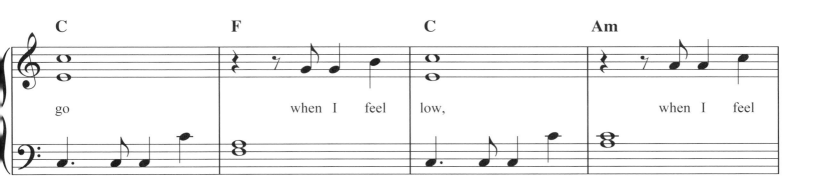

go when I feel low, when I feel

blue, _____ and it's my mind, _____ and there's no

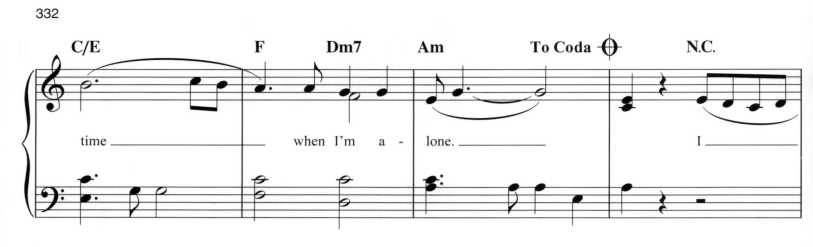

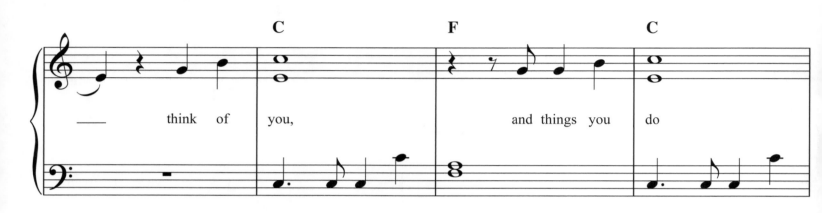

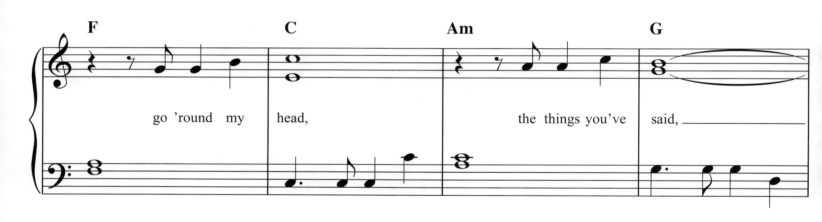

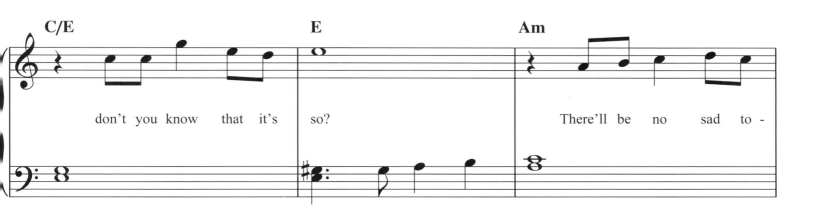

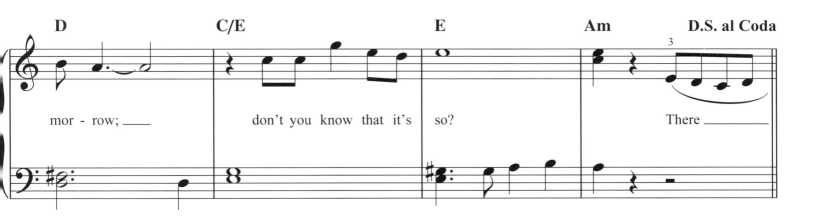

# THINGS WE SAID TODAY

Words and Music by JOHN LENNON
and PAUL McCARTNEY

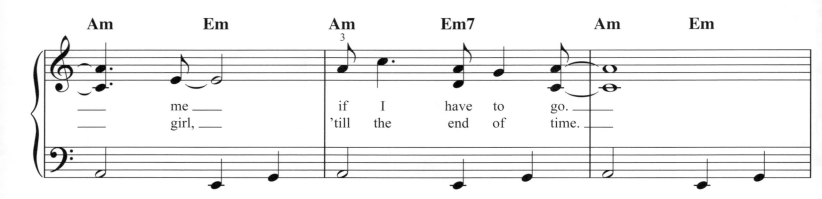

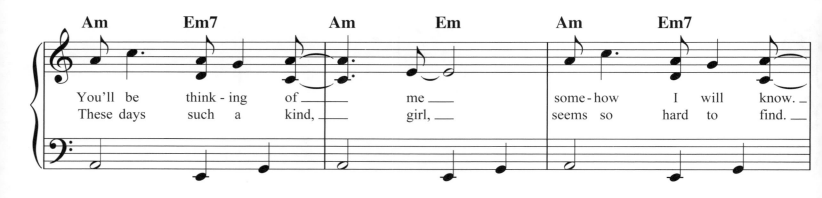

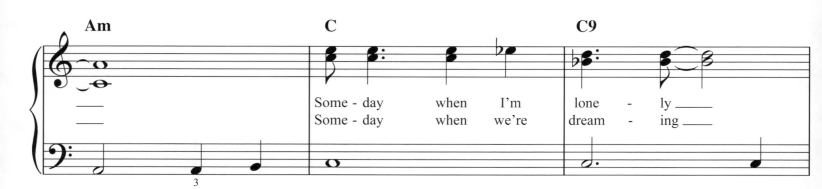

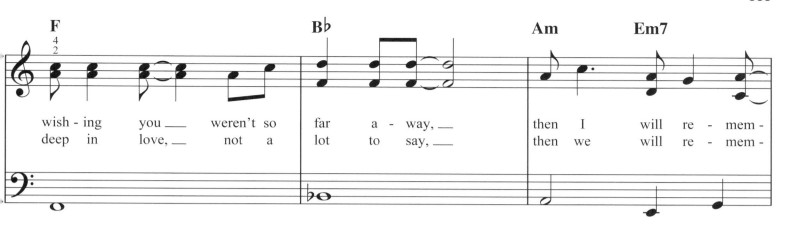

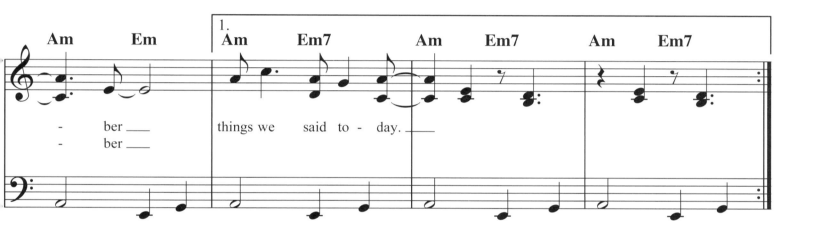

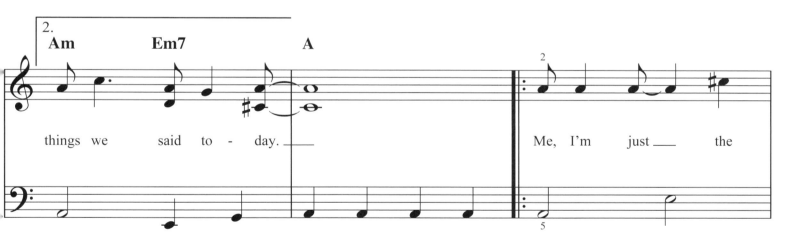

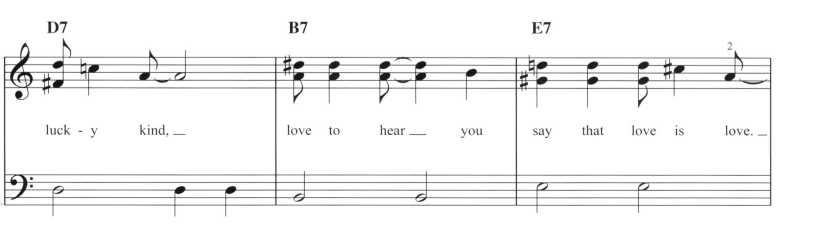

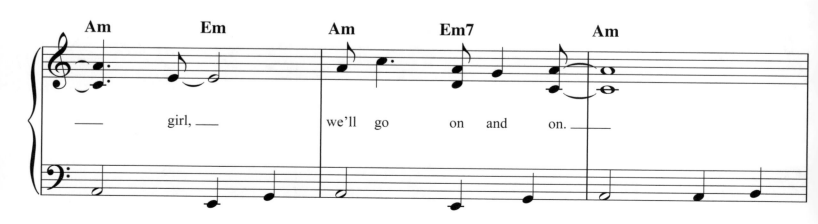

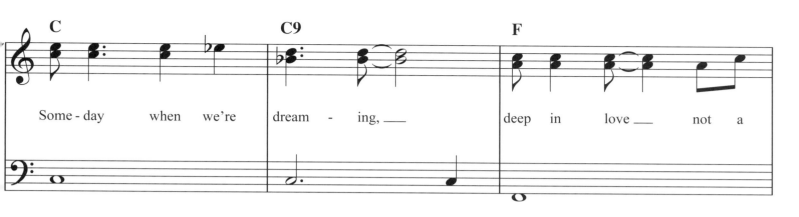

Some - day when we're dream - ing, ___ deep in love ___ not a

lot to say, ___ then we will re - mem - ber ___

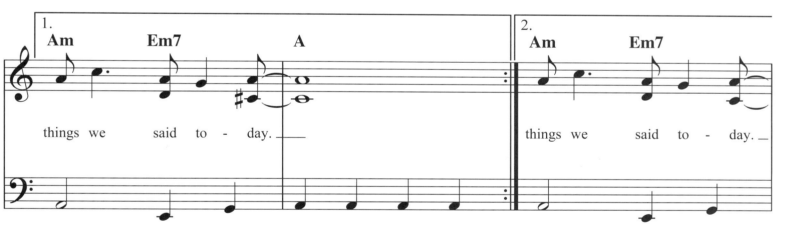

1. things we said to - day. ___

2. things we said to - day. ___

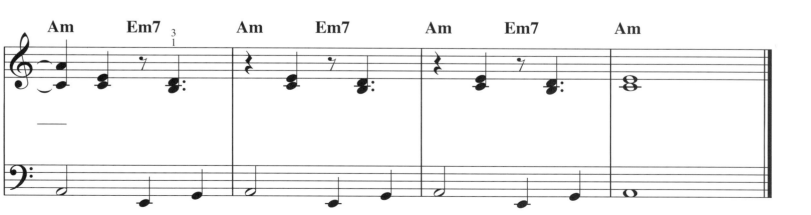

# THIS BOY
## (Ringo's Theme)

Words and Music by JOHN LENNON
and PAUL McCARTNEY

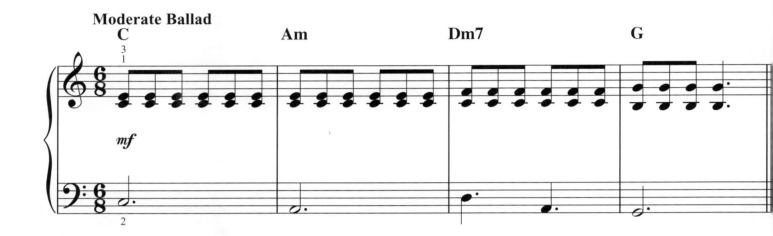

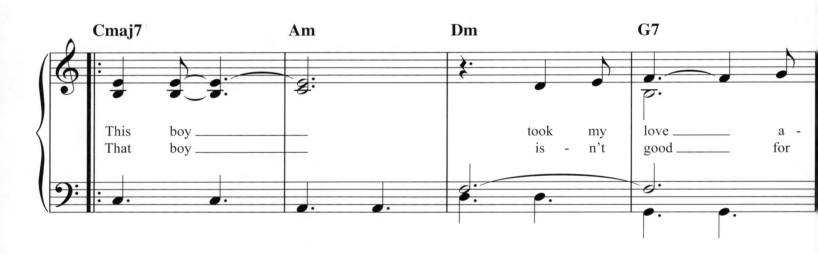

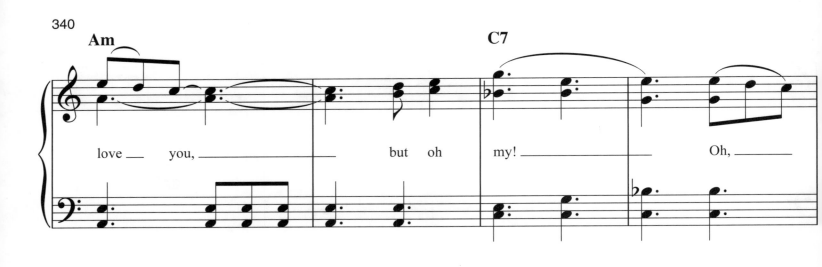

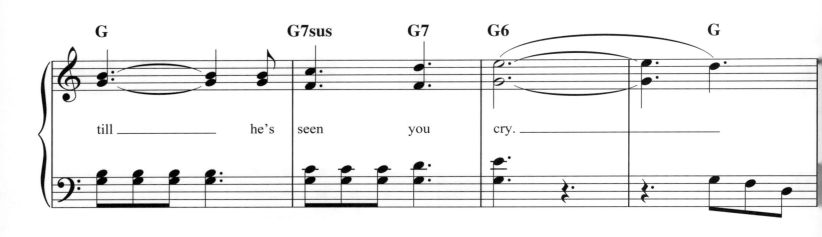

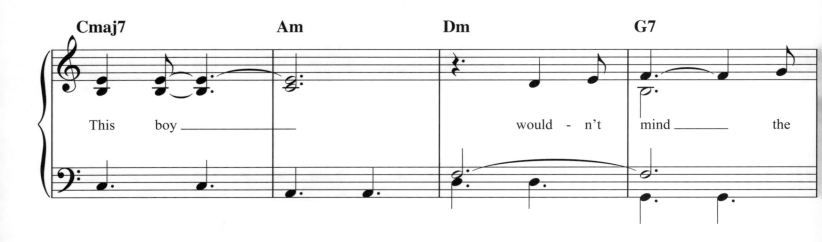

# WHILE MY GUITAR GENTLY WEEPS

Words and Music by
GEORGE HARRISON

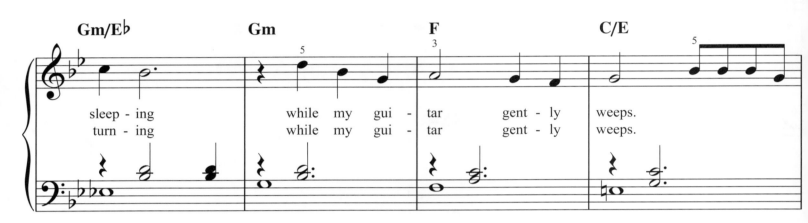

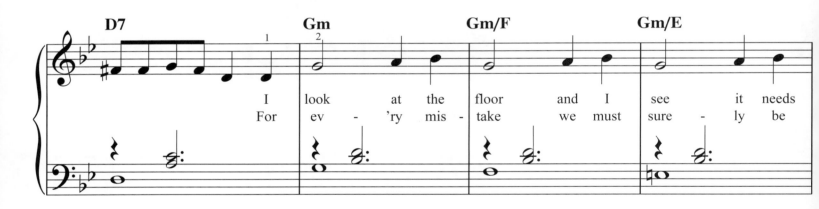

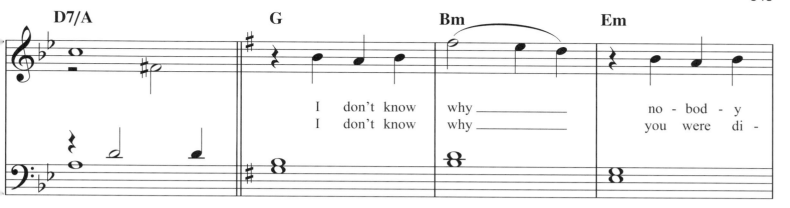

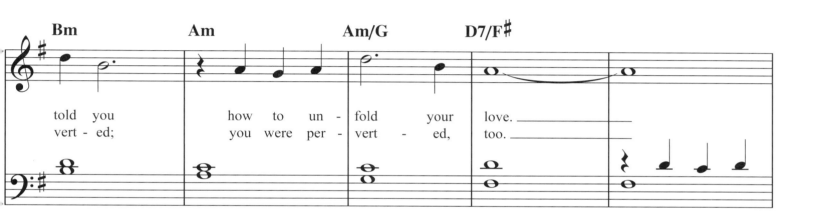

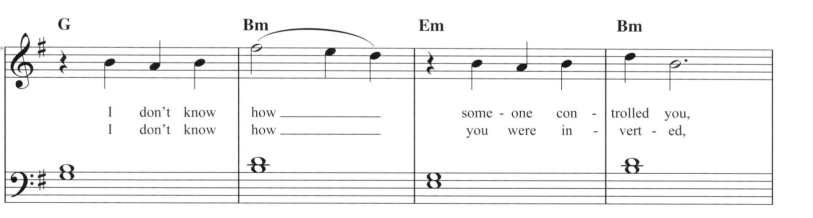

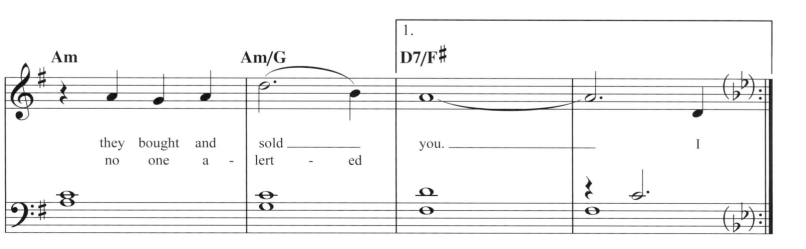

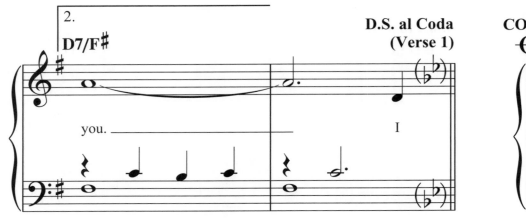

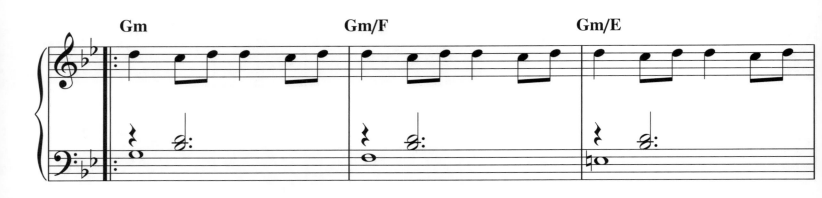

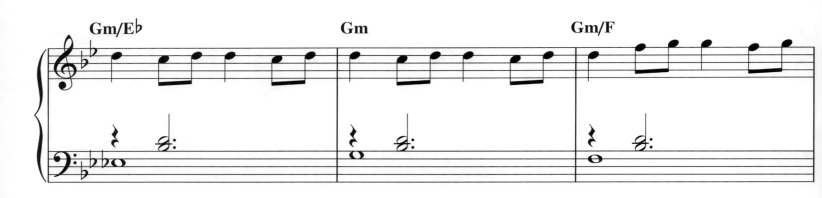

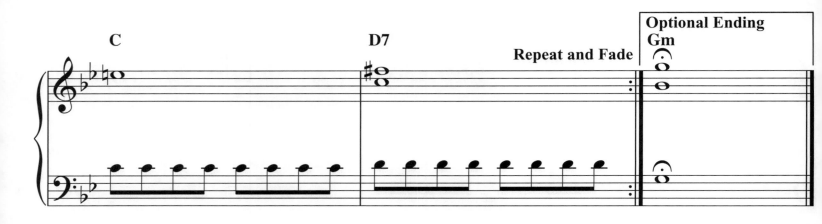

# WE CAN WORK IT OUT

Words and Music by JOHN LENNON
and PAUL McCARTNEY

**Slow and steady**

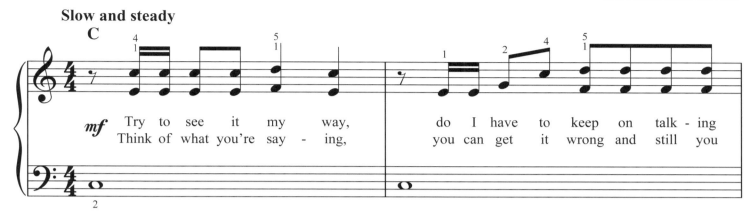

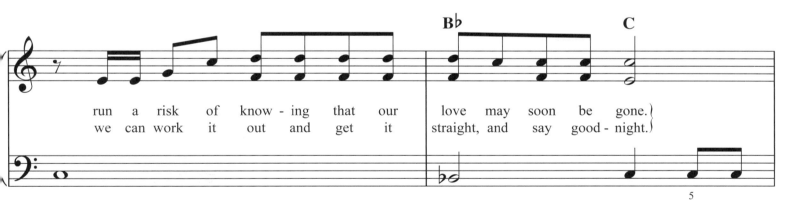

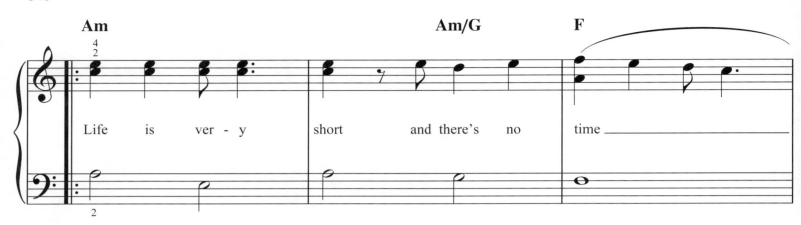

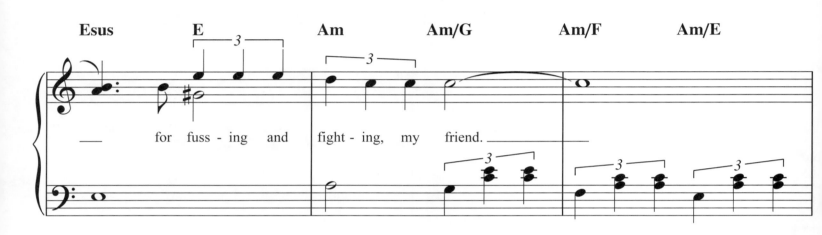

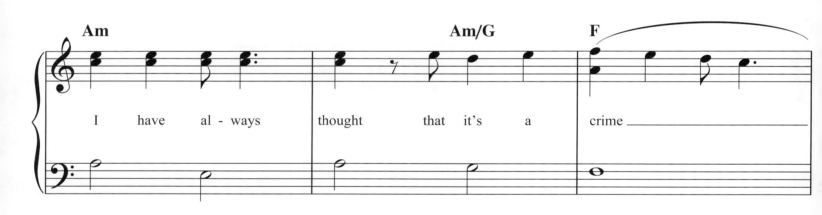

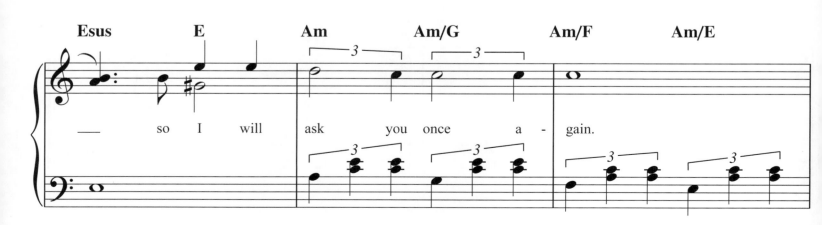

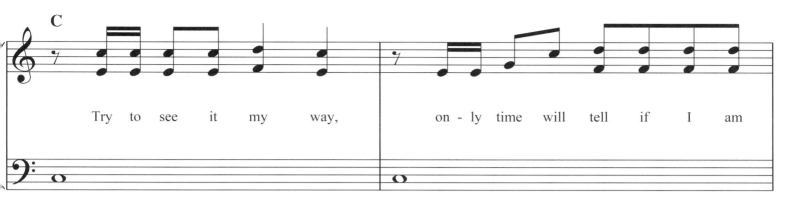

Try to see it my way, on - ly time will tell if I am

right or I am wrong. While you see it your way

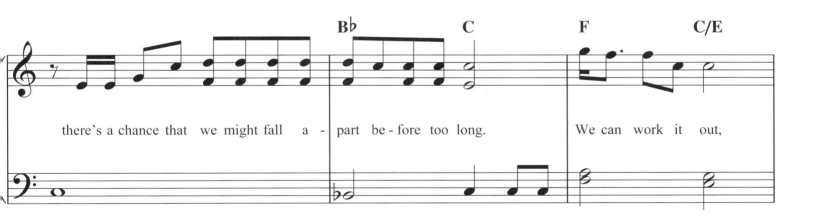

there's a chance that we might fall a - part be - fore too long. We can work it out,

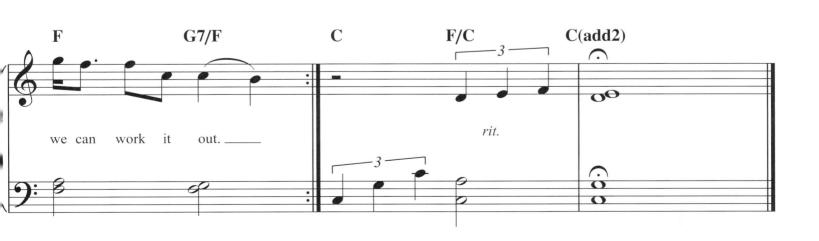

we can work it out. _____

# WHEN I'M SIXTY-FOUR

Words and Music by JOHN LENNON
and PAUL McCARTNEY

When I get old - er, losing my hair, ___
I could be hand - y mend - ing a fuse ___
Send me a post - card, drop me a line, ___

man - y years from now,
when your lights have gone.
stat - ing points of view.

will you still be send - ing me a
You can knit a sweat - er by the
In - di - cate pre - cise - ly what you

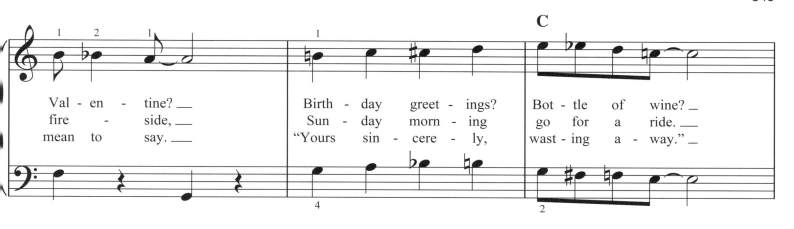

Val - en - tine? ___
Birth - day greet - ings?
Bot - tle of wine? ___

fire - side, ___
Sun - day morn - ing
go for a ride. ___

mean to say. ___
"Yours sin - cere - ly,
wast - ing a - way." ___

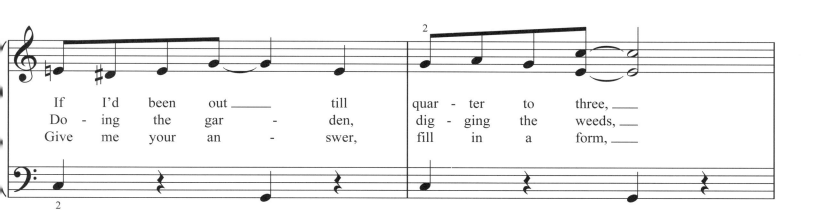

If I'd been out ___ till
Do - ing the gar ___ den,
Give me your an - swer,

quar - ter to three, ___
dig - ging the weeds, ___
fill in a form, ___

would you lock the
who could ask for
mine for - ev - er -

door?
more?
more.

Will you still need ___ me,
Will you still need ___ me,
Will you still need ___ me,

will you still feed ___ me
will you still feed ___ me
will you still feed ___ me

when I'm six - ty -
when I'm six - ty -
when I'm six - ty

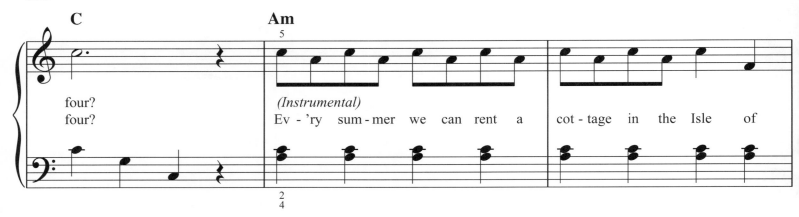

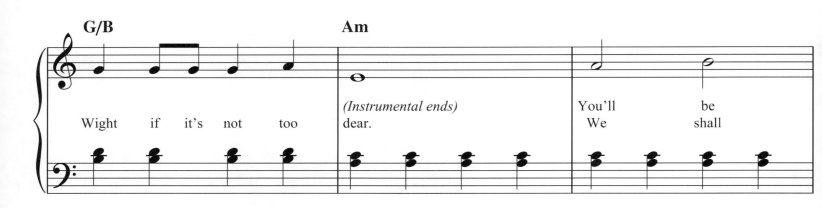

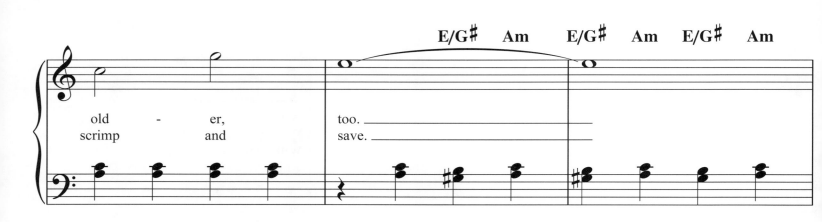

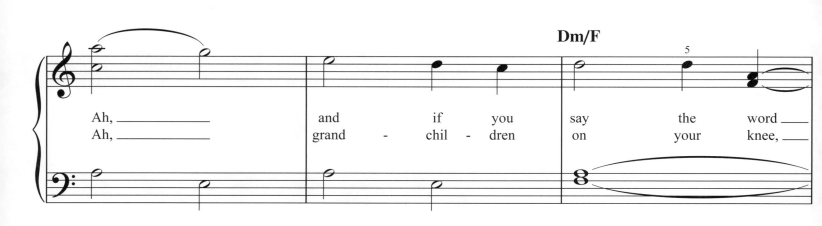

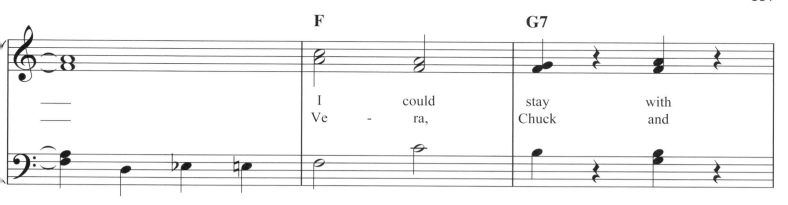

I          could          stay          with
Ve    -    ra,          Chuck          and

you.
Dave.

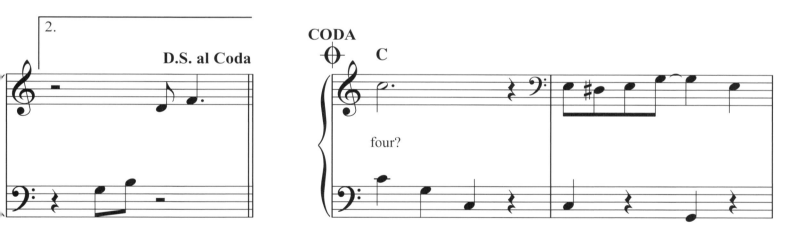

four?

# WITH A LITTLE HELP FROM MY FRIENDS

Words and Music by JOHN LENNON
and PAUL McCARTNEY

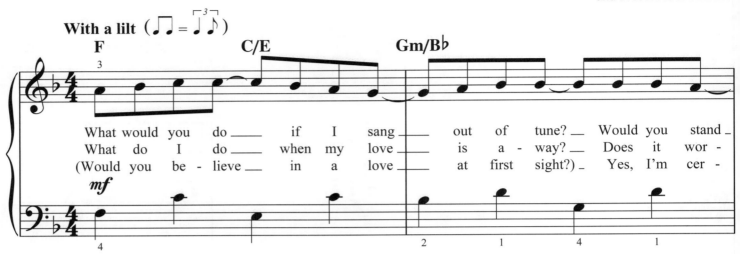

What would you do ___ if I sang ___ out of tune? ___ Would you stand ___
What do I do ___ when my love ___ is a - way? ___ Does it wor -
(Would you be - lieve ___ in a love ___ at first sight?) ___ Yes, I'm cer -

___ up and walk ___ out on me? ___
- ry you to ___ be a - lone?)
- tain that it hap-pens all the time.

Lend me your ears ___ and I'll sing ___
How do I feel ___ by the end ___
(What do you see ___ when you turn

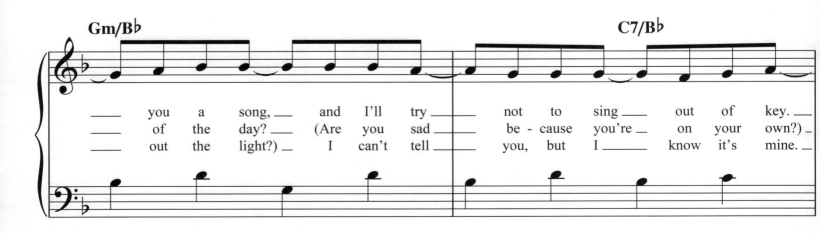

___ you a song, ___ and I'll try ___ not to sing ___ out of key.
___ of the day? ___ (Are you sad ___ be - cause you're ___ on your own?)
___ out the light?) ___ I can't tell ___ you, but I ___ know it's mine. ___

Oh,
No, } I get by ____ with a lit-tle help ____ from my friends, ____
Oh,

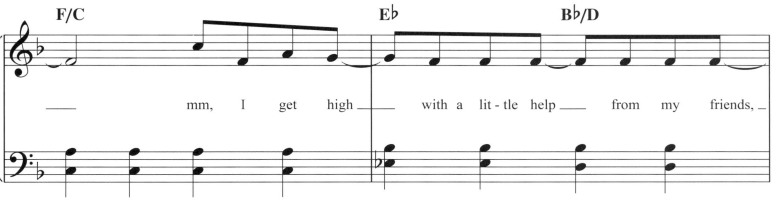

____ mm, I get high ____ with a lit-tle help ____ from my friends, ____

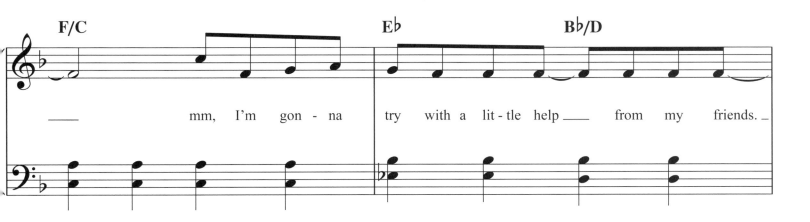

____ mm, I'm gon-na try with a lit-tle help ____ from my friends. ____

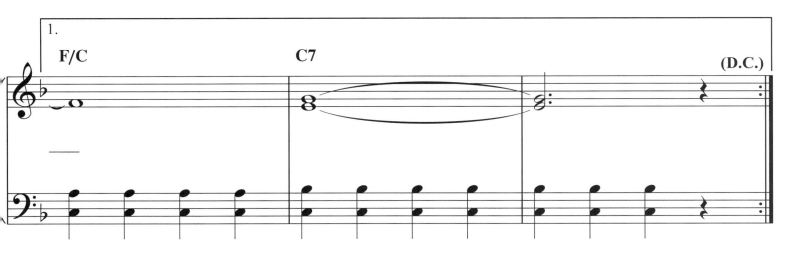

1.
____

(D.C.)

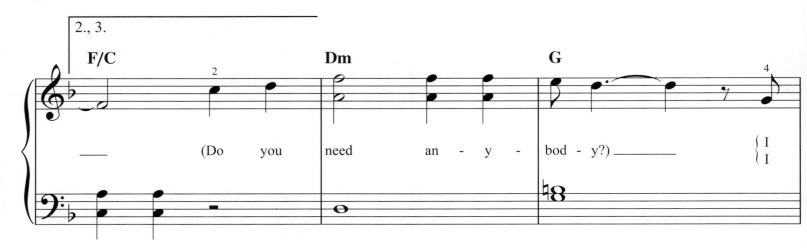

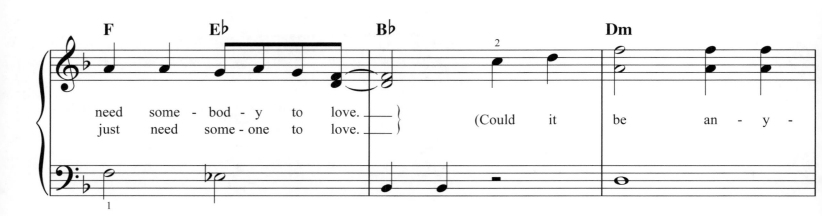

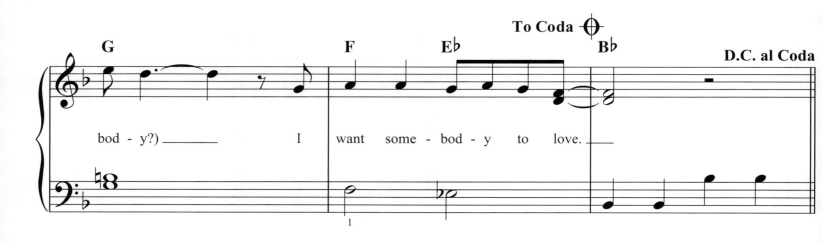

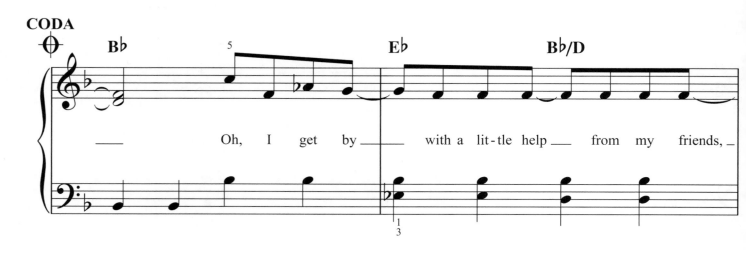

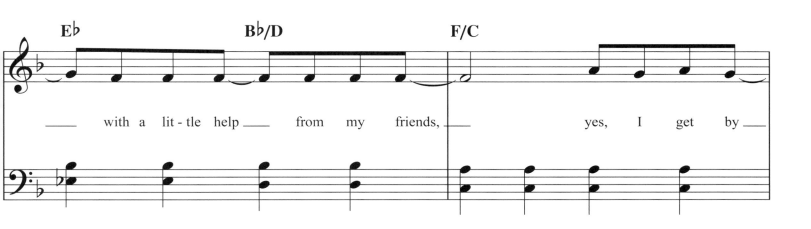

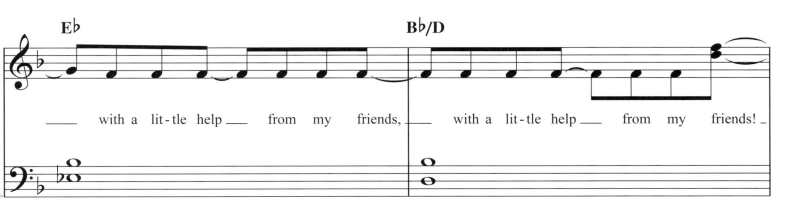

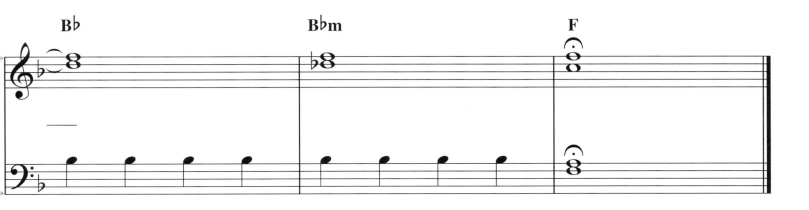

# THE WORD

Words and Music by JOHN LENNON
and PAUL McCARTNEY

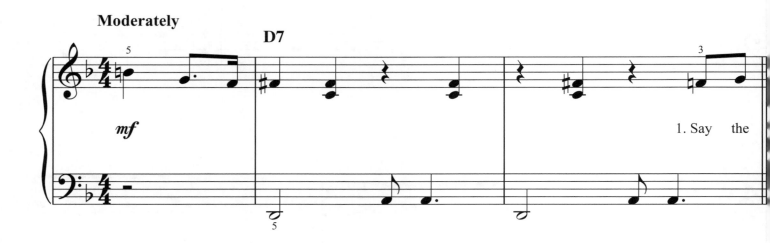

heard? _____ The word is "love." It's so fine, ___ it's

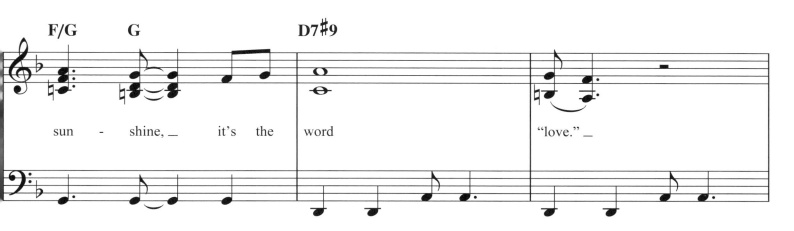

sun - shine, __ it's the word "love." _

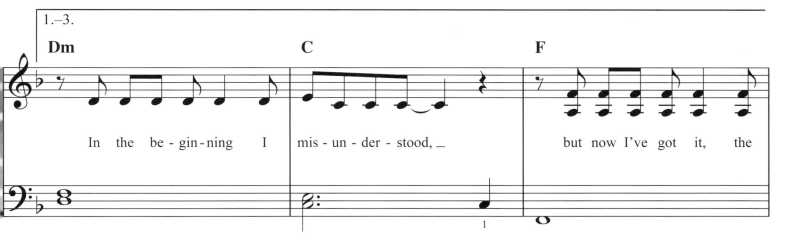

1.–3.

In the be - gin - ning I mis - un - der - stood, __ but now I've got it, the

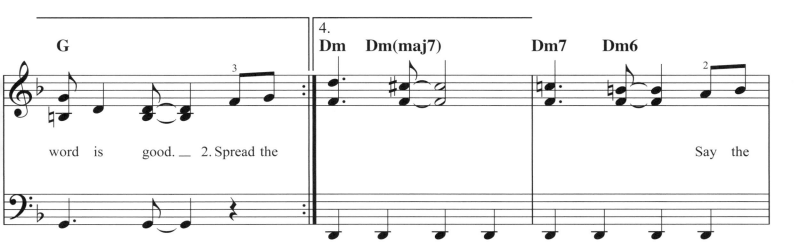

word is good. __ 2. Spread the    Say the

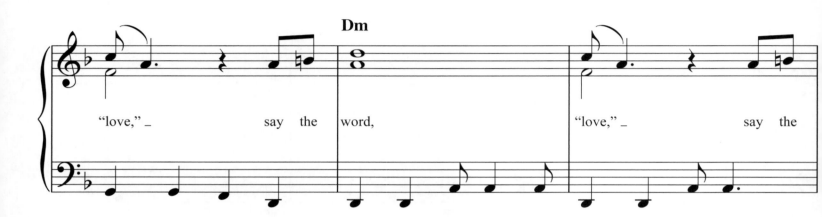

*Additional Lyrics*

2. Spread the word and you'll be free, spread the word and be like me.
   Spread the word I'm thinking of, have you heard? The word is "love."
   It's so fine, it's sunshine, it's the word "love."
   Ev'rywhere I go I hear it said, in the good and the bad books that I have read.

3. Say the word and you'll be free, say the word and be like me.
   Say the word I'm thinking of, have you heard?  The word is "love."
   It's so fine, it's sunshine, it's the word "love."
   In the beginning I misunderstood, but now I've got it, the word is good.

4. Give the word a chance to say, that the word is just the way.
   It's the word I'm thinking of, and the only word is "love."
   It's so fine, it's sunshine, it's the word "love."

# YOU NEVER GIVE ME YOUR MONEY

Words and Music by JOHN LENNON
and PAUL McCARTNEY

You never give me your money,
I never give you my number,

you only give me your
I only give you my

funny paper,
situation,

and in the middle of negotiations you
and in the middle of investigation, I

break down.
break down.

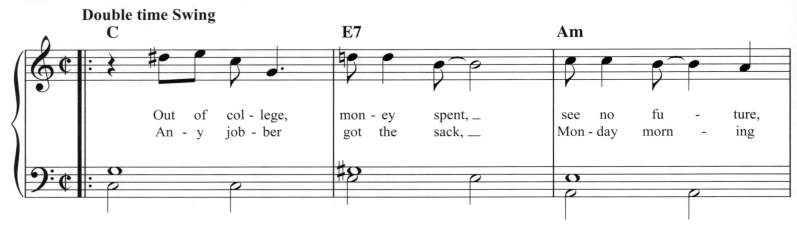

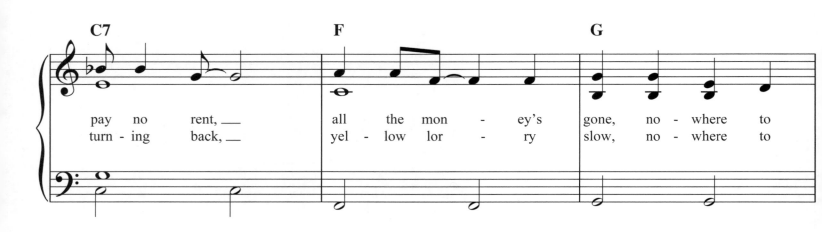

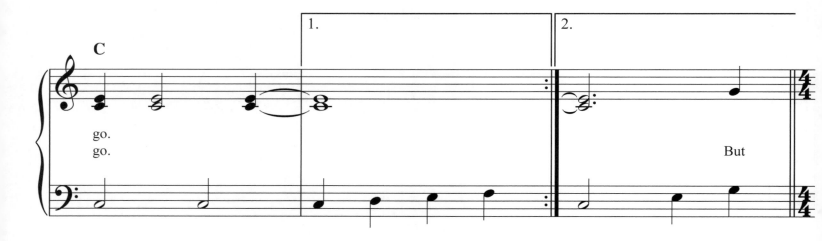

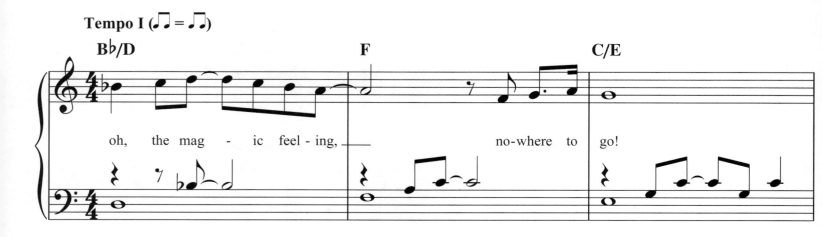

Oh, the mag - ic feel - ing, ___ no - where to go, no-where to go!

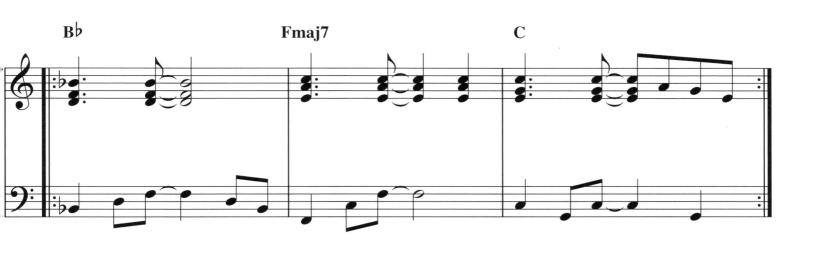

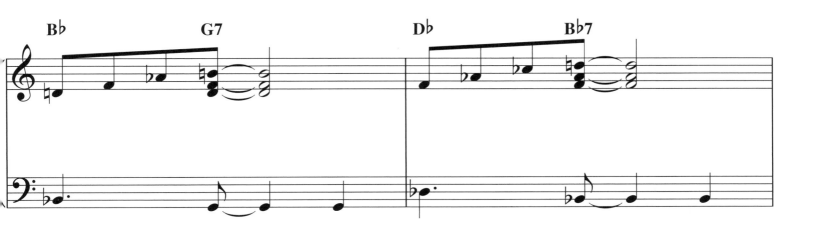

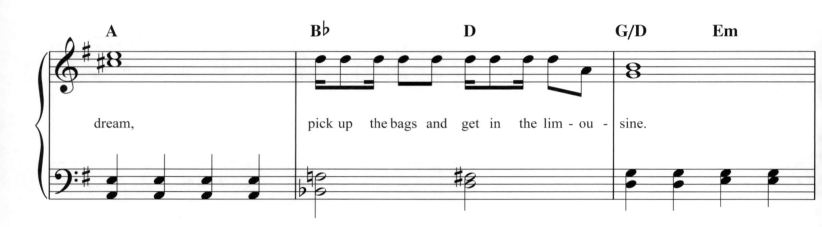

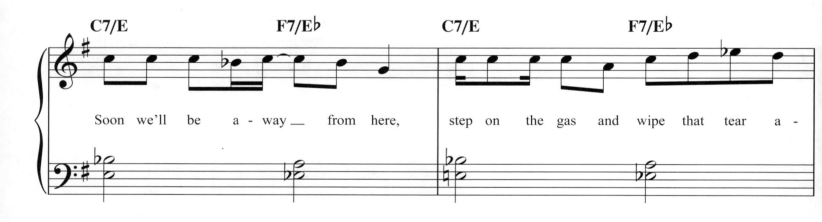

came true ___ to - day, ___ came true ___

to - day. ___

One, two, three, four, five, six, sev - en,

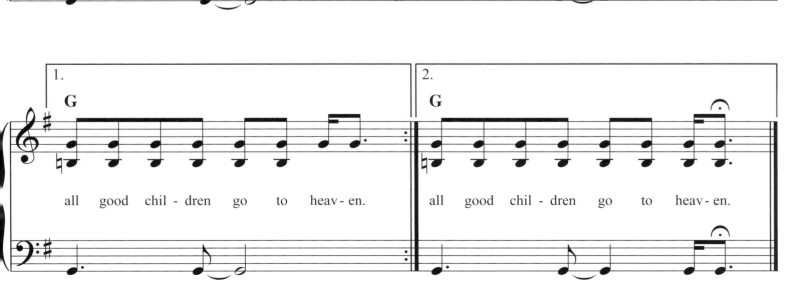

1.

all good chil - dren go to heav - en.

2.

all good chil - dren go to heav - en.

# YELLOW SUBMARINE

Words and Music by JOHN LENNON
and PAUL McCARTNEY

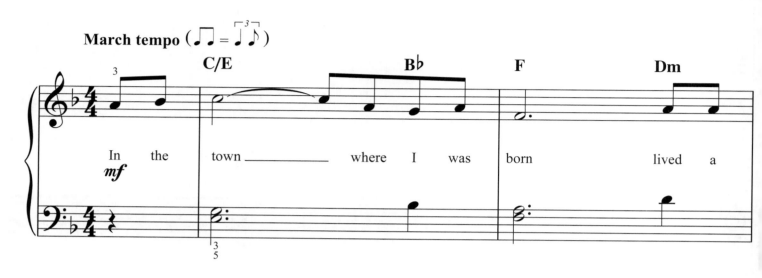

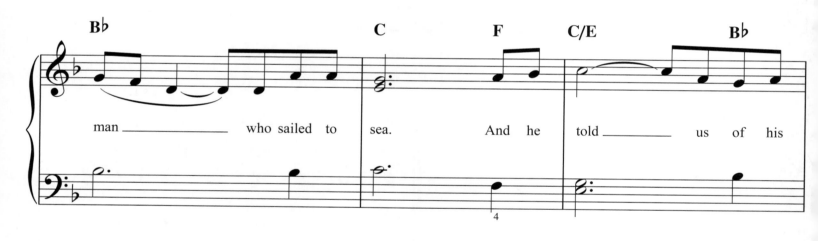

sailed _____ up to the sun till we found _____ the sea of

green, and we lived _____ be - neath the waves in our

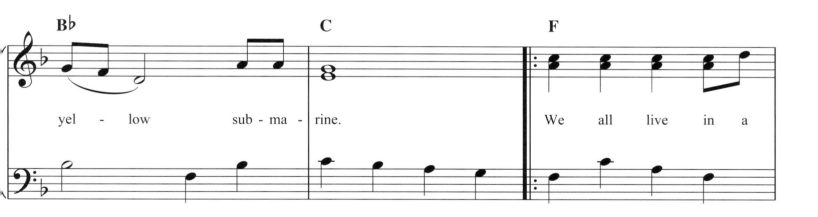

yel - low sub - ma - rine. We all live in a

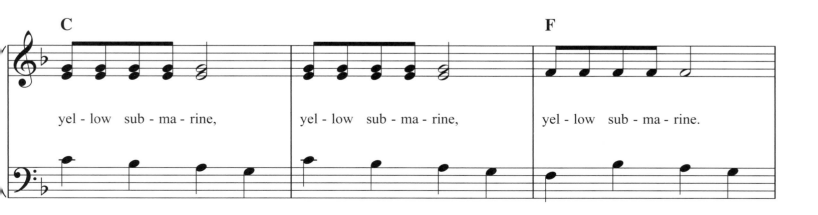

yel - low sub - ma - rine, yel - low sub - ma - rine, yel - low sub - ma - rine.

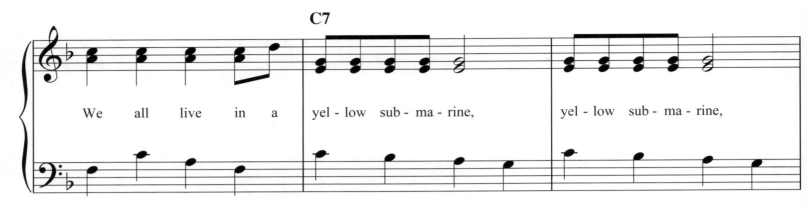

We all live in a yel-low sub-ma-rine, yel-low sub-ma-rine,

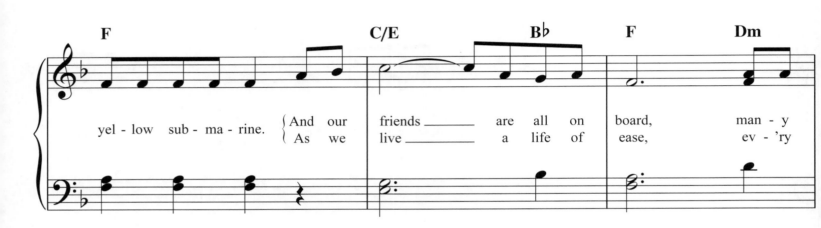

yel-low sub-ma-rine. { And our friends _____ are all on board, man-y ev-'ry
As we live _____ a life of ease,

more of them _____ live next door. And the band _____ be-gins to
one of us _____ has all we need. Sky of blue _____ and sea of

play:

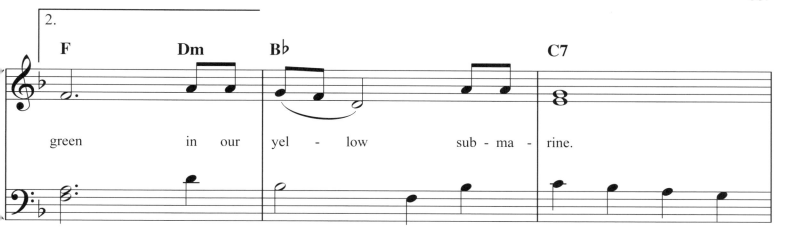

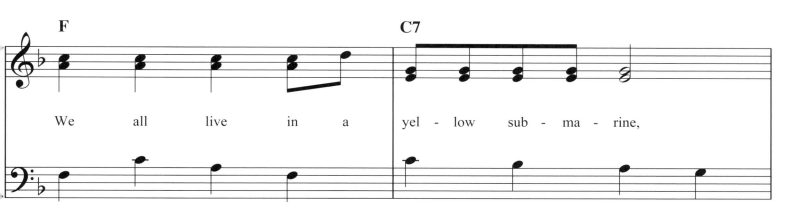

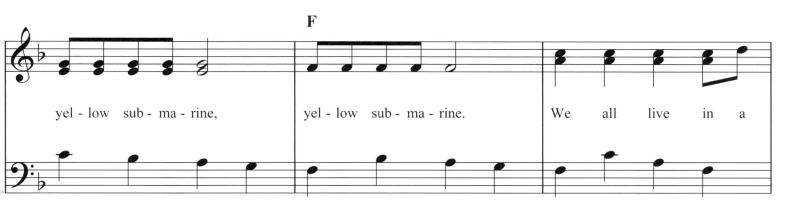

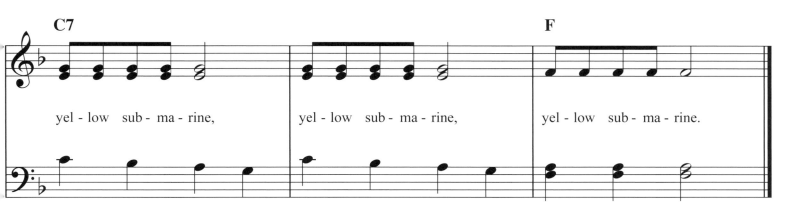

# YESTERDAY

Words and Music by JOHN LENNON
and PAUL McCARTNEY

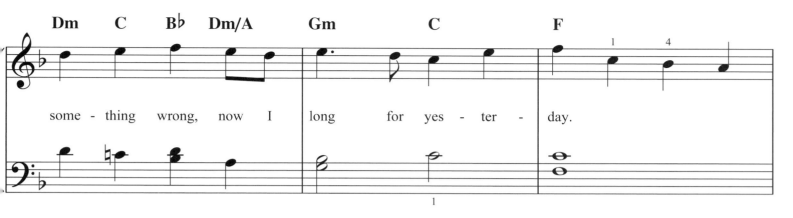

some - thing wrong, now I long for yes - ter - day.

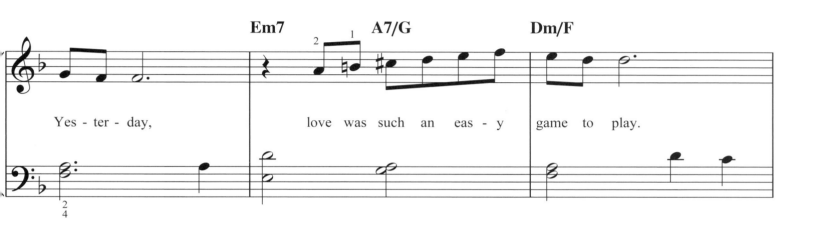

Yes - ter - day, love was such an eas - y game to play.

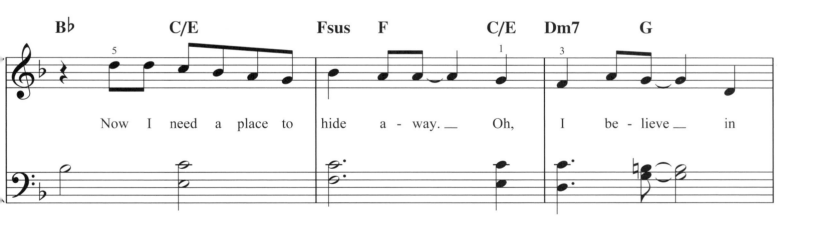

Now I need a place to hide a - way. __ Oh, I be - lieve __ in

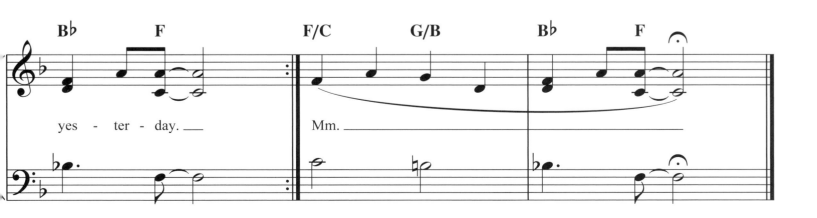

yes - ter - day. __ Mm. __

# YOU CAN'T DO THAT

Words and Music by JOHN LENNON
and PAUL McCARTNEY

Moderately

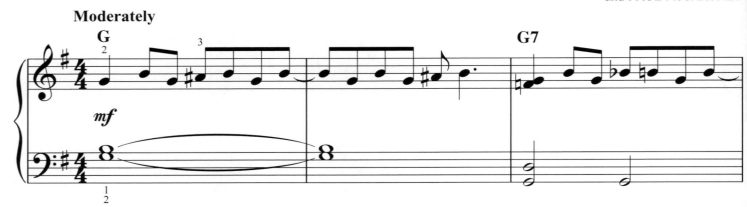

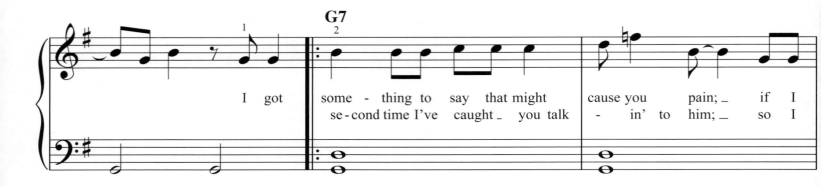

I got some - thing to say that might cause you pain;\_ if I

se - cond time I've caught\_ you talk - in' to him;\_ so I

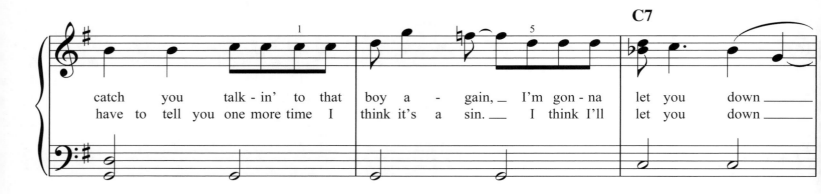

catch you talk - in' to that boy a - gain,\_ I'm gon - na let you down \_\_\_\_\_

have to tell you one more time I think it's a sin.\_ I think I'll let you down \_\_\_\_\_

and leave you flat, \_\_\_\_\_ be - cause I told you be - fore:

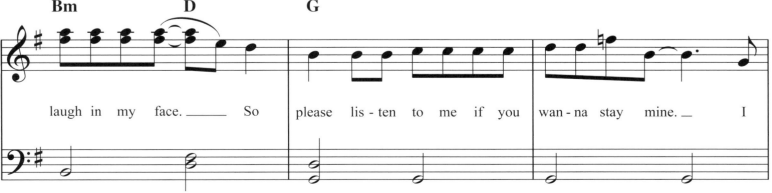

can't help my feel-ings, I'll go out of my mind. I'm gon-na let you down

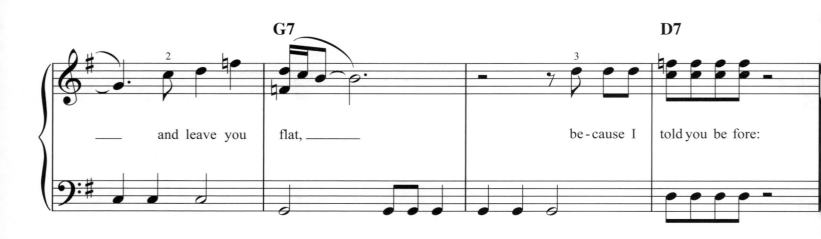

— and leave you flat, be-cause I told you be-fore:

oh, you can't do that.

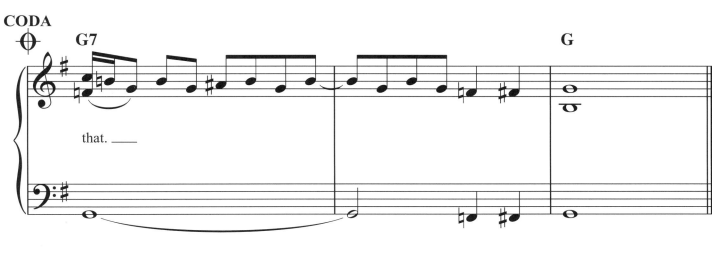

# YOU WON'T SEE ME

Words and Music by JOHN LENNON
and PAUL McCARTNEY

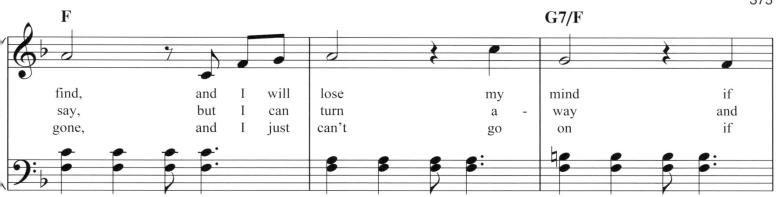

find, and I will lose my mind if
say, but I can turn a - way and
gone, and I just can't go on if

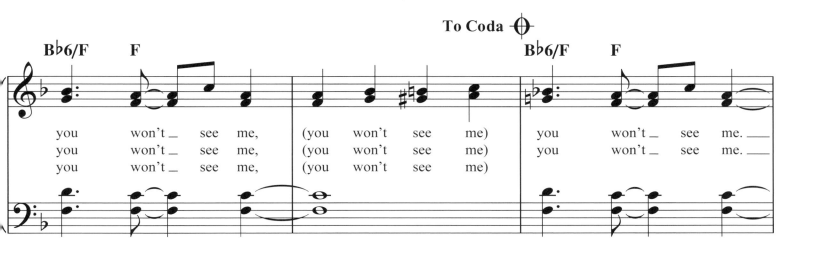

To Coda

you won't __ see me, (you won't see me) you won't __ see me. __
you won't __ see me, (you won't see me) you won't __ see me. __
you won't __ see me, (you won't see me)

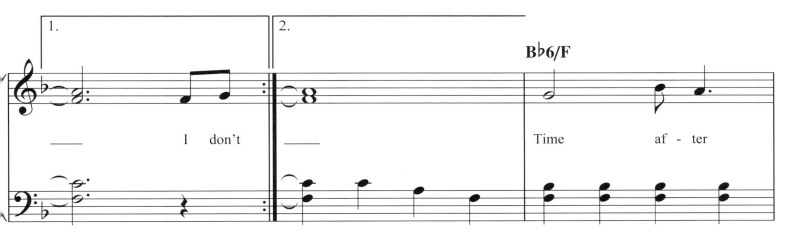

1.
__ I don't

2.
__

Time af - ter

time you re - fuse to e - ven lis - ten;

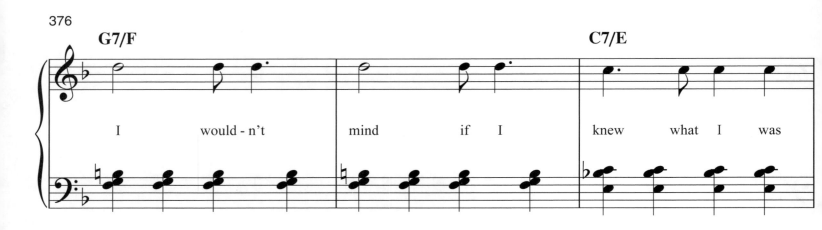

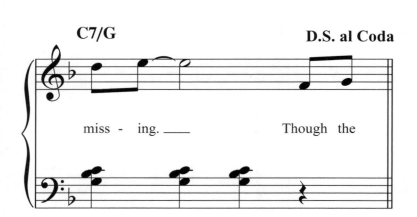

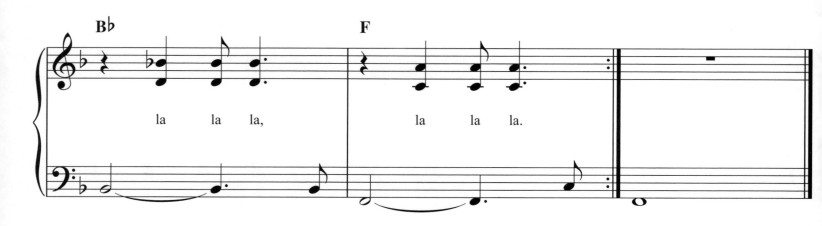

# YOU'VE GOT TO HIDE YOUR LOVE AWAY

Words and Music by JOHN LENNON
and PAUL McCARTNEY

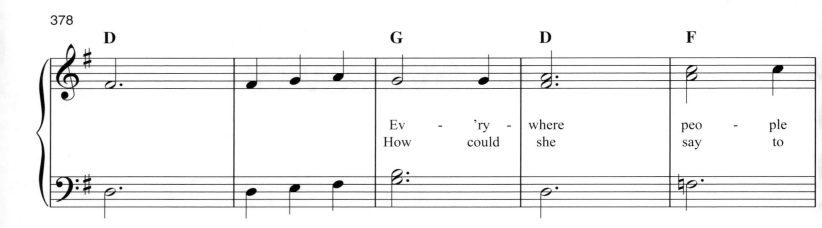

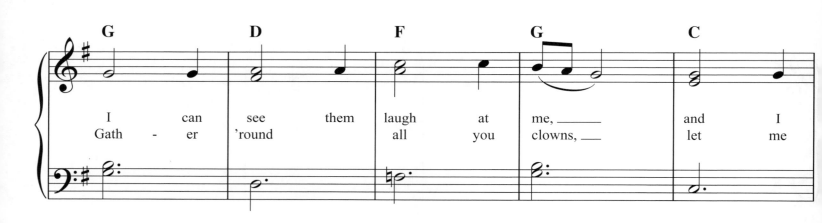

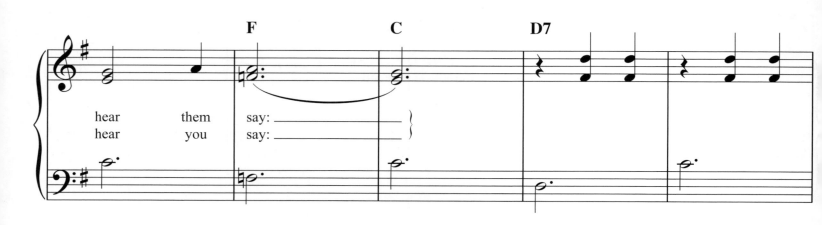

Hey! You've got to hide your _

_ love a - way!

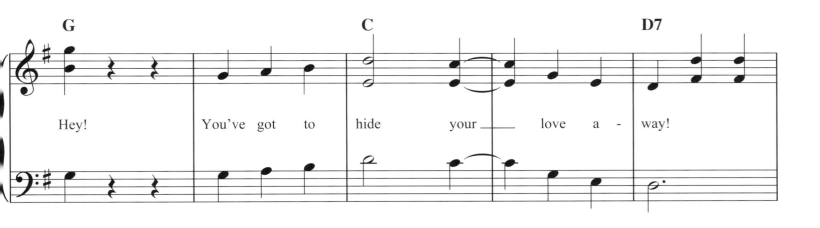

Hey! You've got to hide your ___ love a - way!

# YOUR MOTHER SHOULD KNOW

Words and Music by JOHN LENNON
and PAUL McCARTNEY

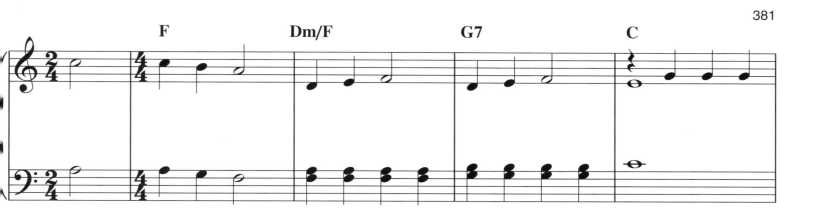

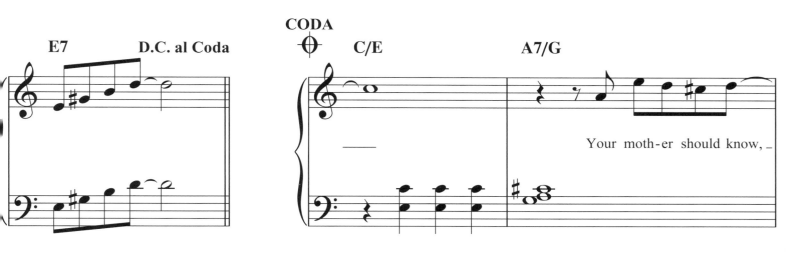

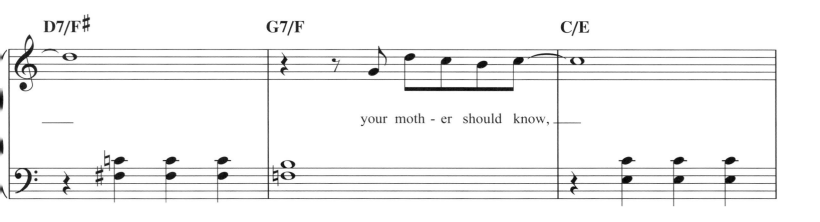

# YOU'RE GOING TO LOSE THAT GIRL

Words and Music by JOHN LENNON
and PAUL McCARTNEY

Moderately

*mf*

You're gon - na lose that girl, ___

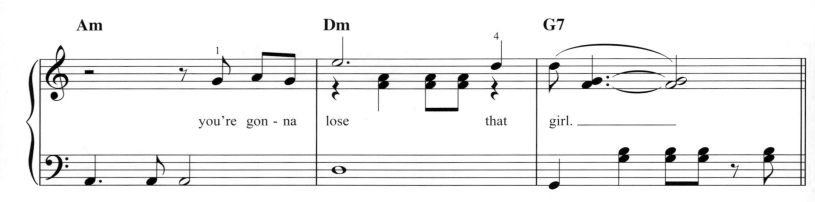

you're gon - na lose that girl. ___

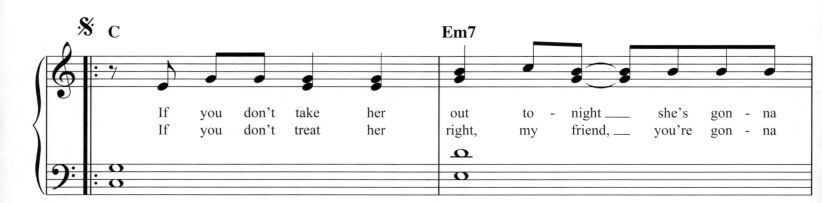

If you don't take her out to - night ___ she's gon - na
If you don't treat her right, my friend, ___ you're gon - na

change her mind, ___ and I will take her
find her gone, ___ 'cause I will treat her

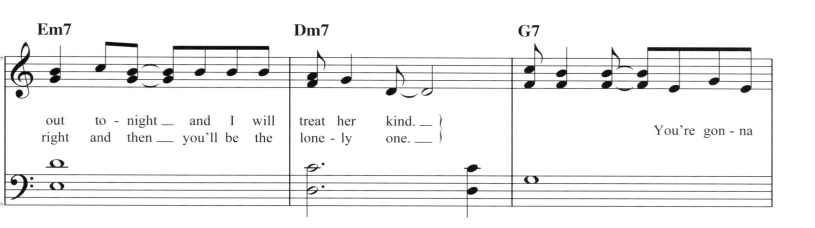

out to - night ___ and I will treat her kind. ___
right and then ___ you'll be the lone - ly one. ___

You're gon - na

**To Coda** ⊕

lose that girl, ___ you're gon - na lose that

1.
girl. _____

2.
girl. ___ You're gon - na lose... _____

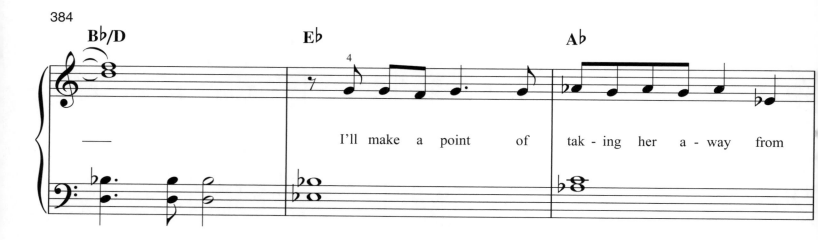

I'll make a point of tak-ing her a-way from

you. Yeah! The way you treat her,

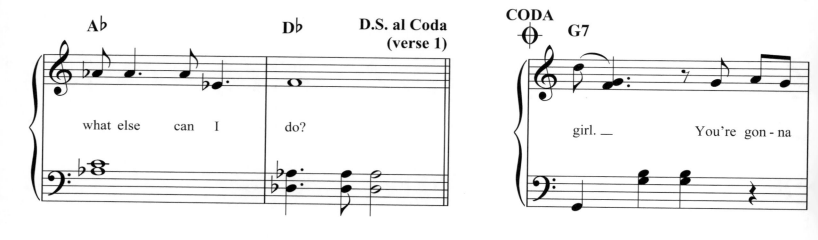

what else can I do? You're gon-na

girl. __ You're gon-na

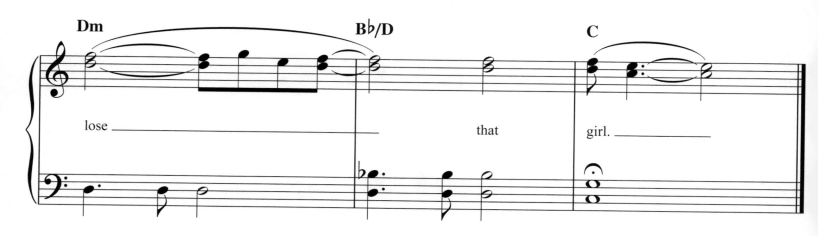

lose __ that girl. __